# WAVES AND RIPPLES
IN
AIR, WATER, AND ÆTHER
(1902)


by J. A. Flemming, M.A. D.Sc, F.R.S.

A CHRISTMAS LECTURE AT THE ROYAL INSTITUTION: "WAVES AND RIPPLES IN THE AIR."

*Drawn by F. C. Dickinson.*]   FIG. 46 (*see* p. 109).   [*From the "Graphic."*

# WAVES AND RIPPLES

IN

## WATER, AIR, AND ÆTHER

BEING

A COURSE OF CHRISTMAS LECTURES DELIVERED
AT THE ROYAL INSTITUTION OF
GREAT BRITAIN

BY

J. A. FLEMING, M.A., D.Sc., F.R.S.

M. INST. E.E., M.R.I., ETC., ETC.

PROFESSOR OF ELECTRICAL ENGINEERING IN UNIVERSITY COLLEGE, LONDON

PUBLISHED UNDER THE DIRECTION OF THE GENERAL LITERATURE
COMMITTEE

LONDON
SOCIETY FOR PROMOTING CHRISTIAN KNOWLEDGE
NORTHUMBERLAND AVENUE, W.C.
43, QUEEN VICTORIA STREET, E.C.
BRIGHTON: 129, NORTH STREET
NEW YORK: E. & J. B. YOUNG AND CO.
1902

# Transcriber's Notes

In the original text, footnotes were designated with symbols such as '*' or '†'. In order to simplify transcription, these were changed to a superscripted number, such as $^5$.

A few obvious misspellings were corrected. Any spaces after an open quote or before a close quote were removed. In the original printing, the decimal point was centred vertically such as 1·08. In this printing, the modern decimal point is used: 1.08. There are a number of spellings that are different from modern practices. These are left with the original spelling. The most notable is 'æther', which, in modern spelling, is 'ether'.

In the original, quoted paragraphs were in the same font, with additional white-space before and after the quote. For convenience, in this version, quoted paragraphs are set in Times New Roman with no additional white-space.

The program used to typeset this book, OpenOffice.org Writer, alphabetizes words in the index somewhat differently from the book. The alphabetization scheme of OpenOffice.org Writer is used.

The page number in the index for the entry "Laplace, calculation of" was incorrect in the original. The correct page is used in this edition. In the original, the index was set in two columns. In this edition, the index is set in one column.

The weight of a cubic yard of water on page 29 was incorrect. The text was left unchanged and a correction placed in a footnote.

The picture on the cover was created by Ackley Road Photos and is licensed.

# PREFACE.

THE Christmas Lectures at the Royal Institution are, by a time-honoured custom, invariably addressed to a "juvenile audience." This term, however, has always been held to be an elastic one, and to include those who are young in spirit as well as those who are young in years. The conditions, therefore, necessarily impose on the Lecturer the duty of treating some subject in such a manner that, whilst not beyond the reach of youthful minds, it may yet possess some elements of interest for those of maturer years. A subject which admits of abundant experimental illustrations is accordingly, on these occasions, a popular one, particularly if it has a bearing upon topics then attracting public attention. The progress of practical invention or discovery often removes at one stroke some fact or principle out of the region of purely scientific investigation, and places it within the purview of the popular mind. A demand then arises for explanations which shall dovetail it on to the ordinary experiences of life. The practical use of æther waves in wireless telegraphy has thus made the subject of waves in general an interesting one. Hence, when permitted the privilege, for a second time, of addressing Christmas audiences in the Royal Institution, the author ventured to indulge the hope that an experimental treatment of the subject of Waves and Ripples in various media would not be wanting in interest. Although such lectures, when reproduced in print, are destitute of the attractions furnished by successful experiments, yet, in response to the wish of many correspondents, they have been committed to writing, in the hope that the explanations given may still be useful to a circle of readers. The author trusts that the attempt to make the operations of visible waves a key to a comprehension of some of the effects produced by waves of an invisible kind may not be altogether without success, and that those who find some of the imperfect expositions in this little book in any degree helpful may thereby be impelled to study the facts more closely from that "open page of Nature" which lies ever unfolded for the instruction of those who have the patience and power to read it aright.

J. A. F.
UNIVERSITY COLLEGE,
LONDON, 1902.

# CONTENTS.

## CHAPTER I.
### WATER WAVES AND WATER RIPPLES.

..............................................................................PAGE

A visit to the seaside—What is a wave?—Wave-motion on water—Definition of a wave—Sea waves—Various forms of wave-motion—Wave length, velocity, and frequency Atlantic waves—Rules for speed of sea waves—Illustrations of wave-motion—A stone falling on water—Production of a wave-train—Wave-energy—Conditions for the production of wave-motion—Distinction between wave-velocity and wave-train velocity—Why a wave breaks—Waves in canals—Rule for speed of a canal wave—Falling bodies—A "bore" Tidal waves—Ripples—Distinction between waves and ripples—Surface tension on liquids—A needle floating on water—Experimental production of ripples—Reflection and refraction of ripples and waves—Interference of waves and ripples—Photography of waves and ripples .......................................1

## CHAPTER II.

### WAVES AND RIPPLES MADE BY SHIPS.

Ship-waves—The viscosity of liquids—How it is demonstrated—Rotational and irrotational motion in fluids—Eddies and whirls—Smoke rings—Vortex motion—Professor Hele-Shaw's experiments—Irrotational or stream-line motion in water—The motion of water round a ship—The motion of water along a pipe—Flow in uniform pipes and non-uniform pipes—Relation between fluid velocity and pressure—Skin resistance and wave-making resistance—The movement of a fish—Motion through a perfect fluid—The waves made by moving objects—Waves made by ducks and swans—Echelon waves—Ship bow waves—The form of ship-waves—Mr. Froude's experiments—Ship-models and experimental tanks—How a ship is designed Froude's laws—Testing ship-models—The design of a racing-yacht—Comparison of British and American yachts—The Cup race—Scott Russell's experiments on canal-boats.................................................................51

## CHAPTER III.

### WAVES AND RIPPLES IN THE AIR.

Air necessary for the production of sound—A sounding body is in vibration—Harmonic motion—The difference between noise and music—The nature of an air wave—The physical qualities of air—Longitudinal or compressional waves—Wave-models to illustrate the nature of sound waves—Quality of a sound—Velocity of an air wave—An illustration on a gigantic scale—The voice of a volcano heard round the world—The effect of temperature on air-wave velocity—Comparison of theory and experiment—Circumstances affecting distance at which sounds can be heard—Funeral guns—Fog-signals and sirens—Effect of wind and density—Sensitive flames as sound-detectors—Inaudible sounds—The reflection and refraction of sound waves—A sound-lens and sound-prism—The interference of sounds—Two sounds producing silence—The phonograph—A soap-bubble film set in vibration by air waves..................................................................91

## CHAPTER IV.

### SOUND AND MUSIC.

The difference between sounds and musical tones—The natural period of vibration of an elastic body—The effect of accumulated impulses—Free and forced vibrations—Breaking down a bridge with a pea-shooter—The vibration of a stretched string —Stationary waves—A string vibrating in segments—Acoustic resonance—Nodes and anti-nodes—The musical scale or gamut—Musical intervals—The natural gamuts and the scale of equal temperament—Concords and discords Musical beats—Helmholtz's theory of discords—Musical instruments—Pipes—Strings and plates—A pan-pipe—An organ-pipe—Open and closed organ-pipes—The distribution of air pressure and velocity in a sounding organ-pipe—Singing flames—Stringed instruments—The violin —the

Stroh violin—The structure of the ear—The ear a wonderful air-wave detector and analyzer..............................................131

## CHAPTER V.

ELECTRIC OSCILLATIONS AND ELECTRIC WAVES.
The conception of an æther—The phenomena of light require the assumption of an æther—The velocity of light—Interference of light—Two rays of light can produce darkness—An electric current—The phenomena of electricity require the assumption of an electro-magnetic medium—Properties and powers of an electric current—Alternating and continuous electric currents—Electromotive force and electric strain—A Leyden jar—The oscillatory discharge of a condenser—Oscillatory sparks—Transformation of electric oscillations—Hertz oscillator—Production of a wave of electric displacement—Detection of electric waves—Metallic filings detectors—The coherer—Inductance and capacity of circuits—Electro-static and electro-magnetic energy—An induction coil—Electric oscillations give rise to electric waves—The electron theory of electricity....................................................................165

## CHAPTER VI.

WAVES AND RIPPLES IN THE JETHER.
The experiments of Heinrich Hertz—Electric radiation—Lecture apparatus for producing and detecting electric radiation—Electric transparency and opacity—Why this difference—The reflection of electric radiation—The refraction of electric rays—An electric prism and an electric lens—The electric refractive index—Interference of electric rays—The velocity of electric radiations identical with that of light—Dark heat rays—Actinic or photographic rays—The cause of colour—The frequency of light waves—The classification of electric or æther waves—The gamut of æther waves—The eye an æther-wave detector of limited power—The electro-magnetic theory of light—Artificial production of light—Use of Hertz waves in wireless telegraphy—Marconi's methods—Mar-

coni's aerial and wave-detector—The Morse alphabet—How a wireless message is sent—The tuning of wireless stations—Communication between ships and shore—The velocity of wireless waves—Conclusion..................................................207

APPENDIX....................................................................255

INDEX..........................................................................261

### USEFUL MEMORANDA.

One statute mile is 5280 feet.

One nautical mile is 6086 feet = $1\frac{1}{6}$ statute mile.

A knot is a speed of 1 nautical mile per hour.

Hence the following rules: –

To convert

Knots to miles per hour multiply by $1\frac{1}{6}$.

Miles per hour to knots multiply by $\frac{6}{7}$.

Feet per second to miles per hour multiply by $\frac{2}{3}$.

Feet per second to knots multiply by $\frac{6}{10}$.

Knots to feet per minute multiply by 100.

CHAPTER I.

# WAVES AND RIPPLES IN WATER, AIR, AND ÆTHER

## CHAPTER I.

## WATER WAVES AND WATER RIPPLES.

WE have all stood many times by the seashore, watching the waves, crested with white foam, roll in and break upon the rocks or beach. Every one has more than once cast a stone upon still water in a lake or pond, and noticed the expanding rings of *ripples*; and some have voyaged over stormy seas, whereon great ships are tossed by mighty *billows* with no more seeming effort than the rocking of a cradle. In all these things we have been spectators of a *wave-motion*, as it is called, taking place upon a water surface. Perhaps it did not occur to us at the time that the *sound* of the splash or thunder of these breaking waves was conveyed to our ears as a wave-motion of another sort in the air we breathe, nay, even that the *light* by which we see these beautiful objects is also a wave-motion of a more recondite description, produced in a medium called the æther, which fills all space.

A progressive study of Nature has shown us that we are surrounded on all sides by wave-motions of various descriptions waves in water, waves in air, and waves in æther and that our most precious senses, our eyes and ears, are really wave-detectors of a very special form. The examination of these waves and their properties and powers has led us to see that waves in water, air, and æther, though differing greatly in detail, have much in common; and many things about them that are difficult to understand become more intelligible when we compare these various wave-motions together. In these lectures, therefore, I shall make use of your familiar experiences concerning sea and water waves to assist you to understand some of the properties of air waves to which we owe our sensations of sound and music; and, as far as possible, attempt an explanation of the nature of æther waves, created in the all-pervading æther, to which are due not only light and sight, but also many electrical effects, including such modern wonders as wireless telegraphy. In all departments of natural science we find ourselves confronted by the phenomena of wave-motion. In the study of earthquakes and tides, telegraphs and telephones, as well as terrestrial temperature, no less than in the examination of water waves and ripples, sound, music, or light and heat, we are bound to consider waves of some particular kind.

Fastening our attention for the moment on surface water waves, the first question we shall ask ourselves is—What is a wave? If we take our station on a high cliff looking down on the sea, on some clear day, when the wind is fresh, we see the waves on its surface like green rounded ridges racing forward, and it appears at first sight as if these elevations were themselves moving masses of water. If, however, we look instead at some patch of seaweed, or floating cork, or seagull, as each wave passes over it, we shall notice that this object is merely lifted up and let down again, or, at most, has a small movement to and fro. We are led, therefore, to infer that, even when agitated by waves, each particle of water never moves far from its position when at rest, and that the real movement of the water is something very different from its apparent motion. If we place on the surface of water a number of corks or pieces of paper, and then watch them as a wave passes over them, we shall notice that the corks or bits of paper rise and fall successively, that is, one after the other, and not all together. A little more careful scrutiny will show us that, in the case of sea waves in deep water, the motion of the floating object as the wave passes over it is a circular one, that is to say, it is first lifted up, then pushed forward, next let down, and, lastly, pulled back; and so it repeats a round-and-round motion, with the plane of the circle in the direction in which the wave is progressing. This may be illustrated by the diagram in Fig. 1, where the circular dotted lines represent the paths described by corks floating on the sea surface when waves are travelling over it.

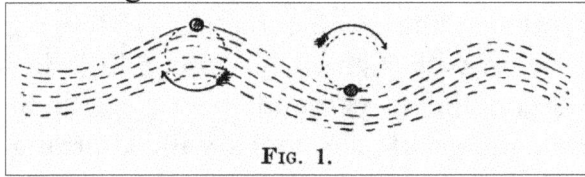

Fig. 1.

Accordingly, we conclude that we have to distinguish clearly between the actual individual motion of each water particle and that general motion called the wave-motion. We may define the latter by saying that to produce a wave-motion, each separate particle of a medium, be it water, or air, or any other fluid, must execute a movement which is repeated again and again, and the several particles along any line must perform this same motion one after the other, that is, lagging behind each other, and not simultaneously. We might illustrate this performance by supposing a row of fifty boys to stand in a line in a playground, and each boy *in turn* to lift up his arm and let it down again, and to continue to perform this action. If all the boys lifted up their arms together, that would not produce a wave-motion; but if each boy did it one after the other in order, along the rank, it would constitute a *wave-motion* travelling along the line of boys. In more learned language, we may define a wave-motion by saying that *a wave-motion exists in any medium when the separate portions of it along any line execute in order any kind of cyclical or repeated motion, the particles along this line performing the movement one after the other, and with a certain assigned delay between each adjacent particle as regards their stage in the movement.*

It will be evident, therefore, that there can be many different kinds of waves, depending upon the sort of repeated motion the several parts perform.

Some of the numerous forms of wave-motion can be illustrated by mechanical models as follows: A board has fastened to it a series of wooden wheels, and on the edge of each wheel is fixed a white knob. The wheels are connected together by endless bands, so that on turning one wheel round they all revolve in the same direction. If the knobs are so arranged to begin with, that each one is a little in advance of its neighbour on the way round the wheel, then when the wheels are standing still the knobs will be arranged along a wavy line (see Fig. 2). On turning round the first wheel, each knob will move in a circle, but every knob will be lagging a little behind its neighbour on one side, and a little in advance of its neighbour on the other side. The result will be to produce a wave-motion, and, looking at the general effect of the moving knobs, we shall see that it resembles a hump moving along, just as in the case of a water wave.

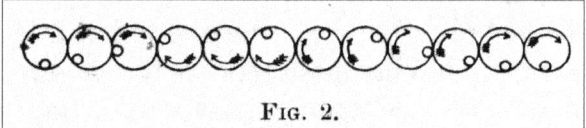

FIG. 2.

The motion of the particles of the water in a deep-sea wave resembles that of the white knobs in the model described. Those who swim will recall to mind their sensations as a sea wave surges over them. The wave lifts up the swimmer, then pushes him a little forward, then lets him down, and, lastly, drags him back. It is this dragging-back action which is so dangerous to persons who cannot swim, when they are bathing on a steep coast where strong waves are rolling in towards the shore.

Two other kinds of wave-motion may be illustrated by the model shown in Fig. 3. In this appliance there are a number of eccentric wheels fixed to a shaft. Each wheel is embraced by a band carrying a long rod which ends in a white ball. The wheels are so placed on the shaft that, when at rest, the balls are arranged in a wavy line. Then, on turning round the shaft, each ball rises and falls in a vertical line, and executes a periodic motion, lagging behind that of its neighbour on one side. The result is to produce a wave-motion along the line of balls.

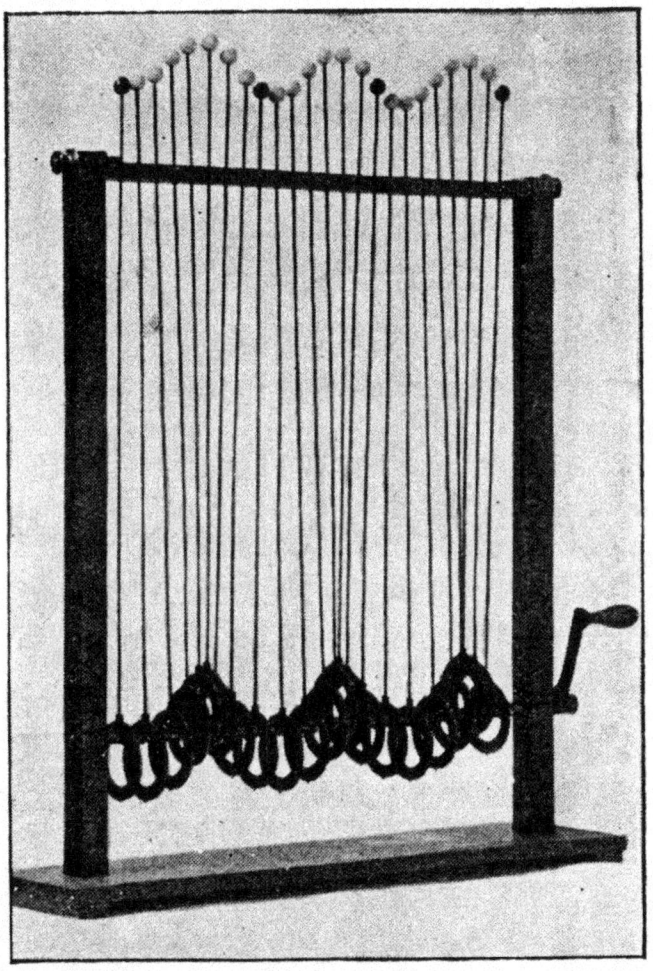

Fig. 3.

By slightly altering the model, each ball can be made to describe a circle in a direction at right angles to the line of the balls, and then we have a sort of corkscrew wave-motion propagated along the line of balls.

Again, another form of wave-motion may be illustrated by the model shown in Fig. 4. In this case a number of golf-balls are hung up by strings, and spiral brass springs are interposed between each ball. On giving a slight tap to the end ball, we notice that its to-and-fro motion is handed on from ball to ball, and we have a wave-motion in which the individual movement of the balls is *in the direction* of the wave-movement, and not across it.

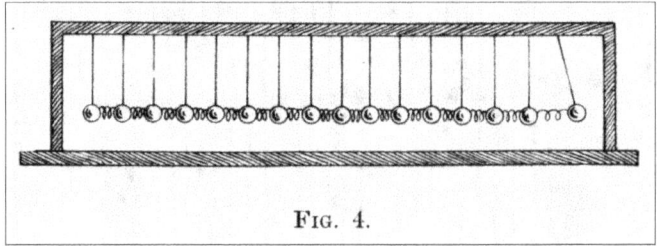

Fig. 4.

The kind of wave illustrated by the model in Fig. 3 is called a *transverse* wave, and that shown in Fig. 4 is called a *longitudinal* wave.

At this stage it may be well to define the meaning of some other expressions which will be much used in these lectures. We have seen that in a wave-motion each part of the medium makes some kind of movement over and over again; and of its neighbours on either side, one is a little ahead of it in its performance, and the other a little in arrear. If we look along the line, we shall see that we can select, portions of it which are exactly in the same stage of movement that is, are moving in the same way at the same time. The distance between these portions is called *one wave-length*. Thus, in the case of sea waves, the distance between two adjacent crests, or humps, is one wave-length.

When we use the expression, *a long wave*, we do not mean a wave which is of great length *in the direction* of the ridge, but waves in which the crests, or humps, are separated far apart, measuring from crest to crest *across* the ridges.

Strictly speaking, the wave-length may be defined as the shortest distance from crest to crest, or hollow to hollow, or from one particle to the next one which is in the same stage of its movement at the same time.

Another way of illustrating the same thing would be to pleat or pucker a sheet of paper into parallel ridges. If we make these pleats very narrow, they would represent what we call *short waves*; but if we make these pleats very far apart, they would represent *long waves*.

Another phrase much used is the term *wave-velocity*. Suppose that a seagull were to fly along over a set of sea waves so as to keep always above one particular hump, or wave-crest; the speed of the gull, reckoned in miles per hour or feet per minute, would be called the speed of the waves. This is something very different from the actual speed of each particle of water.

A third and constantly used expression is the term *wave-frequency*. If we watch a cork floating on a wave-tossed sea, we observe that it bobs up and down so many times in a minute. The number of times per second or per minute that each particle of the medium performs its cycle of motion is called the wave-frequency, or simply *the frequency*.

Again, we employ the term *amplitude* to denote the extreme distance that each individual particle of the medium moves from its mean position, or position of rest. In speaking of sea waves, we generally call the vertical distance between the crest and the hollow the *height* of the wave, and this is twice the amplitude. With regard to the height of sea waves, there is generally much exaggeration. Voyagers are in the habit of speaking of "waves running mountains high," yet a sea wave which exceeds 40 feet in height is a rare sight. Waves have been measured on the Southern Indian Ocean, between the Cape of Good Hope and the Island of St. Paul, and of thirty waves observed the average height was found to be just under 30 feet. The highest was only 37 feet in height. On the other hand, waves of 16 to 20 feet are not uncommon. Travellers who have crossed the Atlantic Ocean in stormy weather will often recount experiences of waves said to be 100 feet high; but these are exceedingly rare, if even ever met with, and unless wave-heights are obtained by some accurate method of measurement, the eye of the inexperienced voyager is apt to be deceived.

In all cases of wave-motion there is a very close connection between the wave-velocity, or speed, the wave-length, and the wave-frequency. This connection is expressed by the numerical law that the velocity is equal to the product of the length and the frequency.

Thus, supposing we consider the case of Atlantic waves 300 feet from crest to crest, which are travelling at the rate of 27 miles an hour, it is required to calculate the frequency or number of times per minute or per second that any floating object, say a boat, will be lifted up as these waves pass over it.

We must first transform a speed of 27 miles per hour into its equivalent in feet per second. Since one mile is 5280 feet, 27 miles per hour is equal to 2376 feet per minute. Accordingly, it is easy to see that the wave-frequency must be 7·92, or nearly 8, because 7·92 times 300 is 2376. The answer to the question is, then, that the floating object will rise and fall eight times a minute. This rule may be embodied in a compact form, which it is desirable to hold firmly in the memory, viz.

---

*Wave-velocity = wave-length x wave-frequency.*

This relation, which we shall have frequent occasion to recall, may be stated in another manner. We call the *period* of a wave the time taken to make one complete movement. The periodic time is therefore inversely proportional to the fre-

## WATER WAVES AND WATER RIPPLES.

quency. Hence we can say that the *wave-length*, divided by the *periodic time*, gives us the *wave-velocity*.

In the case of water waves and ripples, the wave-velocity is determined by the wave-length. This is not the case, as we shall see, with waves in air or waves in æther. In these latter cases, as far as we know, waves of all wave-lengths travel at the same rate. Long sea waves, however, on deep water travel faster than short ones.

A formal and exact proof of the law connecting speed and wave-length for deep-sea waves requires mathematical reasoning of an advanced character; but its results may be expressed in a very simple statement, by saying that, in the case of waves on deep water, the speed with which the waves travel, reckoned in miles per hour, is equal to the square root of 2¼ times the wave-length measured in feet. Thus, for instance, if we notice waves on a deep sea which are 100 feet from crest to crest, then the speed with which those waves are travelling, reckoned in miles per hour, is a number obtained by taking the square root of 2 times 100, viz. 225. Since 15 is the square root of 225 (because 15 times 15 is 225), the speed of these waves is therefore 15 miles an hour.

In the same way it can be found that Atlantic waves 300 feet long would travel at the rate of 26 miles an hour, or as fast as a slow railway train, and much faster than any ordinary ship.[1]

The above rule for the speed of deep-sea waves, viz. *wave-velocity = square root of 2¼ times the wave-length*, combined with the general rule, *wave-velocity = wave-length multiplied by frequency*, provides us with a useful practical method of finding the speed of deep-sea waves which are passing any fixed point. Suppose that a good way out at sea there is a fixed buoy or rock, and we notice waves racing past

---

1   The wave velocity in the case of waves on deep water varies as $\sqrt{\frac{g\lambda}{2\pi}}$

where $\lambda$ is the wave-length. The rule in the text is deduced from this formula.

it, and desire to know their speed, we may do it as follows: Count the number of waves which pass the fixed point per minute, and divide the number into 198; the quotient is the speed of the waves in miles per hour. Thus, if ten waves per minute race past a fixed buoy, their velocity is very nearly 20 miles an hour.[2]

Waves have been observed by the *Challenger* 420 to 480 feet long, with a period of 9 seconds. These waves were 18 to 22 feet high. Their speed was therefore 50 feet per second, or nearly 30 knots. Atlantic storm waves are very often 500 to 600 feet long, and have a period of 10 to 11 seconds. Waves have been observed by officers in the French Navy half a mile in length, and with a period of 23 seconds.

It has already been explained that in the case of deep-sea waves the individual particles of water move in circular paths. It can be shown that the diameter of these circular paths decreases very rapidly with the depth of the particle below the surface, so that at a distance below the surface equal only to one wave-length, the diameter of the circle which is described by each water-particle is only $\frac{1}{535}$ of that at the surface.[3] Hence storm waves on the sea are a purely surface effect. At a few hundred feet down a distance small compared with the depth of the ocean the water is quite still, even when the surface is tossed by fearful storms, except in so far as there may be a steady movement due to ocean currents.

By a more elaborate examination of the propagation of wave-motion on a fluid, Sir George Stokes showed, many

---

2  If V is the velocity of the wave in feet per minute, and V is the V' is the velocity in miles per hour, then $\frac{V' \times 5280}{60} = V$. But $V' = \sqrt{2\frac{1}{4}\lambda}$, and $V = n\lambda$, where $\lambda$ is the wave-length in feet and $n$ the frequency per minute; from which we have $V' = \frac{198}{n}$, or the rule given in the text.

3  The amplitude of disturbance of a particle of water at a depth equal to one wave-length is equal to $\frac{1}{\varepsilon^{2\pi}}$ of its amplitude at the surface. (See Lamb's "Hydrodynamics," p. 189.)

years ago, that in addition to the circular motion of the water-particles constituting the wave, there is also a transfer of water in the direction in which the wave is moving, the speed of this transfer depending on the depth, and decreasing rapidly as the depth increases. This effect, which is known to sailors as the "heave of the sea," can clearly be seen on watching waves on not very deep water. For the crest of the wave will be seen to advance more rapidly than the hollow until the wave falls over and breaks; and then a fresh wave is formed behind it, and the process is repeated. Hence waves break if the depth of water under them diminishes; and we know by the presence of breakers at any place that some shallow or sandbank is located there.

It is necessary, in the next place, to point out the difference between a mere *wave-motion* and a *true wave*. It has been explained that in a wave-motion each one of a series of contiguous objects executes some identical movement in turn. We have all seen the wind blowing on a breezy day across a cornfield, and producing a sort of dark shadow which sweeps along the field. This is clearly caused by the wind bending down, in turn, each row of cornstalks, and as row after row bows itself and springs up again, we are presented with the appearance of a wave-motion in the form of a rift rushing across the field.

A very similar effect can be produced, and another illustration given of a wave-motion, as follows: Coil a piece of brass wire into an open spiral like a corkscrew, and affix to it a small fragment of sealing-wax (see Fig. 5). Hold this in the sun, and let the shadow of it fall upon paper. Then turn it

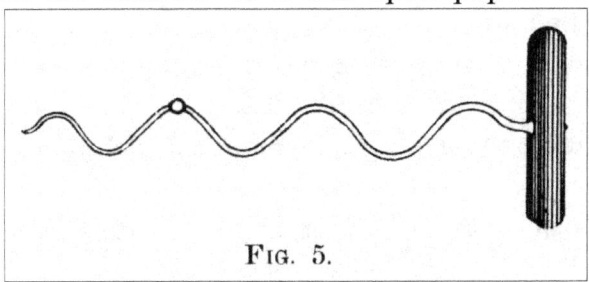

Fig. 5.

round like a screw. "We shall see that the shadow of the spiral is a wavy line, and that, as it is turned round, the humps appear to move along just as do the crests of sea waves, but that the shadow of the little bit of sealing-wax simply moves up and down. Another wave-motion model may be made as follows: Procure a *painter's comb*. This is a thin steel plate, cut into long narrow teeth. Provide also a slip of glass about 3 inches wide and 12 inches long. Paint one side of this glass with black enamel varnish, and when it is quite dry scratch a wavy line upon it (see Fig. 6). Place the glass slip close in front of the comb before the light, and, holding the comb still, move the glass slip to and fro, lengthways. The observer will see a row of dots of light lying in a wavy line, and these, as the glass moves, will rise and fall. If the movement is rapid enough, the appearance of a wave moving along will be seen.[4] In all these exhibitions of wave-motion the movement of the particles is due to a common cause, but the moving particles do not control each other's motion. There is no connection or tie between them. Suppose, however, that we suspend a series of heavy balls like pendulums, and interconnect them by elastic threads (see Fig. 7), then we have an arrangement along which we can propagate a true wave. Draw the end ball to one side, and notice what takes place when it is released. The first ball, being displaced, pulls the second one through a less distance, and that the third one, and the third the fourth, and so on. This happens because the balls are tied together by elastic threads, which resist stretching. When the first ball is released, it is pulled back by the tension of the thread connecting it to its neighbours, and it begins to return to its old position. The ball possesses, however, a quality called *inertia*, and accordingly, when once set in motion, its motion persists until an opposing force brings it to rest. Hence the returning ball overshoots the mark, and passes to the opposite side of its

---

[4] This can easily be shown to an audience by projecting the apparatus on a screen by the aid of an optical lantern.

original position of rest. Then, again, this displacement stretches the elastic threads connecting it to its fellows, and a controlling or retarding force is thus created, which brings it to rest, and forces it again to return on its steps. We see, therefore, that each ball must oscillate, or swing to and fro, and that its movement is gradually communicated to its neigh-

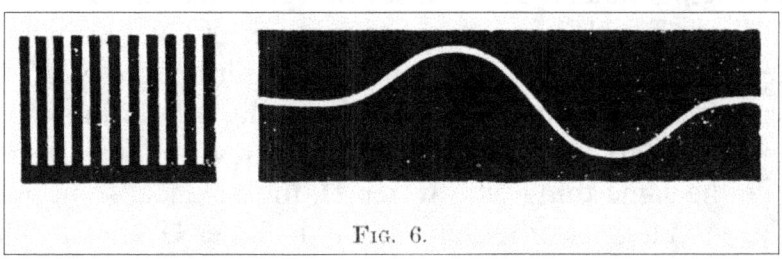

Fig. 6.

bours. A wave-motion is thus started, and a true wave is propagated along the line of balls, in consequence of the presence of *elasticity* and *inertia*. The necessary conditions for the production of a true wave in a medium of any kind are therefore: (1) that the medium must elastically resist some sort of deformation; and (2) when it is deformed at any place, and returns to its original state, it must overshoot the mark or persist in movement, in consequence of inertia, or something equivalent to it.

Briefly speaking, any material or medium in or on which a true self-propagating wave-motion can be made must *resist* and *persist*. It must have an elastic resistance to some change

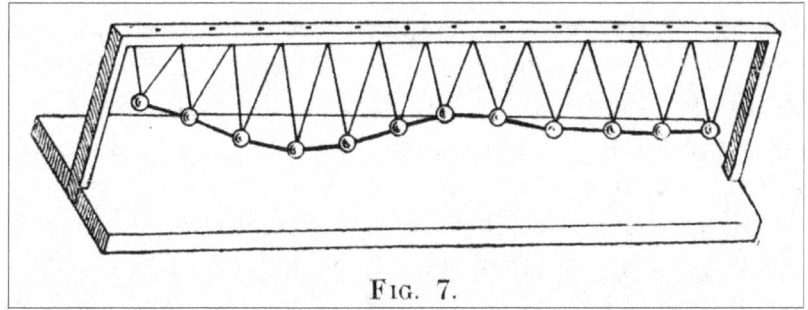

Fig. 7.

or deformation, and it must have an inertia which causes it to persist in movement when once set in motion. These two qualities, or others equivalent to them, must invariably be present if we are to have a true wave produced in a medium.

These things may be best understood by considering, for example, the production of surface waves on water. Let us ask ourselves, in the first place, what alteration or change it is that a water-surface *resists*. The answer is, that, for one thing, it resists being made unlevel. A still water surface is everywhere a level surface. If we attempt to make it unlevel by pouring water on to it at one point, or by heaping it up, the water surface would resist this process. We can dig a hole in sand, or heap up sand to form a hillock, but we know full well we cannot do the same thing with water. If, for instance, some water is placed in a glass tube shaped like the letter U, then it stands at the same level in both limbs. Again, if water is set in motion, being a heavy substance, it cannot be brought to rest instantly. Like every other body, it possesses inertia. Accordingly, if we do succeed by any means in making a depression in a water-surface for an instant, the water would immediately press in to fill up the hole; but more, it would, so to speak, overshoot the mark, and, in consequence of its inertia, it would create a momentary hump, or elevation, in the place on the surface where an instant ago there was a depression.

This elevation would again subside into a hollow, and the process would be continued until the water-motion was brought to rest by friction, or by the gradual dispersion of the original energy. The process by which a wave is started on the surface of water, as a consequence of these two qualities of resistance to being made unlevel and persistence in motion, is beautifully shown by the study of waves made by throwing stones into a pond. The events which give rise to the expanding wave are, however, over so quickly that they can only be studied by the aid of instantaneous photography. The most interesting work on this subject is that of Professor A. M. Worthington, who has photographed, by the exceedingly brief light of an electric spark, the various stages of the events

WATER WAVES AND WATER RIPPLES.

which happen when a drop of water or a stone falls into water.[5] These photographs show us all that happens when the falling object touches the water, and the manner in which it gives rise to the wave or ripple which results. Some of Professor Worthington's results for a drop of water falling into milk are reproduced in the appended diagrams. In the first place (Fig. 8) the drop is seen just entering the water. As it plunges down, it leaves behind it a cavity, or, as it may be called, a hole in the water (see Fig. 9).

This hole, at a certain stage, begins to fill up. The water rushes in on all sides, and the impetus carries up the inrushing water so that it builds up a tall pillar of water in the place where an instant ago there was a hole (see Fig. 10). No one could anticipate such an extraordinary effect; but the instantaneous photographs, taken by the light of an electric spark, which reveal it, cannot but be truthful.

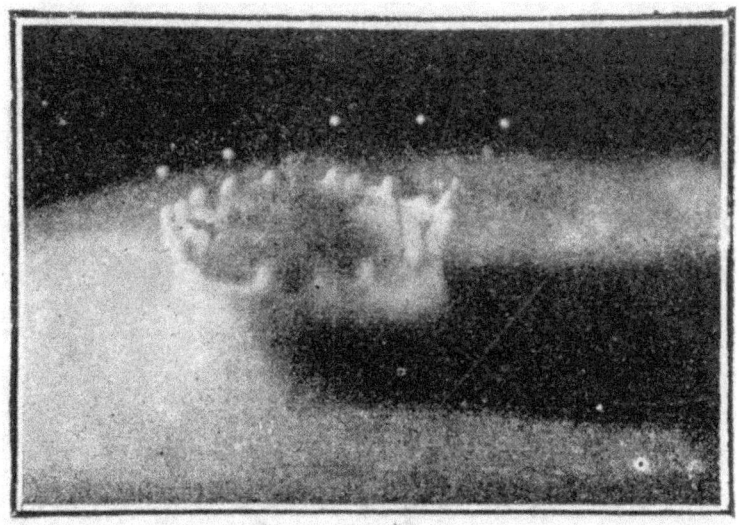

Time after contact = ·0262 sec.

FIG. 8.

---

5  See "The Splash of a Drop," by Professor A. M. Worthington, F.B.S., Romance of Science Series, published by the Society for Promoting Christian Knowledge.

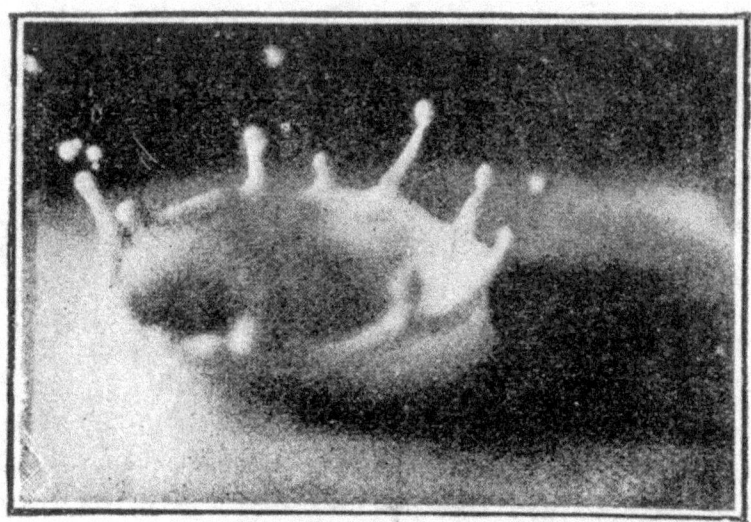

Time after contact = ·0391 sec.

FIG. 9.

The next stage is that this pillar of water breaks up, and falls back again on the surface. Hence the water, at the place where the drop plunges into it, is subjected to two violent impulses—a downward, succeeded by an uplifting, force. The effect of this is exactly analogous to that of giving a blow to the interconnected string of balls in the model shown in Fig. 7

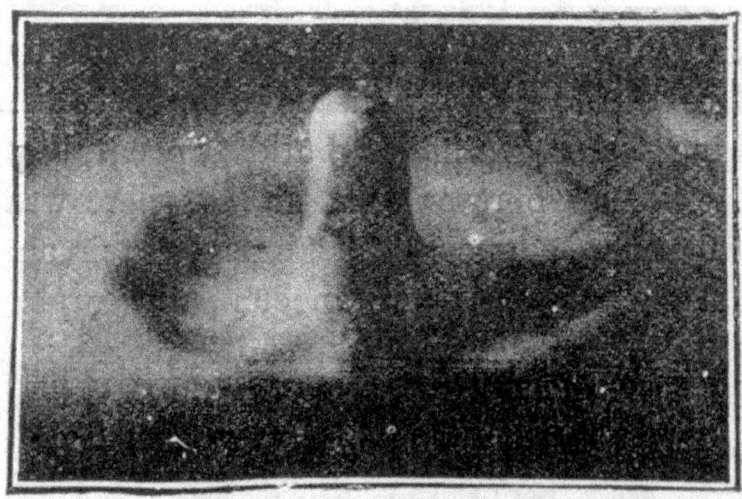

Time after contact = ·101 sec.

FIG. 10.

it propagates a wave. In Fig. 10 is illustrated the next stage, in which this outward-moving initial wave-crest is shown.

So much for the events revealed by the an electric spark; but succeeding these there is a long train of interesting wave-making performance which can be watched with the eye, or the stages photographed with a hand camera. This wave-production is best seen when a large stone is thrown into calm water in a lake or pond.

A story is recorded of the great artist Turner, that he once spent a morning throwing stones into a pond. A friend reproved him for his idleness. "No," said the painter, "I have not been idle; I have learnt how to paint a ripple." If the artist's eye has to be carefully trained to notice all that there is to see when a stone is hurled into a pond, it is not strange that a careless observer cannot grasp at once what really happens to the water in this ordinary occurrence.

The photograph in Fig. 11 will, however, show one stage in the event. As soon as the first wave-crest, the origin of which we have already explained, is formed, it begins to move outwards in a circular form, and as it moves it gives rise to a *wave-train*, that is, it multiplies itself into a series of concentric ripples, or waves, which move outwards, multiplying in number, but getting smaller as they move.

Thus if a large stone is thrown far out into a deep, still lake, after the first splash we shall see a circular wave spreading out from the place where the commotion was made in the water. As we look at this wave we shall see it growing in size and multiplying itself. At first there is but a single wave, then two, four, seven, ten, or more concentric ripples are seen, each circular wave expanding and getting feebler, but seeming to give birth to others as it moves. Moreover, a very careful examination will show us that the whole group of waves, or the wave-train, has an outward motion with a less speed than any individual wave. This observation will serve to initiate the conceptions of a *wave-train* and of a *wave-group velo-*

# WAVES AND RIPPLES

Fig. 11.—Ripples on a lake (Sierre), produced by throwing in a stone.

*city*. At first it is difficult to understand that a *group of waves* may move more slowly than the individual waves which compose it. If, however, we cast a stone into a pond, and look very carefully at what takes place, we shall see that the circular expanding band of ripples has an ill-defined but visible inner and outer edge, and that wavelets or ripples which compose it are being continually brought into existence on its outer edge, and dying away on its inner edge. Waves, so to speak, pass through the ripple band with a greater speed than that at which the whole band of waves moves forward. This rather difficult, but important, idea of the distinction between the velocity of a group of waves and that of an individual wave was first suggested by Sir George Stokes, who set a question in a Cambridge Examination on the subject in 1876, and subsequently it was elucidated by Professor Osborne Reynolds[6] and Lord Rayleigh.

---

6 See Osborne Reynolds, *Nature* vol. 1C, 1877, p. 343, a paper read before the British Association at Plymouth; see also Appendix, Note A.

It can be further explained as follows: Let us consider a wave-motion model such as that represented in Fig. 7, in which a number of suspended heavy balls are connected to one another by elastic threads. Let one ball in the centre be drawn on one side and then released. It will swing to and fro, and will start a wave outwards in both directions. If the row of balls is sufficiently long, it will be seen that the ball by which the wave was started soon comes to rest, and that the wave-motion is confined to a certain group of balls on either side. As time goes on, the wave-motion in each group dies away on the side nearest the origin, and extends on the side furthest away. Hence the particular group of balls which are the seat of the visible wave-motion is continually being shifted along. The rate at which the centre of this active group of vibrating balls is displaced may be called the velocity of the wave-train. The velocity of the wave is, however, something greater, since the waves are all the time moving through the group. This wave-velocity is numerically estimated by taking the product of the wave-length and frequency of the motion.

At this stage it is necessary to explain that waves are not merely a mode of motion; they are a means of conveying energy. It is difficult to give in a compact form any simple definition of what is meant in modern scientific writings by the word *Energy*.

Briefly speaking, we may say that there are two fundamental agencies or things in Nature with which we are in contact, manifesting themselves in many different forms, but of which the total quantity is unchangeable by human operations. One of these is called *Matter*. This term is the collective name given to all the substance or stuff we can see or touch, and which can be weighed or has weight. All known solids, liquids, or gases, such things as ice, water, steam, iron, oil, or air, are called material substances, and they have in common the two qualities of occupying space or taking up room, and of having weight. Experiment has shown that there are some eighty different kinds of simple matter which cannot be transformed into each other, and these forms are called *the Elements*. Any other material substance is made up of mixtures or combinations of these elements. The elementary substances are therefore like the *letters* of the alphabet, which, taken in groups, make up *words*, these last corresponding to compound chemical bodies. Exact research has shown that no chemical changes taking place in a closed space can alter the total weight or amount of gravitating matter in it. If a chemist and numerous chemicals were enclosed in a great glass ball, and the ball balanced on a gigantic but very sensitive pair of scales, no operations which the chemist could conduct in the interior of his crystal laboratory would alter, by the ten-thousandth part of a grain, the total weight of it all. He might analyze or combine his chemicals, burn or mix them as he pleased, but as long as nothing entered or escaped from the ball, the total gravitating mass would remain precisely the same. This great fact is called the *Law of Conservation of Matter*, and it teaches us that although a scuttle of coal may seem to disappear when burnt, yet the weight of the ashes and of all the gaseous products of combustion are together equal to the weight of the original coal and the air required to burn it.

In addition to various material substances we find that we have to recognize different forms of something called *Energy*, associated with Matter. Thus an iron ball may be more or less hot, more or less electrified or magnetized, or moving with more or less speed. The production of these states of heat, electrification, magnetization, or movement, involves the transfer to the iron of Energy, and they are themselves forms of Energy. This Energy in all its various forms can be evaluated or measured in terms of Energy of movement. Thus the Energy required to heat a ball of iron weighing one imperial pound from a temperature of the melting point of ice to that of boiling water, is nearly equal to the Energy required to impart to it a speed of 1000 feet a second.

In the same way, every definite state of electrification or magnetization can be expressed in its *mechanical equivalent*, as it is called. Moreover, it is found that we can never create any amount of heat or mechanical motion or other form of energy without putting out of existence an equivalent of energy in some other form. We are therefore compelled to consider that *Energy* stands on the same footing as *Matter* in regard to our inability to create or destroy it, and its constancy in total amount, as far as we can ascertain, gives it the same character of permanence. The difference, however, is that we cannot, so to speak, ear-mark any given quantity of energy and follow it through all its transformations in the same manner in which we can mark and identify a certain portion of Matter. The moment, however, that we pass beyond these merely quantitative ideas and proceed to ask further questions about the nature of Energy and Matter, we find ourselves in the presence of inscrutable mysteries. We are not able as yet to analyze into anything simpler this "something" we call Energy which presents itself in the guise of heat or light, electricity or magnetism, movement or chemical action. It is protean in form, intangible, yet measurable in magnitude, and all its changes are by definite equivalent amount and value. There is a most rigid system of book-keeping in the transactions of the physical universe. You may have anything you like in the way of Energy served out to you, but the amount of it is debited to your account immediately, and the bill has to be discharged by paying an equivalent in some other form of Energy before you can remove the goods from the counter.

Matter in its various forms serves as the vehicle of Energy. We have no experience of Energy apart from Matter of some kind, nor of Matter altogether devoid of Energy. We do not even know whether these two things can exist separately, and we can give no definition of the one which does not in some way presuppose the existence of the other. Returning, then, to the subject of waves, we may say that a true wave can only exist when Energy is capable of being associated with a medium in two forms, and the wave is a means by which that Energy is transferred from place to place.

It has already been explained that a true wave can only be created in a medium which elastically resists some kind of deformation, and persists in motion in virtue of inertia. When any material possesses such a quality of resistance to some kind of strain or deformation of such a character that the deformation disappears when the force creating it is withdrawn, it is called an *elastic material*. This elasticity may arise from various causes. Thus air resists being compressed, and if the compressing force is removed the air expands again. It possesses so-called elasticity of bulk. In the case of water having a free surface there is, as we have seen, a resistance to any change of level in the surface. This may be called an elasticity of surface form. Whenever an elastic material is strained or deformed, energy has to be expended on it to create the deformation. Thus to wind up a watch-spring, stretch a piece of indiarubber, compress some air, or bend a bow, requires an energy expenditure.

As long as the material is kept strained, it is said to have *potential energy* associated with it. This term is not a very expressive one, and it would be better to call it Energy of strain, or deformation. If, however, we relax the bent bow or release the compressed air, the Energy of Strain disappears, and we have it replaced by Energy of Motion. The arrow which flies from a bow carries with it, as energy of motion, some part of the energy of strain associated with the bent bow.

A little examination of wave-motion shows us, therefore, that we always have at any instant associated with the material in which the wave is being propagated, both Energy of Strain and Energy of Motion. It can be shown that in a true wave of permanent type, the whole energy at any one moment is half energy of strain and half energy of motion, or, as it is called, half potential and half kinetic.

Thus if we consider a wave being propagated along a line of balls elastically connected, at any one moment some of the balls are moving with their greatest velocity, and some are at the extremity of their swing. The former have energy of motion, and the latter energy of strain.

Or, look at a train of sea waves. Some parts of the water are at any moment lifted high above the average level of the sea, or are much below it, but are otherwise nearly at rest. These portions possess what is called potential energy, or energy of position. Other parts of the water are at the average level of the sea, but are moving with considerable velocity, and these portions possess energy of motion. Every other part of the wave has in some degree both energy of motion and energy of position, and it can be shown that the energy of the whole wave is half of one kind and half of the other.

As a wave progresses over the surface, wave-energy is continually being imparted to portions of the water in front, and it is transferred away from others in the rear. In the very act of setting a fresh particle of water in oscillation, the portions already vibrating must diminish their own motion. They may hand on the *whole* of their energy or only a *part* of it to their neighbours. This distinction is a very important one, and it determines whether a single act of disturbance shall create a *solitary wave* or *wave-train* in a medium.

The difference may be illustrated as follows: Consider a row of glass or steel balls suspended by threads so hung as to be quite close to each other (see Fig. 12). Withdraw the first ball, and let it fall against the second one. The result is that the last ball of the row flies off with a jerk. In this case the whole energy imparted to the first ball is transmitted along the row of balls. The first ball, on falling against the second one, exerts on it a pressure which slightly squeezes both out of shape. This pressure is just sufficient to bring the first ball to rest. The second ball, in turn, expands after the blow and squeezes the third, and so on. Hence, in virtue of Newton's Third Law of Motion, that "action and reaction are equal and opposite," it follows that the pressure produced by the blow of the first ball is handed on from ball to ball, and finally causes the last ball to fly off.

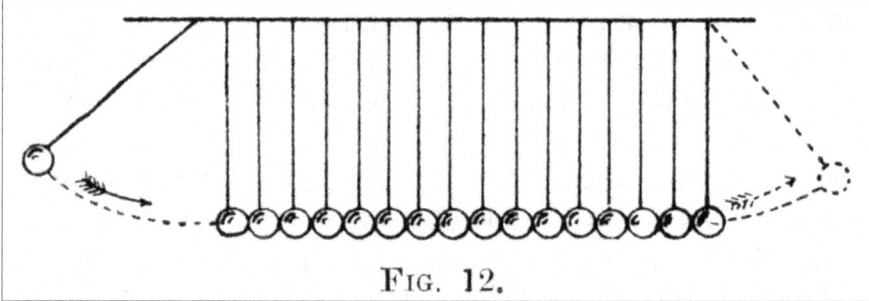

FIG. 12.

In this case, owing to the rigid connection between the elastic balls, each one hands on to its neighbour the whole of the energy it receives. Supposing, however, that we separate the balls slightly, and give the first ball a transverse, or side-to-side swing. Then, owing to the fact that there is no connection between the balls, the energy imparted to the first ball would not be handed on at all, and no wave would be propagated.

Between these two extremes of the whole energy transferred and a solitary wave produced, and no energy transferred and no wave produced, we have a condition in which an initial disturbance of one ball gives rise to a wave-train and part of the energy is transferred.

For if we interconnect the balls by loose elastic threads, and then give, as before, a transverse or sideways impulse to the first ball, this will pull the second one and set it swinging, but it will be pulled back itself, and will be to some extent deprived of its motion. The same sharing or division of energy will take place between the second and third, and third and fourth balls, and so on. Hence the initial solitary vibration of the first ball draws out into a wave-train, and the originally imparted energy is spread out over a number of balls, and not concentrated in one of them. Accordingly, as time goes on, the wave-train is ever extending in length and the oscillatory motion of each ball is dying away, and the original energy gets spread over a wider and wider area or number of balls, but is propagated with less speed than the wave-velocity for that medium.

There need be no difficulty in distinguishing between the notion of a wave-velocity and a wave-train velocity, if we remember that the wave travels a distance equal to a wavelength in the time taken by one oscillation. Hence the wave-velocity is measured by taking the quotient of the wave-length by the time of one complete vibration.

If, for example, the wave-length of a water wave is 4 inches, and we observe that twelve waves pass any given point in 3 seconds, we can at once infer that the wave-velocity is 16 inches per second. The transference of energy may, however, take place so that the whole group of waves moves forward much more slowly. They move forward because the waves are dying out in the rear of the group and being created in the front, and the rate of movement of the group is, in the case of deep-water waves, equal to half that of the single-wave velocity.

A very rough illustration of this difference between a group velocity and an individual velocity may be given by supposing a barge to be slowly towed along a river. Let a group of boys run along the barge, dive over the bows, and reappear at the stern and climb in again. Then the velocity of the group of boys on the barge is the same as the speed of the barge, but the speed of each individual boy in space is equal to the speed of the barge added to the speed of each boy relatively to the barge. If the barge is being towed at 3 miles an hour, and the boys run along the boat also at 3 miles an hour, then the velocity of the group of boys is only half that of the individual boy, because the former is 3 miles an hour and the latter is 6 miles an hour.

Before leaving the subject of sea waves there are two or three interesting matters which must be considered. In the first place, the breaking of a wave on the shore or on shallow water calls for an explanation. If we watch a sea wave rolling in towards the beach, we shall notice that, as it nears the shore, it gets steeper on the shore side, and gradually curls over until it falls and breaks into spray. The reason is because, as the wave gets into the shallow water, the top part of the wave advances more rapidly than the bottom portion. It has already been explained that the path of the water-particle is a circle, with its plane vertical and perpendicular to the wave-front or line.

Accordingly, if the wave is moving in shallow water, the friction of the water against the bottom retards the backward movement at the lowest position of the water, but no such obstacle exists to the forward movement of the water at its highest position. An additional reason for the deformation of the wave on a gently sloping shore may be found in the fact that the front part of the wave is then in shallower water, and hence moves more slowly than the rearward- portion in deeper water. From both causes, however, the wave continually gets steeper and steeper on its landward side until it curls over and tumbles down like a house which leans too much on one side. The act of curling over in a breaking wave is a beautiful thing to watch, and one which attracts the eye of every artist who paints seascapes and storm waves, or of any lover of Nature who lingers by the shore.

Another matter of interest is the origin of sea waves. Undoubtedly they are due originally to the action of the wind upon the water. Whenever two layers of fluid lie in contact with each other, and one moves faster than the other, the faster-moving layer will throw the other into waves. This is seen, not only in the action of moving air or wind upon water, but even in the action of air upon air or water upon water. From the tops of high mountains we may sometimes look down upon a flat surface of cloud beneath. On one occasion the author enjoyed a curious spectacle from the summit of an Alpine peak. The climb up had been through damp and misty air, but on reaching the summit the clouds were left behind, and a canopy of blue sky and glorious sunshine were found overhead. Beneath the clouds lay closely packed like a sea of white vapour, and through this ocean of cloud the peaks of many high mountains projected and stood up like islands. The surface of this sea of white cloud, brilliantly illuminated by the sunshine, was not, however, perfectly smooth. It was tossed into cloud waves and billows by the action of currents of air blowing over its upper surface, and it had a striking resemblance to the surface of a rough sea. When such a cloud layer is not too thick, the ruffling of its upper or under surface into cloud waves may thin it away into regular cloud rolls, and these cloud rollers may then be cut up again by cross air-currents into patches, and we have the appearance known as a "mackerel sky."

Another familiar phenomenon is that known as the "ripple-mark" on wet sand. As the tide ebbs out over a smooth bank of sea-sand, it leaves the surface ploughed into regular rounded ridges and furrows, which are stationary waves on the sand. This is called the ripple-mark. It is due to the fact that the sand, when covered by the water, forms a surface which in a certain sense is fluid, being saturated and filled with water, but the movement of this bottom sand-logged water is hindered by the sand, and hence the layer of overlying water moves over it at a different speed in ebbing out, and carves it into what are virtually sand waves.

Even a dry sand or snow surface may in this manner be moulded into a wave-form by the wind, and very curious effects of this kind have been noticed and described by Dr.

Vaughan Cornish, who has made a great study of the science of waves.[7]

The production of waves on water by means of a current of air blowing over it is easily exhibited on a small scale by blowing through an indiarubber pipe, the end of which is held near the surface of the water in a tub or tank. The exact manner in which the moving air gets a grip of the water is not quite plain, but it is clear that, if once an inequality of level is set up, the moving air has then an oblique surface against which it can press, and so increase the inequality by heaping up the water in some places, and hollowing it out in others.

Hence oscillations of the water-surface are set up, which go on accumulating. These waves then travel away with a speed depending upon their wave-length, and we may have great disturbances of the sea-surface at places where there is no actual storm-wind. These "echoes of a far-off storm" are known as a "ground swell." In some localities the inhabitants are able to apprise themselves of the coming of a storm by noticing movements of the sea which indicate the arrival of waves which have travelled more quickly than the storm-centre itself.

Every visitor to the seaside will have noticed occasions on which the sea is violently disturbed by waves, and yet the air in the locality is tolerably calm. In this case the waves have been propagated from some point of disturbance at a distance.

A study of breaking waves shows us that the cause of their great power to effect damage to coast structures, such as piers, harbour works, and shipping in harbours, is really due to the forward motion of the water as the wave is breaking. Every cubic foot of water weighs 63½ lbs., so that a cubic

---

7 A very interesting article on "Kumatology, or the Science of Waves," appeared in a number of Pearson's Magazine for July, 1901. In this article, by Mr. Marcus Tindal, many interesting facts about, and pictures of, sea waves are given.

## WATER WAVES AND WATER RIPPLES.

yard of water weighs about three-quarters† of a ton. If this water is moving with a speed of many feet per second in a forward direction, the energy of motion stored up in it is tremendous, and fully sufficient to account for the destructive power of storm waves on a coast.

The total volume of water which is comprised in the space occupied by even one sea-storm wave of moderate dimensions may have a mass of many hundreds of tons, and its energy of motion may easily amount to that of an express train in motion. Hence when, in the last stage of its career, this mass of water is hurled forward on the shore, its destructive effects are not a matter for surprise.

We must now leave the subject of waves in the open sea on a large level surface, and consider that of waves in narrow channels, such as canals or rivers. The laws which govern water-wave production in a canal can best be studied by placing some water in a long tank with glass sides. If at one end we insert a flat piece of wood and give it a push forward, we shall start what is called a long wave in the tank. The characteristic of this kind of wave is that the oscillatory motion is chiefly to-and-fro, and not up-and-down. This may be very easily seen by placing some Iran in the water, or floating in it some glass balls which have been adjusted so as to just float anywhere in the water. When this is done, and a wave started in the tank, it runs up and down, being reflected at each end (see Fig. 13).

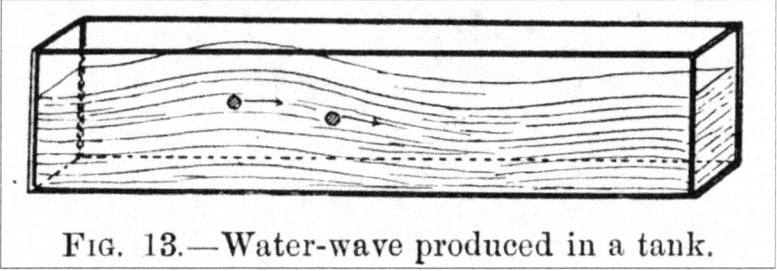

Fig. 13.—Water-wave produced in a tank.

---

† Transcriber's note: Since 63½ pounds per cubic foot × 9 cubic feet per cubic yard = 571.5 pounds per cubic yard, this should read 'one-quarter ton'.

From the motion of the bran we can see that the water swings backwards and forwards in a horizontal line with a pendulum-like motion, but its up-and-down or vertical motion is much more restricted. A wave of this kind travels along a canal with a speed which depends upon the depth of the canal. If waves of this kind are started in a very long trough, the wave-length being large compared with the depth of the trough,[8] it can be shown that the speed of the wave is equal to the velocity which would be gained by a stone or other heavy body in falling through half the depth of the canal. Hence, the deeper the water, the quicker the wave travels. This can be shown as an experimental fact as follows: Let two galvanized iron tanks be provided, each about 6 feet long and 1 foot wide and deep.

At one end of each tank a hollow cylinder, such as a coffee-canister or ball made water-tight, is floated, and it may be prevented from moving from its place by being attached to a hinged rod like the ball-cock of a cistern. The two tanks are placed side by side, and one is filled to a depth of 6 inches, and the other to a depth of 3 inches, with water. Two pieces of wood are then provided and joined together as in Fig. 14, so

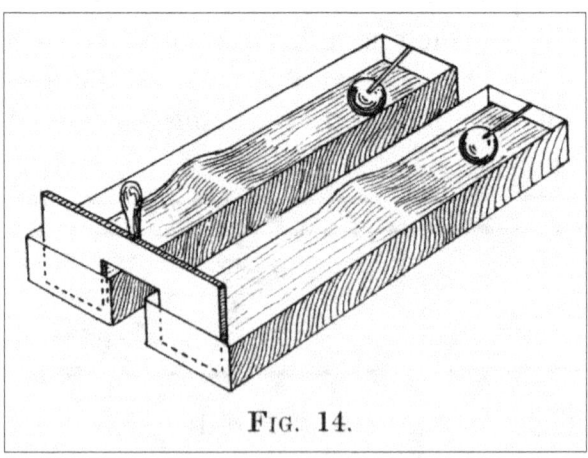

FIG. 14.

---

8 Lord Kelvin (see lecture on " Ship Waves," Popular Lectures, vol. iii. p. 468) says the wave-length must be at least fifty times the depth of the canal.

as to form a double paddle. By pushing this through the water simultaneously in both tanks at the end opposite to that at which the floating cylinders are placed, it is possible to start two solitary waves, one in each tank, at the same instant. These waves rush up to the other end and cause the floats to bob up. It will easily be seen that the float on the deeper water bobs up first, thus showing that the wave on the deeper water has travelled along the tank more quickly than the wave .on the shallower water.

In order to calculate the speed of the waves, we must call to mind the law governing the speed of falling bodies. If a stone falls from a height its speed increases as it falls. It can be shown that the speed in feet per second after falling from any height is obtained by multiplying together the number 8 and a number which is the square root of the height in feet.

Thus, for instance, if we desire to know the speed attained by falling from a height of 25 feet above the earth's surface, we multiply 8 by 5, this last number being the square root of 25. Accordingly, we find the velocity to be 40 feet per second, or about 26 miles an hour.

The force of the blow which a body administers and suffers on striking the ground depends on the energy of motion it has acquired during the fall, and as this varies as the square of the speed, it varies also as the height fallen through.

Let us apply these rules to calculate the speed of a long wave in a canal having water 8 feet deep in it. The half-depth of the canal is therefore 4 feet. The square root of 4 is 2; hence the speed of the wave is that of a body which has fallen from a height of 4 feet, and is therefore 16 feet per second, or nearly 11 miles an hour. When we come to consider the question of waves made by ships, in the next chapter, a story will be related of a scientific discovery made by a horse employed in dragging canal-boats, which depended on the fact that the speed of long waves in this canal was nearly the same as the trotting speed of the horse.

It may be well, as a little digression, to point out how the law connecting height fallen through and velocity acquired by the falling body may be experimentally illustrated for teaching purposes.

The apparatus is shown in Fig. 15. It consists of a long board placed in a horizontal position and held with the face vertical. This board is about 16 feet long. Attached to this board is a grooved railway, part of which is on a slope and part is horizontal. A smooth iron ball, A, about 2 inches in diameter, can run down this railway, and is stopped by a movable buffer or bell, B, which can be clamped at various positions on the horizontal rail. At the bottom of the inclined plane is a light lever, T, which is touched by the ball on reaching the bottom of the hill. The trigger releases a pendulum, P, which is held engaged on one side, and, when released, it takes one swing and strikes a bell, G. The pendulum occupies half a second in making its swing. An experiment is then performed in the following manner: The iron ball is placed at a distance, say, of 1 foot up the hill and released. It rolls down, detaches the pendulum at the moment it arrives at the bottom of the hill, and then expends its momentum in running along the flat part of the railway. The buffer must be so placed by trial that the iron ball hits it at the instant when the pendulum strikes the bell. The distance which the buffer has to be placed from the bottom of the hill is a measure of the velocity acquired by the iron ball in falling down the set distance

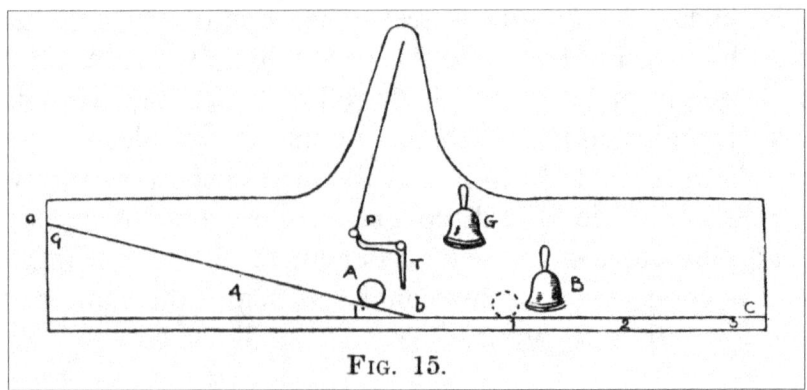

Fig. 15.

along the hill. The experiment is then repeated with the iron ball placed respectively four times and nine times higher up the hill, and it will be found that the distances which the ball runs along the flat part in one half- second are in the ratio of 1, 2, and 3, when the heights fallen through down the hill are in the ratio of 1, 4, and 9.

The inference we make from this experiment is that the velocity acquired by a body in falling through any distance is proportional to the square root of the height. The same law holds good, no matter how steep the hill, and therefore it holds good when the body, such as a stone or ball, falls freely through the air.

The experiment with the ball rolling down a slope is an instructive one to make, because it brings clearly before the mind what is meant by saying, in scientific language, that one thing "varies as the square root" of another. We meet with so many instances of this mode of variation in the study of physics, that the reader, especially the young reader, should not be content until the idea conveyed by these words has become quite clear to him or her.

Thus, for instance, the time of vibration of a simple clock pendulum "varies as the square root of the length;" the velocity of a canal wave "varies as the square root of the depth of the canal;" and the velocity or speed acquired by a falling ball "varies as the square root of the distance fallen through." These phrases mean that if we have pendulums whose lengths are in the ratio of 1 to 4 to 9, then the respective times of their vibration are in the ratio of 1 to 2 to 3. Also a similar relation connects the canal-depth and wave-velocity, or the ball-velocity and height of fall.

Returning again to canal waves, it should be pointed out that the real path of a particle of water in the canal, when long waves are passing along it, is a very flat oval curve called an ellipse. In the extreme cases, when the canal is very wide and deep, this ellipse will become nearly a circle; and, on the other hand, when narrow and shallow, it will be nearly a straight line. Hence, if long waves are created in a canal which is shallow compared with the length of the wave, the water-particles simply oscillate to and fro in a horizontal line. There is, however, one important fact connected with wave-propagation in a canal, which has a great bearing on the mode of formation of what is called a "bore." As a wave travels along a canal, it can be shown, both experimentally and theoretically, that the crest of the wave travels faster than the hollow, and as a consequence the wave tends to become steeper on its front side, and its shape then resembles a saw-tooth.

A very well known and striking natural phenomenon is the so-called "bore" in certain tidal rivers or estuaries. It is well seen on the Severn in certain states of the tide and wind. The tidal wave returning along the Severn channel, which narrows rapidly as it leaves the coast, becomes converted into a "canal wave," and travels with great rapidity up the channel. The front side of this great wave takes an almost vertical position, resembling an advancing wall of water, and works great havoc with boats and shipping which have had the misfortune to be left in its path. To understand more completely how a "bore" is formed, the reader must be reminded of the cause of all tidal phenomena. Any one who lives by the sea or an estuary knows well that the sea-level rises and falls twice every 24 hours, and that the average interval of time between high water and high water is nearly 12½ hours. The cause of this change of level in the water-surface is the attraction exerted by the sun and moon upon the ocean. The earth is, so to speak, clothed with a flexible garment of water, and this garment is pulled out of shape by the attractive force of our luminaries; very roughly speaking, we may say that the ocean-surface is distorted into a shape called an ellipsoid, and that there are therefore two elevations of water which march across the sea-covered regions of the earth as it revolves on its axis. These elevations are called the *tidal waves*. The effects, however, are much complicated by the fact that the ocean does not cover all parts of the earth. There is no difficulty in showing that, as the tidal wave progresses round the earth across each great ocean, it produces an elevation of the sea-surface which is not simultaneous at all places. The time when the crest of the tidal wave reaches any place is called the "time of high tide." Thus if we consider an estuary, such as that of the Thames, there is a marked difference between the time of high tide as we ascend the estuary.

Taking three places, Margate, Gravesend, and London Bridge, we find that if the time of high tide at Margate is at noon on any day, then it is high tide at Gravesend at 2.15 p.m., and at London Bridge a little before three o'clock. This difference is due to the time required for the tidal wave to travel up the estuary of the Thames.

When an estuary contracts considerably as it proceeds, as is the case with the Bristol Channel, then the range of the tide or the height of the tidal wave becomes greatly increased as it travels up the gradually narrowing channel, because the wave is squeezed into a smaller space. For example, the range of spring tides at the entrance of the Bristol Channel is about 18 feet, but at Chepstow it is about 50 feet.[9] At oceanic ports in open sea the range of the tide is generally only 2 or 3 feet.

If we look at the map of England, we shall see how rapidly the Bristol Channel contracts, and hence, as the tidal wave advances from the Atlantic Ocean, it gets jambed up in this rapidly contracting channel, and as the depth of the channel in which it moves rapidly shallows, the rear portion of this tidal wave, being in deeper water, travels faster than the front part and overtakes it, producing thus a flat or straight-fronted wave which goes forward with tremendous speed.[10]

---

9 See article "Tides," by G. H. Darwin, "Encyclopaedia Britannica," 9th edit., vol. 23, p. 353.
10 The progress of the Severn "bore" has been photographed and repro-

## WAVES AND RIPPLES

We must, in the next place, turn our attention to the study of water ripples. The term "ripple" is generally used to signify a very small and short wave, and in ordinary language it is not distinguished from what might be called a wavelet, or little wave. There is, however, a scientific distinction between a wave and a ripple, of a very fundamental character.

It has already been stated that a wave can only exist, or be created, in or on a medium which resists in an elastic manner some displacement. The ordinary water-surface wave is termed a *gravitation wave*, and it exists because the water-surface resists being made unlevel. There is, however, another thing which a water-surface resists. It offers an opposition to small stretching, in virtue of what is called its *surface tension*. In a popular manner the matter may thus be stated: The surface of every liquid is covered with a sort of skin which, like a sheet of indiarubber, resists stretching, and in fact contracts under existing conditions so as to become as small as possible. We can see an illustration of this in the case of a soap-bubble. If a bubble is blown on a rather wide glass tube, on removing the mouth the bubble rapidly shrinks up, and the contained air is squeezed out of the tube with sufficient force to blow out a candle held near the end of the tube.

Again, if a dry steel sewing-needle is laid gently in a horizontal position on clean water, it will float, although the metal itself is heavier than water. It floats because the weight of the needle is not sufficient to break through the surface film. It is for this reason that very small and light insects can run freely over the surface of water in a pond.

This surface tension is, however, destroyed or diminished by placing various substances on the water. Thus if a small disc of writing-paper the size of a wafer is placed on the surface of clean water in a saucer, it will rest in the middle. The surface film of the water on which it rests is, however,

---

duced by a kinematograph by Dr. Vaughan Cornish. For a series of papers bearing on this sort of wave, by Lord Kelvin, see the *Philosophical Magazine* for 1886 and 1887.

strained or pulled equally in different directions. If a wire is dipped in strong spirits of wine or whisky, and one side of the wafer touched with the drop of spirit, the paper shoots away with great speed in the opposite direction. The surface tension on one side has been diminished by the spirit, and the equality of tension destroyed.

These experiments and many others show us that we must regard the surface of a liquid as covered with an invisible film, which is in a state of stretch, or which resists stretching. If we imagine a jam-pot closed with a cover of thin sheet indiarubber pulled tightly over it, it is clear that any attempt to make puckers, pleats, or wrinkles in it would involve stretching the indiarubber. It is exactly the same with water. If very *small* wrinkles or pleats, as waves, are made on its surface, the resistance which is brought into play is that due to the surface tension, and not merely the resistance of the surface to being made unlevel. Wavelets so made, or due to the above cause, are called *ripples*.

It can be shown by mathematical reasoning[11] that on the free surface of a liquid, like water, what are called *capillary ripples* can be made by agitations or movements of a certain kind, and the characteristic of these surface-tension waves or capillary ripples, as compared with gravitation waves, is that the velocity of propagation of the capillary ripple is *less* the greater the wave-length, whereas the velocity of gravitation on ordinary surface waves is *greater* the greater the wave-length.

It follows from this that for any liquid, such as water, there is a certain length of wave which travels most slowly. This slowest wave is the dividing line between what are properly called ripples, and those that are properly called waves. In the case of water this slowest wave has a wave-length of

---

[11] See Lord Kelvin, "Hydrokinetic Solutions and Observations," *Philosophical Magazine*, November, 1871.

about two-thirds of an inch (0.68 inch), and a speed of travel approximately of 9 inches (0.78 foot) per second.

More strictly speaking, the matter should be explained as follows: Sir George Stokes showed, as far back as 1848, that the surface tension of a liquid should be taken into account in finding the pressure at the free surface of a liquid. It was not, however, until 1871 that Lord Kelvin discussed the bearing of this fact on the formation of waves, and gave a mathematical expression for the velocity of a wave of oscillatory type on a liquid surface, in which the wave-length, surface tension, density, and the acceleration of gravity were taken into account. The result was to show that when waves are very short, viz. a small fraction of an inch, they are principally due to surface tension, and when long are entirely due to gravity.

It can easily be seen that ripples run faster the smaller their wave-length. If we take a thin wire and hold it perpendicularly in water, and then move it quickly parallel to itself, we shall see a stationary pattern of ripples round the wire which moves with it. These ripples are smaller and closer together the faster the wire is moved.

Ripples on water are formed in circular expanding rings when rain-drops fall upon the still surface of a lake or pond, or when drops of water formed in any other way fall in the same manner. On the other hand, a stone flung into quiet and deep water will, in general, create waves of wave-length greater than two-thirds of an inch, so that they are no longer within the limits entitling them to be called ripples. Hence we have a perfectly scientific distinction between a ripple and a wave, and a simple measurement of the wave-length will decide whether disturbances of oscillatory type on a liquid surface should be called ripples or waves in the proper sense of the words.

The production of water ripples and their properties, and a beautiful illustration of wave properties in general, can be made by allowing a steady stream of water from a very small jet to fall on the surface of still water in a tank. In order to see the ripples so formed, it is necessary to illuminate them in a particular manner.

The following is a description of an apparatus, designed by the author for exhibiting all these effects to a large audience:

The instrument consists essentially of an electric lantern. A hand-regulated or self-regulating arc lamp is employed to produce a powerful beam of light. This is collected by a suitable condensing-lens, and it then falls upon a mirror placed at an angle of 45, which throws it vertically upwards. The light is then concentrated by a plain convex lens placed horizontally, and passes through a trough of metal having a plane† glass bottom. This trough is filled to a depth of half an inch with water, and it has an overflow pipe to remove waste water. Above the tank, at the proper distance, is placed a focussing-lens, and another mirror at an angle of 45 to throw an image of the water-surface upon a screen. The last lens is so arranged that ripples on the surface of the water appear like dark lines flitting across the bright disc of light which appears upon the screen. Two small brass jets are also arranged to drop water into the tank, and these jets must be supplied with water from a cistern elevated about 4 feet above the trough. The jets must be controlled by screw-taps which permit of very accurate adjustment. These jets should work on swivels, so that they may be turned about to drop the water at any point in the tank.

The capillary ripples which are produced on the water-surface by allowing water to drop on it from a jet, flit across the surface so rapidly that they cannot be followed by the eye. They may, however, be rendered visible as follows: A zinc disc, having holes in it, is arranged in front of the focussing-lens, and turned by hand or by means of a small electric motor. This disc is called a stroboscopic disc. When turned

---

† Transcriber's note: spelling is correct.

round it eclipses the light at intervals, so that the image on the screen is intermittent. If, now, one of the water-jets is adjusted so as to originate at the centre of the tank a set of diverging circular ripples, they can be projected as shadows upon the screen. These ripples move at the rate of 1 or 2 feet per second, and their shadows move so rapidly across the field of view that we cannot well observe their behaviour. If, however, the metal disc with holes in it is made to revolve and to intermittently obscure the view, it is possible to adjust its speed so that the interval of time between two eclipses is just equal to that required by the ripples to move forward through one wave-length. When this exact speed is obtained, the image of the ripples on the screen becomes stationary, and we see a series of concentric dark circles with intermediate bright spaces (see Fig. 16), which are the shadows of the ripples. In this manner we can study many of their effects. If, for instance, the jet of water is made to fall, not in the centre of the trough, but nearer one side, we shall notice that there are two sets of ripples which intersect one of these is the direct or original set, and the other is a set produced by the reflection of the original ripples from the side of the trough. These direct and reflected ripple-shadows intersect and produce a cross-hatched pattern. If a slip of metal or glass is inserted into the trough, it is very easy to show that when a circular ripple meets a plane hard surface it is reflected, and that the reflected ripple is also a circular one which proceeds as if it came from a point, Q, on the opposite side of the boundary, just as far behind that boundary as the real centre of disturbance or origin of the ripple P is in

Fig. 16.

front of it (see Fig. 17). In the diagram the dotted curves represent the reflected ripple-crests.

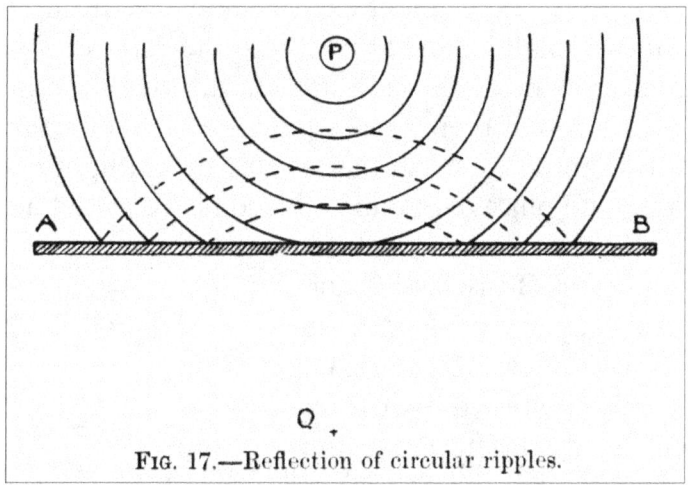

Fig. 17.—Reflection of circular ripples.

If we make two sets of ripples from origins P and Q (see Fig. 18), at different distances from a flat reflecting boundary, it is not difficult to trace out that each set of ripples is reflected independently, and according to the above-mentioned rule. We here obtain a glimpse of a principle which will come before us again in speaking of æther waves, and furnishes an explanation of the familiar optical fact that when we view our

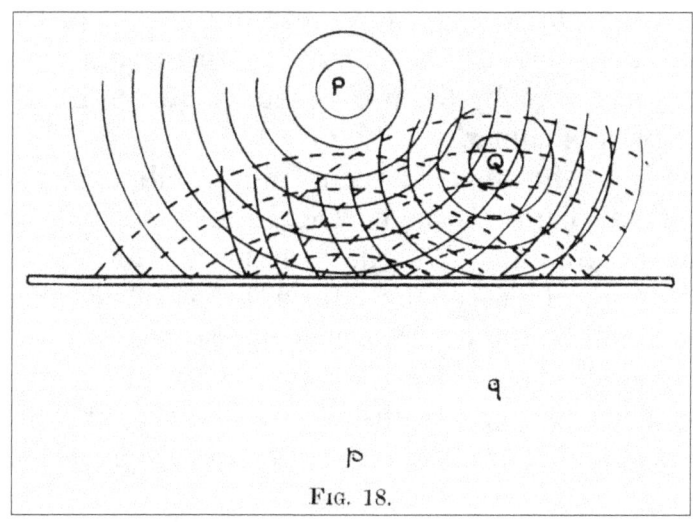

Fig. 18.

## WAVES AND RIPPLES

own reflection in a looking-glass, the image appears to be as far behind the glass as we are in front of it.

A very pretty experiment can be shown by fitting into the trough an oval band of metal bent into the form of an ellipse. If two pins are stuck into a sheet of card, and a loop of thread fitted loosely round them, and a pencil employed to trace out a curve by using it to strain the loop of thread tight and moving it round the pin, we obtain a closed curve called an ellipse (see Fig. 19). The positions of the two pins A and B are called the *foci*. It is a property of the ellipse that the two lines AP and BP, called *radii vectores*, drawn from the foci to any point P on the curve, make equal angles with a line TT' called a tangent, drawn to touch the selected point on the ellipse. If we draw the tangent

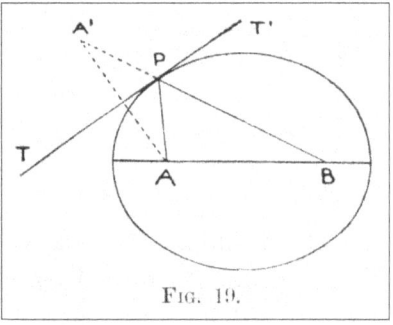

Fig. 19.

TT' to the ellipse at P, then it needs only a small knowledge of geometry to see that the line PB is in the same position and direction as if it were drawn through P from a false focus A', which is as far behind the tangent TT' as the real focus A is in front of it. Accordingly, it follows that circular ripples diverging from one focus A of an ellipse must, after reflection at the elliptical boundary, be converged to the other focus B. This can be shown by the use of the above described apparatus in a pretty manner.

A strip of thin metal is bent into an elliptical band and placed in the lantern trough. The band is so wide that the water in the trough is about halfway up it. At a point corresponding to one focus of the ellipse, drops of water are then allowed to fall on the water-surface and start a series of divergent ripples. When the stroboscopic disc is set in revolution and its speed properly adjusted, we see that the divergent ripples proceeding from one focus of the ellipse are all con-

## WATER WAVES AND WATER RIPPLES.

verged or concentrated to the other focus. In fact, the ripples seem to set out from one focus, and to be, as it were, swallowed up at the other. When, in a later chapter, we are discussing the production and reflection of sound waves in the air, you will be able to bring this statement to mind, and it will be clear to you that if, instead of dealing with waves on water, we were to create waves in air in the interior of a similar elliptically shaped room, the waves being created at one focus, they would all be collected at the other focus, and the tick of a watch or a whisper would be heard at the point corresponding to the other focus, though it might not be heard elsewhere in the room.

With the appliances here described many beautiful effects can be shown, illustrating the independence of different wave-trains and their interference. If we hurl two stones into a lake a little way apart, and thus create two sets of circular ripples (see Fig. 20), we shall notice that these two ripple-trains pass freely through each other, and each behave as if the other did not exist. A careful examination will, however,

FIG. 20.—Intersecting ripples produced on a lake by throwing in simultaneously two stones.

show that at some places the water-surface is not elevated or disturbed at all, and at others that the disturbance is increased.

If two sets of waves set out from different origins and arrive simultaneously at the same spot, then it is clear that if the crests or hollows of both waves reach that point at the same instant, the agitation of the water will be increased. If, however, the crest of a wave from one source reaches it at the same time as the hollow of another equal wave from the other origin, then it is not difficult to see that the two waves will obliterate each other. This mutual destruction of wave by wave is called interference, and it is a very important fact in connection with wave-motion. It is not too much to say that whenever we can prove the existence of interference, that alone is an almost crucial proof that we are dealing with wave-motion. The conditions under which interference can take place must be examined a little more closely. Let us suppose that two wave-trains, having equal velocity, equal wavelength, and equal amplitude or wave-height, are started from two points, A and B (see Fig. 21). Consider any point, P. What is the condition that the waves from the two sources shall destroy each other at that point? Obviously it is that the difference of the distances AP and BP shall be an odd number of half wavelengths. For if in the length AP there are 100 waves, and in the distance BP there are 100 waves, or 101½ or 103½, etc., waves, then the crest of a wave from A will reach P at the same time as the hollow of a wave from B, and there will be no wave at all at the point P. This is true for all such positions of P that the difference of its distances from A and B are constant.

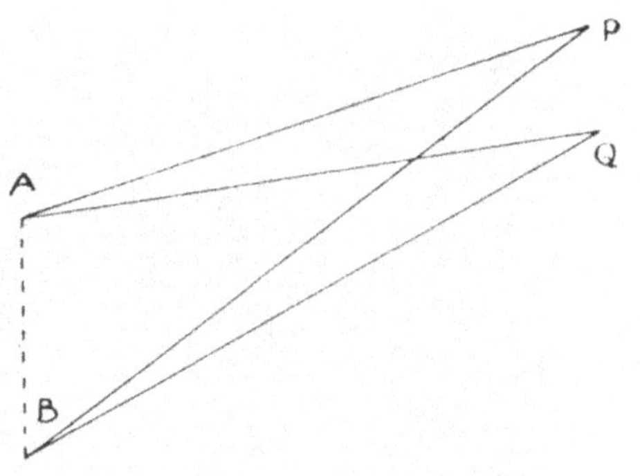

FIG. 21.

But again, we may choose a point, Q, such, that the difference of its distances from A and B is equal to an even number of half wave-lengths, so that whilst in the length AQ there are, say, 100 waves, in the distance BQ there are 101, 102, 103, etc., waves. When this is the case, the wave-effects will conspire or assist each other at Q, and the wave-height will be doubled. If, then, we have any two points, A and B, which are origins of equal waves, we can mark out curved lines such that the difference of the distances of all points on these lines from these origins is constant. These curves are called *hyperbolas* (see Fig. 22). All along each hyperbola the disturbance due. to the combined effect of the waves is either doubled or annulled when compared with that due to each wave-train separately.

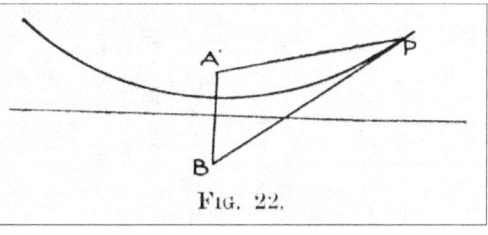

Fig. 22.

With the apparatus described, we can arrange to create and adjust two sets of similar water ripples from origins not far apart, and on looking at the complicated shadow-pattern due to the interference of the waves, we shall be able to trace out certain white lines along which the waves are annulled, these lines being hyperbolic curves (see Fig. 23). With the same appliances another characteristic of wave-motion, which is equally important, can be well shown.

We make one half of the circular tank in which the ripples are generated much more shallow than the other half, by placing in it a thick semicircular plate of glass. It has already been explained that the speed with which long waves travel in a canal increases with the depth of the water in the canal. The same is true, with certain restrictions, of ripples produced in a confined space or tank, one part of which is much shallower than the rest. If waves are made by dropping water on to the water-surface in the deeper part of the tank, they will travel more quickly in this deeper part than in the shallower portion.

Fig. 23.—Interfering ripples on a mercury surface, showing interference along hyperbolic lines (Vincent).

We can then adjust the water-dropping jet in such a position that it creates circular ripples which originate in deep water, but at certain places pass over a boundary into a region of shallower water (see Fig. 24). The left-hand side of the circular tank represented in the diagram is more shallow than the right-hand side.

When this is done, we notice two interesting facts, viz. that the wave-lines are bent, or *refracted*, where they pass over the boundary, and that the waves are shorter or nearer together in the shallower region. This bending, or refraction, of a wave-front in passing the boundary line between two districts in which the wave has different velocities is an exceedingly important characteristic of wave-motion, and we shall have brought before us the analogous facts in speaking of waves in air and waves in æther.

## WATER WAVES AND WATER RIPPLES.

It is necessary to explain a little more in detail how it comes to pass that the wave-line is thus bent. Imagine a row of soldiers, *marching over smooth grass, but going towards a very rough field*, the line of separation SS between the smooth and the rough field being oblique to the line of the soldiers (see Fig. 25). Fur-

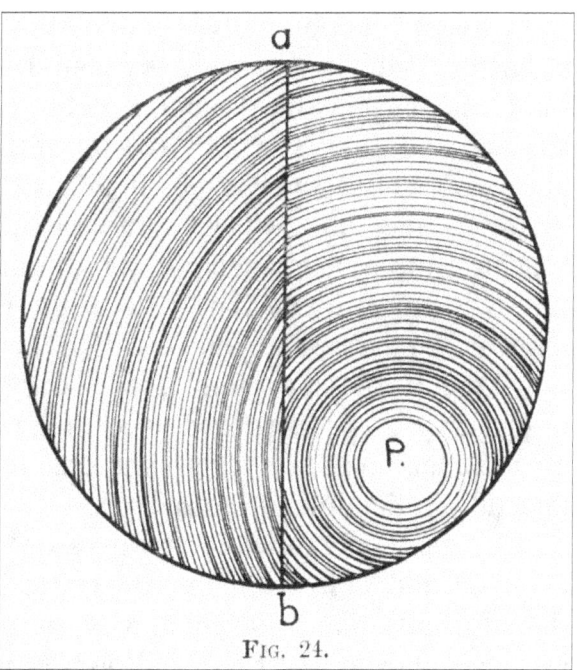

Fig. 24.

thermore, suppose the soldiers can march 4 miles an hour over the smooth grass, but only 3 miles an hour over the rough field. Then let the man on the extreme left of the line be the first to step over the boundary. Immediately he passes into a region where his speed of marching is diminished, but his comrade on the extreme right of the row is still going easily on smooth grass. It is accordingly clear that the direction of the line of soldiers will be swung round because, whilst the soldier on the extreme left marches, say, 300 feet, the one on the extreme right will have gone 400 feet forward; and hence by the time all the men have stepped over the boundary, the row of soldiers will no longer be going in the same direction as before it will have become bent, or refracted.

This same action takes place with waves.

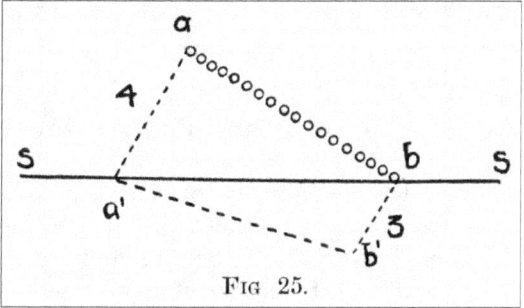

Fig. 25.

47

If a wave meets obliquely a boundary separating two regions, in one of which it moves slower than in the other, then, for the same reason that the direction of the row of soldiers in the above illustration is bent by reason of the retardation of velocity experienced by each man in turn as he steps over the dividing line, so the wave-line or wave-front is bent by passing from a place where it moves quickly to a place where it moves more slowly. The ratio of the velocities or speeds of the wave in the two regions is called the *index of refraction*.

We can, by arranging suitably curved reflecting surfaces or properly shaped shallow places in a tank of water, illustrate all the facts connected with the change in wave-fronts produced by reflection and refraction.

We can generate circular waves or ripples diverging from a point, and convert them, by reflection from a parabolic reflector, into plane waves; and again, by means of refraction at a curved or lens-shaped shallow, converge these waves to a focus.

Interesting experiments of this kind have been made by means of capillary ripples on a mercury surface by Mr. J. H. Vincent, and he has photographed the ripples so formed, and given examples of their reflection and refraction, which are well worth study.[12]

We do not need, however, elaborate apparatus to see these effects when we know what to look for.

A stone thrown into a lake will create a ripple or wave-train, which moves outwards at the rate of a few feet a second. If it should happen that the pond or lake has an immersed wall as part of its boundary, this may form an effective reflecting surface, and as each circular wave meets the wall it will be turned back upon itself as a reflected wave. At the edge of an absolutely calm sea, at low tide, the author

---

[12] "On the Photography of Ripples," by J. H. Vincent, *Philosophical Magazine*, vol. 43, 1897, p. 411, and also vol. 48, 1899. These photographs of ripples have been reproduced as lantern slides by Messrs. Newton and Co., of Fleet Street, London.

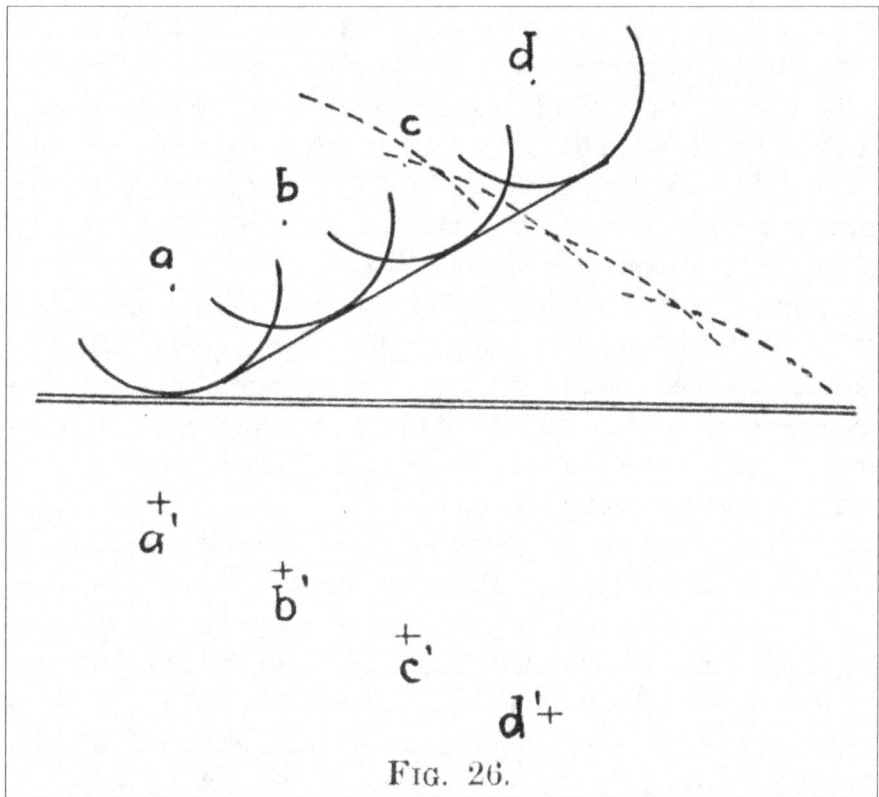

Fig. 26.

once observed little parallel plane waves advancing obliquely to the coast; the edge of the water was by chance just against a rather steep ledge of hard sand, and each wavelet, as it met this reflecting surface, was turned back and reflected at an angle of reflection equal to that of incidence.

It is well to notice that a *plane wave*, or one in which the wave front or line is a straight line, may be considered as made up out of a number of circular waves diverging from points arranged closely together along a straight line. Thus, if we suppose that $a$, $b$, $c$, $d$, etc. (see Fig. 26), are source-points, or origins, of independent sets of circular waves, represented by the firm semicircular lines, if they send out simultaneous waves equal in all directions, the effect will be nearly equivalent to a plane wave, represented by the straight thick black line, provided that the source-points are very numerous and close together.

Supposing, then, we have a boundary against which this plane wave impinges obliquely, it will be reflected and its subsequent course will be exactly as if it had proceeded from a series of closely adjacent source-points, *a*, *b*, *c*, *d*, etc., lying behind the boundary, each of which is the image of the corresponding real source-points, and lies as far behind the boundary as the real point lies in front of it.

An immediate consequence of this is that the plane reflected wave-front makes the same angle with the plane reflecting surface as does the incident or arriving wave, and we thus establish the law, so familiar in optics, that the angle of incidence is equal to the angle of reflection when a plane wave meets a plane reflecting surface.

At the sea- side, when the tide is low and the sea calm or ruffled only by wavelets due to a slight wind, one may often notice trains of small waves, which are reflected at sharp edges of sand, or refracted on passing into sudden shallows, or interfering after passing round the two sides of a rock. A careful observer can in this school of Nature instruct himself in all the laws of wave-motion, and gather a fund of knowledge on this subject during an hour's dalliance at low tide on some sandy coast, or in the quiet study of sea- side pools, the surface of which is corrugated with trains of ripples by the breeze.

# CHAPTER II.

# WAVES AND RIPPLES MADE BY SHIPS.

IT is impossible for the most careless spectator to look at a steam-vessel making her way along a lake, a boy's boat skimming across a pond, or even a duck paddling on a stream, without noticing that the moving body is accompanied in all cases by a trail of waves or ripples, which diverge from it and extend behind. In the case of a steamer there is an additional irregular wave-motion of the water caused by the paddle-wheels or screw, which churn it up, and leave a line of rough water in the steamer's wake. This, however, is not included in the true ship-wave effect now to be discussed. We can best observe the proper ship-wave disturbance of the water in the case of a yacht running freely before the wind when the sea is fairly smooth. The study of these ship-waves has led to most important and practical improvements in the art of ship-designing and shipbuilding, and no treatment of the subject of waves and ripples on water would be complete in which all mention of ship-waves was omitted.

In order that we may explain the manner in which these waves are formed, and their effect upon the motion of the ship, and the power required to move it forward, we must begin by a little discussion of some fundamental facts concerning liquids in motion.

Every one is aware that certain liquids are, as we say *sticky*, or, to use the scientific term, *viscous*. A request to mention sticky liquids would call up the names of such fluids as tar, treacle, gum-water, glycerine, and honey. Very few people would think of including pure water, far less spirits of wine, in a list of sticky, or viscous liquids; and yet it is quite easy to show by experiment that even these fluids possess some degree of stickiness, or viscosity. An illustration may be afforded as follows: We provide several very large glass tubes, nearly filled respectively with quicksilver, water, alcohol, glycerine, and oil. A small space is left in each tube containing a little air, and the tubes are closed by corks. If we suddenly turn all the tubes upside down, these bubbles of air begin to climb up from the bottom of the tube to the top. We notice that in the quicksilver tube it arrives at the top in a second or two, in the water tube it takes a little longer, in the oil tube longer still, and in the tube filled with glycerine it is quite a minute or more before the bubble of air has completed its journey up the tube. This experiment, properly interpreted, shows us that water possesses in some degree the quality of viscosity. It can, however, be more forcibly proved by another experiment.

To a whirling-table is fixed a glass vessel half full of water. On this water a round disc of wood, to which is attached a long wire carrying a paper flag, is made to float. If we set the basin of water slowly in rotation, at first the paper flag does not move. The basin rotates without setting the contained water in rotation, and so to speak slips round it. Presently, however, the flag begins to turn slowly, and this shows us that the water has been gradually set in rotation. This happens because the water sticks slightly to the inner surface of the basin, and the layers of water likewise stick to one another. Hence, as the glass vessel slides round the water it gradually forces the outer layer of water to move with it, and this again the inner layers of water one by one, until at last the floating block of wood partakes of the motion, and the basin and its contents turn round as one mass. This effect could not take place unless the water possessed some degree of viscosity, and also unless so-called *skin friction* existed between the inside of a glass vessel and the water it contains.

We may say, however, at once that no real liquid with which we are acquainted is entirely destitute of stickiness, or viscosity. We can nevertheless imagine a liquid absolutely free from any trace of this property, and this hypothetical substance is called a *perfect fluid*.

It is clear that this ideal perfect liquid must necessarily differ in several important respects from any real fluid, such as water, and some of these differences we proceed to examine. We must point out that in any liquid there may be two kinds of motion, one called *irrotational* motion, and the other called *rotational* or *vortex* motion.

Consider any mass of water, such as a river, in motion in any way; we may in imagination fix our attention upon some small portion of it, which at any instant we will consider to be of a spherical shape. If, as this sphere of liquid moves along embedded in the rest of the liquid, it is turning round an axis in any direction as well as being distorted in shape, the motion of that part of the fluid is called *rotational*. If, however, our little sphere of liquid is merely being stretched or pulled into an ovoid or ellipsoidal shape without any rotation or spinning motion, then the motion of the liquid is said to be *irrotational*. We might compare these small portions of the liquid to a crowd of people moving along a street. If each person moves in such a way as always to keep his face in the same direction, that movement would be an irrotational movement. If, however, they were to move like couples dancing in a ball-room, not only moving along but turning round, their motion would be called rotational. Examples of rotational, or vortex motion are seen whenever we empty a washbasin by pulling up the plug. We see the water swirl round, or rotate, forming what is called an *eddy*, or whirlpool. Also eddies are seen near the margin of a swiftly flowing river, since the water is set in rotation by friction against objects on the banks. Eddies are likewise created when two streams of water flow over each other with different speeds. A beautiful instance of this may be viewed at an interesting place a mile or two out of the city of Geneva. The Rhone, a rapid river, emerges as a clear blue stream from the Lake of Geneva. At a point called *Junction d'eaux* it meets the river Arve, a more sluggish and turbid glacier stream, and the two then run together in the same channel. The waters of the Rhone and Arve do not at once mix, but the line of separation is marked by a series of whirlpools or eddies set up by the flow of the rapid Rhone water against the slower Arve water in contact with it.

Again, it is impossible to move a solid body through a liquid without setting up eddy-motion. The movement of an oar through the water, or even of a teaspoon through tea, is seen to be accompanied by little whirls which detach themselves from the oar or spoon, and are really the ends of vortices set up in the liquid. The two facts to notice particularly are that the production of eddies in liquids always involves the expenditure of energy, or, in mechanical language, it necessitates *doing work*. To set in rotation a mass of any liquid requires the delivery to it of *energy*, just as is the case when a heavy wheel is made to rotate or a heavy train set in movement. This energy must be supplied by or absorbed from the moving solid or liquid which creates the eddies.

In the next place, we must note that eddies or vortices set up in an imperfect fluid, such as water, are ultimately destroyed by fluid friction. Their energy is frittered down into heat, and a mass of water in which eddies have been created by moving through it a paddle, is warmer after the eddies have subsided than before. It is obvious, from what has been said, that if a really perfect fluid did exist, it would be impossible by mechanical means to make eddies in it; but if they were created, they would continue for ever, and have something of the permanence of material substances.

A vortex motion in water may be either a terminated vortex, in which case its ends are on the surface, and are seen as eddies, or whirls; or it may be an endless vortex, in which case it is called a *vortex ring*. Such a ring is very easily made in the air as follows: A cubical wooden box about 18 inches in the side has a hole 6 inches in diameter made in the bottom (see Fig. 27). The open top of the box is covered tightly with elastic cloth. The box is then filled with the white vapour of ammonium chloride, by leading into it at the same time dry hydrochloric acid gas and dry ammonia gas. When quite full of dense white fumes, we give the cloth cover of the box a sharp blow with the fist, and from the round hole a white smoke ring leaps out and slides through the air. The experi-

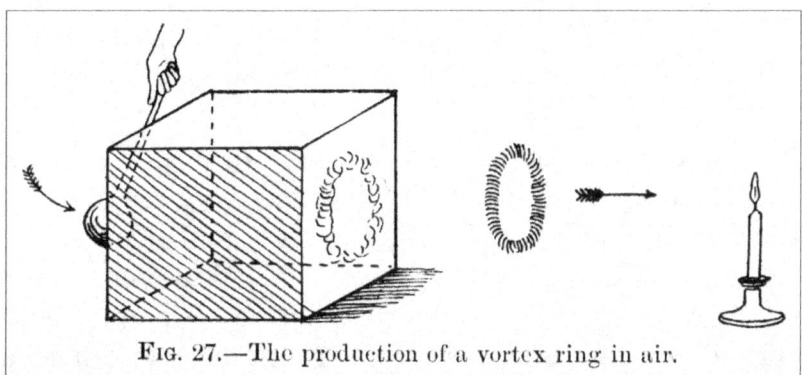

FIG. 27.—The production of a vortex ring in air.

ment may be made on a smaller scale by using a cardboard box and filling it with the smoke of brown paper or tobacco.[13] If we look closely at the smoke ring as it glides through the air, we shall see that the motion of the air or smoke particles composing the ring is like that of an indiarubber umbrella-ring fitted tightly on a round ruler and pushed along. The ring turns itself continually over and over, the rotation being

---

13 Sonic smokers can blow these smoke rings from their mouth, and they may sometimes be seen when a gun is fired with black old-fashioned gunpowder, or from engine-funnels.

round the circular ring axis line. This rotatory motion is set up by the friction of the smoky air against the edge of the hole in the box, as the puff of air emerges from it when the back of the box is thumped. A simple but striking experiment may be made without filling the box with smoke. Place a lighted candle at a few feet away from the opening of the above-described box, and strike the back. An invisible vortex ring of air is formed and blows out the candle as it passes over it. Although it is quite easy to make a rotational motion in an imperfect fluid, and in fact difficult not to do it, yet of late years a very interesting and valuable discovery has been made by Professor Hele-Shaw, of a method of creating and rendering visible a motion in an imperfect liquid like water, which is irrotational. This discovery was that, if water is made to flow in a thin sheet between two plates, say of flat glass, not more than a fiftieth of an inch or so apart, the motion of the water is exactly that of a perfect fluid, and is irrotational. No matter what objects may be placed in the path of the water, it then flows round them just as if all fluid friction or viscosity was absent.

This interesting fact can be shown by means of an apparatus designed by Professor Hele-Shaw.[14] Two glass plates are held in a frame, and separated by a very small distance. By means of an inlet-pipe water is caused to flow between the plates. A metal block pierced with small holes is attached to the end of one plate, and this serves to introduce several small jets of coloured water into the main sheet. In constructing the apparatus great care has to be exercised to make the holes in

---

14 For details and illustrations of these researches, the reader is referred to papers by Professor H. S. Hle-Shaw, entitled, "Investigation of the Nature of Surface-resistance of Water, and of Stream-line Motion under Experimental Conditions," Proceedings of the Institution of Naval Architects) July, 1897, and March, 1898. A convenient apparatus for exhibiting these experiments in lectures has been designed by Professor Hele-Shaw, and is manufactured by the Imperial Engineering Company, Pembroke Place, Liverpool.

the above-mentioned block very small (not more than $\frac{1}{100}$ inch in diameter) and placed exactly at the right slope.

The main water inlet-pipe is connected by a rubber tube with a cistern of water placed about 4 feet above the level of the apparatus. The frame and glass plates are held vertically in the field of an optical lantern so as to project an image of the plates upon the screen. The side inlet-pipe leading to the pierced metal block is connected to another reservoir of water, coloured purple with permanganate of potash (Condy's fluid), and the flow of both streams of water controlled by taps. The clear water is first allowed to flow down between the plates, so as to exclude all air-bubbles, and create a thin film of flowing water between two glass plates. The jets of coloured water are then introduced, and, after a little adjustment, we shall see that the coloured water flows down in narrow, parallel streams, not mixing with the clear water, and not showing any trace of eddies. The regularity of these streams of coloured water, and their sharp definition, shows that the liquid flow between the plates is altogether irrotational.

The lines marked out by the coloured water are called *stream-lines*, and they cut up the whole space into uniform *tubes of flow*. The characteristic of this flow of liquid is that the clear water in the space between two coloured streams of water never passes over into an adjacent tube. Hence we can divide up the whole sheet of liquid into tubular spaces called tubes of flow, by lines called stream-lines.

If now we dismount the apparatus and place between the glass a thin piece of indiarubber sheet—cut, say, into the shape of a ship, and of such thickness that it fills up the space between the glass plates—we shall be able to observe how the water flows round such an obstacle.

If the air is first driven out by the flow of the clear water, and then if the jets of coloured water are introduced, we see that the lines of liquid flow are delineated by coloured streams or narrow bands, and that these stream-lines bend round and enclose the obstructing object.

The space all round the ship-shaped solid body is thus cut up into tubes of flow by stream-lines, but these tubes of flow are now no longer straight, and no longer of equal width at all points.

They are narrower opposite the middle part of the obstruction than near either end.

At this point we must make a digression to explain a fundamental law concerning fluid flow in tubes. Suppose we have a uniform horizontal metal tube, through which water is flowing (see Fig. 28). At various points along the tube let vertical glass pipes be inserted to act as gauge or pressure-tubes. Then when the fluid flows along the horizontal pipe it will stand up a certain height in each pressure-tube, and this height will be a measure of the pressure in the horizontal pipe at the point where the pressure-tube is inserted. We shall notice that when the water flows in the horizontal pipe, the water in the gauge-pipes stands at different heights, indicating a fall in pressure along the horizontal pipe. We also notice that a line joining the tops of all the liquid columns in the pressure-pipes is a straight, sloping line, which is called the *hydraulic gradient*. This experiment proves to us that when fluid flows along a uniform-sectioned pipe there is a uniform fall or decrease in pressure along the pipe. The force which is driving the liquid

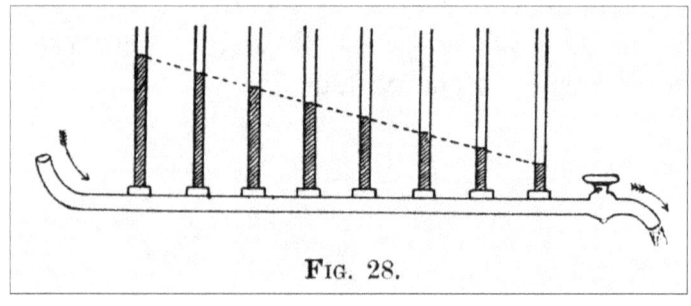

Fig. 28.

along the horizontal pipe is measured by the difference between the pressures at its extreme ends, and the same is true of any selected length of the horizontal pipe.

It will also be clear that, since water is not compressible to any but the very slightest extent, the quantity of water, reckoned, say in gallons, which passes per minute across any section of the pipe must be the same.

In the next place, suppose we cause water to flow through a tube which is narrower in some places than in others (see Fig. 29). It will be readily admitted that in this tube also the same quantity of water will flow across every section, wide or

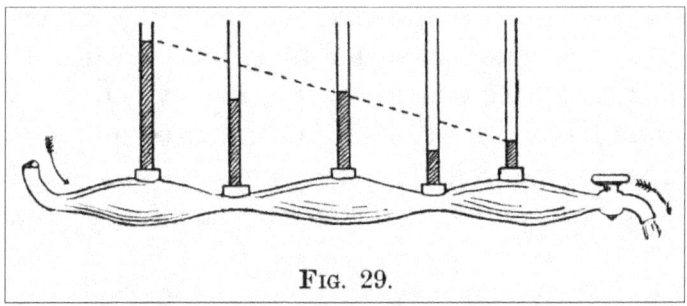

Fig. 29.

narrow, of the tube. If, however, we ask Where, in this case, will there be the greatest pressure? it is certain that most persons would reply In the narrow portions of the tube. They would think that the water-particles passing through the tube resemble a crowd of people passing along a street which is constricted in some places like the Strand. The crowd would be most tightly squeezed together, and the pressure of people would therefore be greater, in the narrow portions of the street. In the case of the water flowing through the tube of variable section this, however, is not the case. So far from the pressure being greatest in the narrow portions of the tube, it can be shown experimentally that it is precisely at those places it is least.

This can be demonstrated by the tube shown in Fig. 29. If water is allowed to flow through a tube constricted in some places, and provided with glass gauge-pipes at various points to indicate the pressure in the pipe at those places, it is found that the pressure, as indicated by the height of the water in the gauge-glasses at the narrow parts of the tube, is less than that which it would have at those places if the tube were of uniform section and length, and passed the same quantity of water. We can formulate this fact under a general law which controls fluid motion also in other cases, viz. that *where the velocity of the liquid is greatest, there the pressure is least*. It is evident, since the tube is wider in some places than in others, and as a practically incompressible liquid is being passed through it, that the speed of the liquid must be greater in the narrow portions of the tube than in the wider ones. But experiment shows that after allowing for what may be called the proper hydraulic gradient of the tube, the pressure is least in those places, viz. the constricted portions, where the velocity of the liquid is greatest. This general principle is of wide application in the science of hydraulics, and it serves to enable us to interpret aright many perplexing facts met with in physics.

We can, in the next place, gather together the various facts concerning fluid flow which have been explained above, and apply them to elucidate the problems raised by the passage through water of a ship or a fish. Let us consider, in the first place, a body totally submerged, such as a fish, a torpedo or a submarine boat, and discuss the question why a resistance is experienced when an attempt is made to drag or push such a body through water. The old-fashioned notion was that the water has to be pushed out of the way to make room for the fish to move forward, and also has to be sucked in to fill up the cavity left behind. Most persons who have not been instructed in the subject, perhaps even now have the idea that this so-called "head resistance" is the chief cause of the resistance experienced when we make a body of any shape move through water. A common assumption is also that the object of making a ship's bows sharp is that they may cut into the water like a wedge, and more easily push it out of the way.

Scientific investigation has, however, shown that both of these notions are erroneous. The resistance felt in pulling or pushing a boat through the water is not due to resistance offered by the water in virtue of its inertia. No part of this resistance arises from the exertion required to displace the water or push it out of the way.

The Schoolmen of the Middle Ages used to discuss the question how it was that a fish could move through the water. They said the fish could not move until the water got out of the way, and the water could not get out of the way until the fish moved. This and similar perplexities were not removed until the true theory of the motion of a solid through a liquid had been developed.

Briefly it may be said that there are three causes, and only three, for the resistance which we feel and have to overcome when we attempt to drag a boat or ship through the water. These are: First, *skin friction*, due to the friction between the ship-surface and the water; secondly, *eddy-resistance*, due to the energy lost or taken up in making water eddies; and thirdly, *wave-resistance*, due to energy taken up in making surface-waves. The skin friction and the eddy-resistance both arise from the fact that water is not a perfect fluid. The wave-resistance arises, as we shall show, from the unavoidable formation of waves by the motion of the boat through the water.

In the case of a wholly submerged body, like a fish, the only resistance it has to overcome is due to the first two causes. The fish, progressing through the water wholly under the surface, makes no waves, but the water adheres to its skin, and there is friction between them as he moves. Also he creates eddies in the water, which require energy to produce them, and whenever mechanical work has to be done, as energy drawn off from a moving body, this implies the existence of a resistance to its motion which has to be overcome.

Accordingly Nature, economical on all occasions in energy expenditure, has fashioned the fish so as to reduce the power it has to expend in moving through water as much as possible. The fish has a smooth slippery skin. (We say "as slippery as an eel.") It is not covered either with fur or feathers, but with shiny scales, so as to reduce to a minimum the skin friction. The fish also is regular and smooth in outline. It has no long ears, square shoulders, or projecting limbs or organs, which by giving it an irregular outline, would tend to produce eddies in the water as it moves along. Hence, when we wish to design a body to move quickly under the water, we must imitate in these respects the structure of a fish. Accordingly, a Whitehead torpedo, that deadly instrument employed in naval warfare, is made smooth and fish-shaped, and a submarine boat is made cigar-shaped and as smooth as possible, for the same reason.

If the floating object is partly above the surface, yet nevertheless, as far as concerns the portion submerged, there is skin friction, and the production of eddy-resistance. Hence, in the construction of a racing-yacht, the greatest care has to be taken to make its surface below water of polished metal or varnished wood, or other very smooth material, to diminish as far as possible the skin friction. In the case of bodies as regular in outline as a ship or fish, the proportion of the driving power taken up in making eddies in the water is not large, and we may, without sensible error, say that in their case the whole resistance to motion is comprised under the two heads of skin friction and wave-making resistance. The proportion which these two causes bear to each other will depend upon the nature of the surface of the body which moves over the water, and its shape and speed.

At this point we may pause to notice that, if we could obtain a perfect fluid in practice, it would be found that an object of any shape wholly submerged in the fluid could be moved about in any way without experiencing the least resistance. This theoretical deduction is, at first sight, so opposed to ordinary preconceived notions on the subject, that it deserves a little attention. It is difficult, as already remarked, for most people who have not carefully studied the subject, to rid their minds of the idea that there is a resistance to the motion of a solid through a liquid arising from the effort required to push the liquid out of the way. But this notion is, as already explained, entirely erroneous.

In the light of the stream-line theory of liquid motion, it is easy to prove, however, the truth of the above statement.

Let us begin by supposing that a solid body of regular and symmetrical shape, say of an oval form (see Fig. 30), is moved through a fluid destitute of all stickiness or viscosity, which therefore does not adhere to the solid.

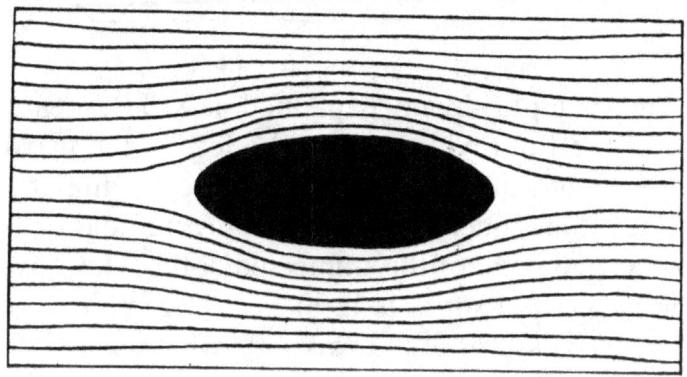

FIG. 30.—Stream-lines round an ovoid.

Then, if the solid is wholly submerged in this fluid, the mutual action of the liquid and the solid will be the same, whether we suppose the liquid to be at rest and the solid to move through it, or the solid body to be at rest and the liquid to flow past it.

If, then, we suppose the perfect fluid to flow round the obstacle, it will distribute itself in a certain manner, and its motion can be delineated by stream-lines. There will be no eddies or rotations, because the liquid is by assumption perfect. Consider now any two adjacent stream-lines (see Fig. 31). These define a tube of flow, represented by the shaded portion, which is narrower in the middle than at the ends. Hence the liquid, which we shall suppose also to be incompressible, must flow faster when going past the middle of the obstacle where the stream-tubes are narrow, than at the ends where the stream-tubes are wider.

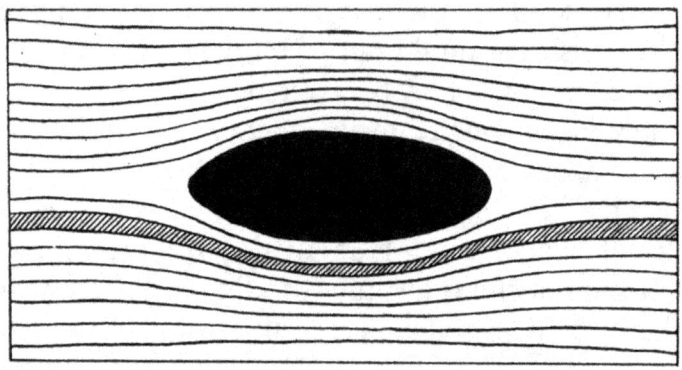

Fig. 31.—Tube of flow in a liquid.

By the principle already explained, it will be clear that the pressure of the fluid will therefore be less in the narrow portion of the stream-tube, and from the perfect symmetry of the stream-lines it is evident there will be greater and equal pressures at the two ends of the immersed solid. The flow of the liquid past the solid subjects it, in fact, to a number of equal and balanced pressures at the two ends which exactly equilibrate each other. It is not quite so easy to see at once that if the solid body is not symmetrical in shape the same thing is true, but it can be established by a strict line of reasoning. The result is to show that when a solid of *any* shape is immersed in a perfect liquid, it cannot be moved by the liquid flowing past it, and correspondingly would not require any force to move it against and through the liquid. In short, there is no resistance to the motion of a solid of any shape when pulled through a perfect or frictionless liquid. When dealing with real liquids not entirely free from viscosity, such resistance as does exist is due, as already mentioned, to skin friction and eddy formation. In the next place, leaving the consideration of the movement of wholly submerged bodies through liquids whether perfect or imperfect, we shall proceed to discuss the important question of the resistance offered by water to the motion through it of a floating object, such as a ship or swan. We have in this case to take into consideration the wave-making properties of the floating solid.

We have already pointed out that to make a wave on water requires an expenditure of energy or the performance of mechanical work. If a wave is made and travels away over water, it carries with it energy, and hence it can only be created if we have a store of energy to draw upon. If we suppose that skin friction is absent, and that the ship floats upon a perfect fluid, it would nevertheless be true that, if the moving object creates waves, it will thereby reduce its own movement and require the application of force to it to keep it going. We may say therefore that if any floating object creates waves on a liquid over which it moves, these waves rob the floating body of some of its energy of motion. The creation of the waves will bring it to rest in time, unless it is continually urged forward by some external and impressed force, and wave-generation is a reason for a part at least of the resistance we experience when we attempt to push it along.

Accordingly, one element in the problem of designing a ship is that of finding a form which will make as little wave-disturbance as possible in moving over the liquid. It is comparatively easy to find a shape for a floating solid which shall make a considerable wave-disturbance on the water when it is pulled over it, but it is not quite so easy to design a shape which will not make waves, or make but very small ones.

If we look carefully at a yacht gliding along before a fresh breeze on a sea or lake surface which is not much ruffled by other waves, it is possible to discover that a ship, when going through the water, creates *four distinct systems of waves*. Two of these are very easy to see, and two are more difficult to identify. These wave-systems are called respectively the oblique bow and stern waves, and the transverse and rear waves. We shall examine each system in turn.

The most important and easily observed of the four sets of waves is the oblique bow wave. It is most easily seen when a boy's boat skims over the surface of a pond, and readily observed whenever we see a duck paddling along on the water. Let any one look, for instance, at a duck swimming on a pond. He will see two trains of little waves or ripples, which are inclined at an angle to the direction of the duck's line of motion. Both trains are made up of a number of short waves, each of which extends beyond or overlaps its neighbour (see Fig. 32). Hence, from a common French word, these waves

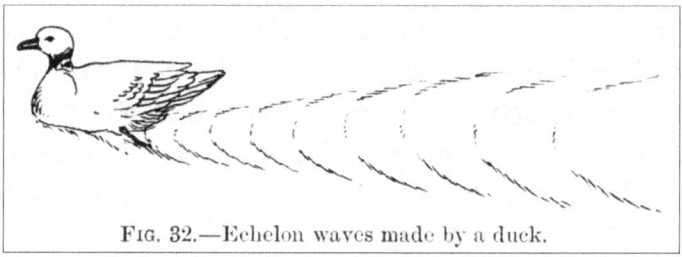

FIG. 32.—Echelon waves made by a duck.

have been called echelon waves[15] and we shall so speak of them. On looking at a boy's model yacht in motion on the water, the same system of waves will be seen; and on looking at any real yacht or steamer in motion on smooth water, they are quite easily identified (see Fig. 33).

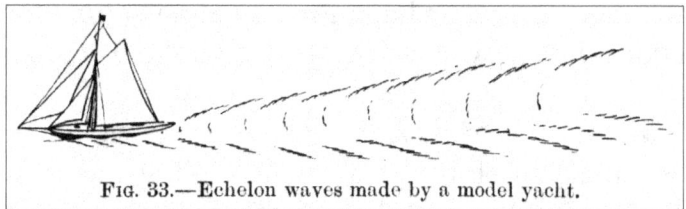

FIG. 33.—Echelon waves made by a model yacht.

The complete explanation of the formation of these bow or echelon waves is difficult to follow, but in a general way

---

15 The French word *échelon* means a step-ladder-like arrangement; but it is usually applied to an arrangement of rows of objects when each row extends a little beyond its neighbour. Soldiers are said to march in *echelon* when the ranks of men are so ordered.

## WAVES AND RIPPLES MADE BY SHIPS.

their formation can be thus explained: Suppose we have a flat piece of wood, which is held upright in water, and to which we give a sudden push. We shall notice that, in consequence of the inertia of the liquid, it starts a wave which travels away at a certain speed over the surface of the water. The sudden movement of the wood elevates the water just in front of it, and this displacement forms the crest of a wave which is then handed on or propagated along the surrounding water-surface. If two pieces of wood are fastened together obliquely, as in Fig. 34, and held in water partly submerged, we shall find that when this wood is suddenly thrust forward like a wedge, it starts two oblique waves which move off parallel to the inclined wooden sides. The bows of a ship, roughly speaking, form such a wedge.

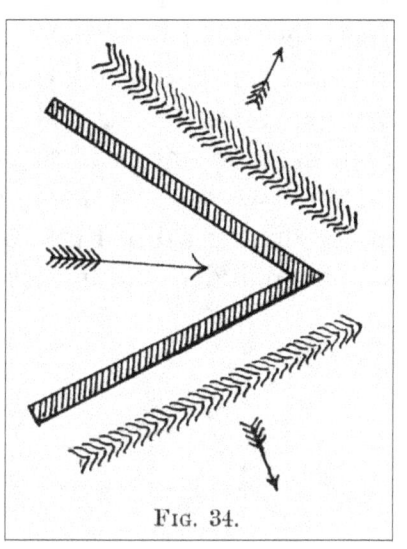

Fig. 34.

Hence, if we consider this wedge or the bows of a ship to be placed in still water and then pushed suddenly forward, they will start two inclined waves, which will move off parallel to themselves.

If we then consider the wedge to leap forward and repeat the process, two more inclined waves will be formed in front of the first; and again we may suppose the process repeated, and a third pair of waves formed. The different positions of the ship's bows are shown in the diagram at 1, 2, and 3 in Fig. 35; and c, e, and f are the three corresponding sets of echeloned waves. For the sake of simplicity, the waves are shown on one side only. If, then, we imagine the ship to move uniformly forwards, its bows are always producing new inclined waves, which move with it, and it is always, so to speak, leaving the old ones behind. All these echelon waves produced by the bow of the ship are included within two sloping lines which each make with the direction of the

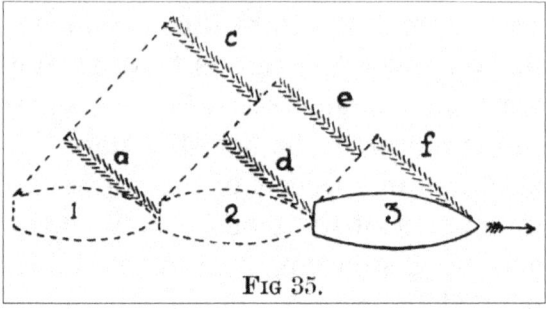

FIG 35.

ship's line of movement, an angle of 19°28'.[16] This angle can be thus set off: Draw a circle (see Fig. 36), and produce the diameter BC of this circle for a distance, CA, equal to its own length. From the end A of the produced diameter draw a pair of lines, AD, AD', called tangents, to touch the circle. Then each of these lines will make an angle of 19°28' with the diameter. If we suppose a ship to be placed at the point marked A in the diagram (see Fig. 36), all the echelon waves it makes will be included within these lines AD, AD'.

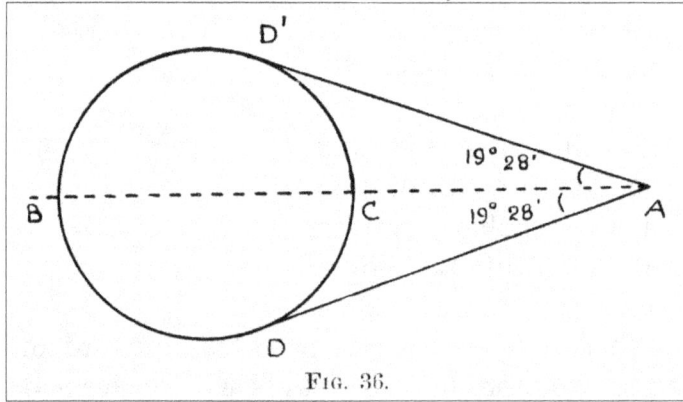

FIG. 36.

Moreover, the angle of the lines will not alter, whether the ship goes fast or slow. This is easily seen in the case of a duck swimming on a lake. Throw bits of bread to a duck so as to induce it to swim faster or slower, and notice the system of inclined or echelon ripples made by the duck's body as it swims. It will be seen that the angle at which the two lines,

---

16 See Lord Kelvin on "Ship Waves," Popular Lectures, vol. iii. p. 482.

including both the trains of echelon ripples meet each other is not altered as the duck changes its speed.

This echelon system of inclined waves is really only a part of a system of waves which is completed by a transverse group in the rear of the vessel. A drawing has been given by Lord Kelvin, in his lecture on "Ship Waves," of the complete system of these waves, part of which is as represented by the firm lines in Fig. 37. This complete system is difficult to see in the case of a real ship moving over the water. The inclined rear system of waves can sometimes be well seen from the deck of a lake steamer, such as those on the large Swiss or Italian lakes, and may sometimes be photographed in a snapshot taken of a boy's yacht skimming along on a pond.

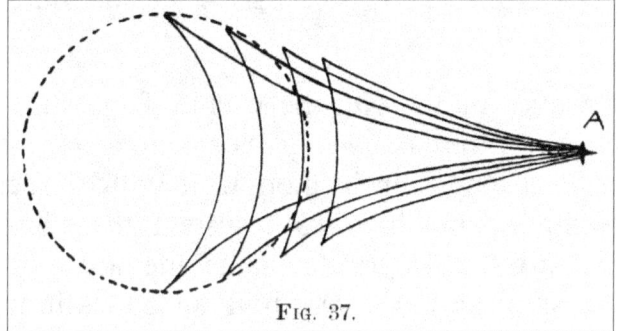

Fig. 37.

In addition to the inclined bow waves, there is a similar system produced by the stern of a vessel, which is, however, much more difficult to detect. The other two wave-systems produced by a ship are generally called the transverse waves. There is a system of waves whose crest-lines are at right angles to the ship, and they may be seen in profile against the side of any ship or yacht as it moves along. These transverse waves are really due to the unequal pressures resulting from the distribution of the stream-lines delineating the movement of the water past the ship.

If we return again to the consideration of the flow of a perfect fluid round an ovoid body, it will be remembered that it was shown that, in consequence of the fact that the stream-lines are wider apart near the bow and stern than they are opposite the middle part of the body, the pressure in the fluid was greater near the bow and stern than at the middle. When a body is not wholly submerged, but floats on the surface as does a ship, these excess pressures at the bow and stern reveal themselves by forcing up the water-surface opposite the ends of the vessel and lowering it opposite the middle. This may be seen on looking at any yacht in profile as it sails. The yacht appears to rest on two cross-waves, one at the bow and one at the stern, and midships the water is depressed (see Fig. 38).

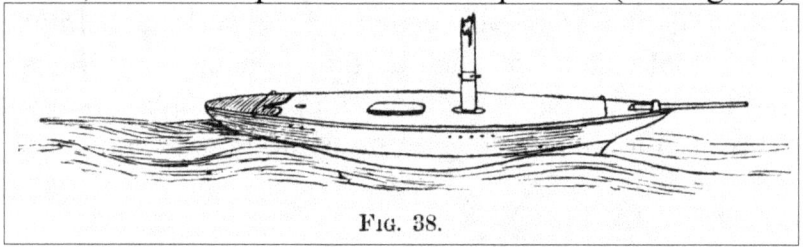

Fig. 38.

These waves move with the yacht. If the ship is a long one, then each of these waves gives rise to a wave-train; and on looking at a long ship in motion, it will be seen that, in addition to the inclined bow wave-system, there is a series of waves which are seen in profile against the hull.

When a ship goes at a very high speed, as in the case of torpedo-boat destroyers, the bow of the vessel is generally forced right up on to the top of the front transverse waves, and the boat moves along with its nose entirely out of water (see Fig. 39). In fact, the boat is, so to speak, always going uphill, with its bows resting on the side of a wave which advances with it, and its stern followed by another wave, whilst behind it is left a continually lengthening trail of

Fig. 39.

## WAVES AND RIPPLES MADE BY SHIPS.

waves, which are produced by those which move with the boat.

The best way to see all these different groups of ship-waves is to tow a rather large model ship without masts or sails in fact, a mere hulk over smooth water in a canal or lake. Let one person carry a rather long pole, to the end of which a string is tied; and by means of the string let the model ship be pulled through the water. Let this person run along the banks of the canal or lake, and tow the ship steadily through the water as far as possible at a constant speed. Let another person, provided with a hand camera, be rowed in a boat after the model, and keep a few yards behind. The second observer will be able to photograph the system of ship-waves made by the model, and secure various photographs when the model ship is towed at different rates. The echelon and transverse waves should then be clearly visible, and if the water is smooth and the light good, it is not difficult to secure many useful photographs.

By throwing bits of bread to ducks and swans disporting themselves on still water, they also may be induced to take active exercise in the right direction, and expose themselves and the waves or ripples that they make to the lens of a hand camera or pocket kodak. From a collection of snap-shot photographs of these objects the young investigator will learn much about the form of the waves made by ships, and will see that they are a necessary accompaniment of the movement of every floating object on water. By conducting experiments of the above kind under such conditions as will enable the exact speed of the model to be determined, and the resistance it experiences in moving through the water, information has been accumulated of the utmost value to ship-builders.

Our scientific knowledge of the laws of ship-resistance we owe chiefly to the labours of two great engineers, Mr. Scott Russell and Mr. William Froude. Mr. Froude's work was begun privately at Torquay about the year 1870, and was subsequently continued by him for the British Admiralty. Mr. Froude was the first to show the value and utility of experiments made with model ships dragged through the water. He constructed at Torquay an experiment tank about 200 feet in length, which was a sort of covered swimming-bath, and he employed for his experiments model ships made of wood or paraffin wax, the latter being chosen because the model could be so easily cut to the desired shape, and all the chips and the model itself could be melted up and used over again for subsequent experiments. Without detailing in historic order his discoveries, suffice it to say that, as the outcome of his work, Mr. Froude was able to state two very important laws which relate to the relative resistance experienced when two models of different sizes are dragged through the water at different speeds.

The first of these relates to what is called the "*corresponding speeds.*" Suppose we have a real ship 250 feet long, and we make an exact model of this ship 10 feet long, then the ship is twenty-five times longer than the model. Mr. Froude's law of corresponding speeds is as follows:—

If the above model and the ship are both made to move over still water, the ship going five times as fast as the model, the system of waves made by the model will exactly reproduce on a smaller scale the system of waves made by the ship. In other words, if we were to take a couple of photographs, one of the ship going at 20 miles an hour, and one of the model one twenty-fifth of its size going at 4 miles an hour, and reduce the two photographs to the same size, they would be exactly alike in every detail.

Expressed in more precise language, the first law of Froude is as follows: When a ship and a model of it move through smooth water at such speeds that the speed of the ship is to the speed of the model as the square root of the length of the ship is to the square root of the length of the model, then these speeds are called "*corresponding speeds.*"

At corresponding speeds the wave-making power of the model resembles that of the ship on a reduced scale. If we call L and l the lengths of the ship and the model, and S and s the speeds of the ship and the model, then we have

$$\frac{S}{s} = \sqrt{\frac{L}{l}}$$

where S and s are called corresponding speeds.

Mr. Froude then established a second law of equal importance, relating to that part of the whole resistance due to wave-making experienced by a ship and a model, or by two models when moving at corresponding speeds.

Mr. Froude's second law is as follows: If a ship and a model are moving at "corresponding speeds," then the resistances to motion due to wave-making are proportional to the cube of their lengths. To employ the example given above, let the ship be 250 feet long and the model 10 feet long, then, as we have seen, the corresponding speeds are as 5 to 1, since the lengths are as 25 to 1. If, therefore, the ship is made to move at 20 miles an hour, and the model at 4 miles an hour, the resistance experienced by the ship due to wave-making is to that experienced by the model as the cube of 25 is to the cube of 1, or in ratio of 15,625 to 1. In symbols the second law may be expressed thus: Let R be the resistance due to wave-making experienced by the ship, and r that of the model when moving at corresponding speeds, and let L and l be their lengths as before; then

$$\frac{R}{r} = \frac{L^3}{l^3}.$$

Before these laws could be applied in the design of real ships, it was necessary to make experiments to ascertain the skin friction of different kinds of surfaces when moving through water at various speeds.

Mr. Froude's experiments on this point were very extensive. For example, he showed that the skin friction of a clean copper surface such as forms the sheathing of a ship may be taken to be about one quarter of a pound per square foot of wetted surface when moving at 600 feet a minute. This is equivalent to saying that a surface of 4 square feet of copper moved through water at the rate of 10 feet a second experiences a resisting force equal to the weight of 1 lb. due entirely to skin friction. Very roughly speaking, this skin resistance increases as the square of the speed.[17] Thus at 20 feet per second the skin friction of a surface of 4 square feet of copper would be 4 lbs., and at 30 feet per second it would be 9 lbs. Any roughness of the copper surface, however, greatly increases the skin friction, and in the case of a ship the accumulation of barnacles on the copper sheathing has an immense effect in lowering the speed of the vessel by increasing the skin friction. Hence the necessity for periodically cleaning the ship's bottom by scraping off these clinging growths of seaweed and barnacles.

Mr. Froude also made many experiments on surfaces of paraffin wax, because of this material his ship models were made. It may suffice to say that the skin friction in this case, in fresh water, is such that a surface of 6 square feet of paraffin wax, moving at a speed of 400 feet per minute, would experience resistance equal to the weight of 1 lb. There are, however, certain corrections which have to be applied in practice to these rules, depending upon the length of the immersed surface. The mean speed of the water past the model or ship-surface depends on the form of the stream-lines next to it, and it has already been shown that the velocity of the water next to the ship is not the same at all points of the ship-surface. It is greater near the centre than at the ends. Hence the longer the model, the less is the mean resistance per square foot of wetted surface due to skin friction when the model is moved at some constant speed through the water.

---

17 More accurately, as the 1.83 power of the speed.

The above explanations will, however, be sufficient to enable the reader to understand in a general way the problem to be solved in designing a ship, especially one intended to be moved by steam-power.

If a shipbuilder accepts a contract to build a steamer say a passenger-steamer for cross-Channel services he is put under obligation to provide a ship capable of travelling at a stated speed. Thus, for instance, he may undertake to guarantee that the steamer shall be able to do 20 knots in smooth water. In order to fulfil this contract he must be able to ascertain beforehand what engine-power to provide. For, if the engine-power is insufficient, he may fail to carry out his contract, and the ship may be returned on his hands. Or if he goes to the opposite extreme and supplies too large a margin of power, he may lose money on the job, or else he may again violate his contract by providing an engine and boiler too extravagant in fuel.

It is in solving the above kind of practical problem that Mr. Froude's methods of experimenting with models in a tank are of such immense value. The first thing that the naval architect does in designing a ship is to prepare a series of drawings, showing the form of the hull of the vessel. From these drawings a model is constructed exactly to scale. In England, following Mr. Froude's practice, these models are usually made of paraffin wax, about 12 or 14 feet long and 1 inch in thickness. In the United States wood is used. These models are constructed with elaborate care and by the aid of special machinery, and are generally 10 or 12 feet in length, and some proper fraction of the length of the real vessel they represent. The models are then placed in a tank and experiments are made, the object of which is to ascertain the force or "pull" required to drag the model through the water at various speeds.

The tank belonging to the British Admiralty is at Haslar, Gosport, near Portsmouth, and the experiments are now conducted there by Mr. E. Edmund Froude, who continues the scientific work and investigations of his distinguished father, Mr. William Froude. This Admiralty tank at Haslar is 400 feet in length. The well-known firm of shipbuilders, Messrs. Denny Bros., of Dumbarton, Scotland, have also a private experimental tank of the same kind. The Government of the United States of America have a similar tank at Washington, the Italian Government have one at Spezzia, and the Russian Admiralty has also made one. These tanks resemble large swimming-baths, which are roofed over (see Fig. 40).

Fig. 40.—An experimental tank for testing ship models (Washington).*

[18]Over the water-surface is arranged a pair of rails, on which runs a light carriage or platform. This carriage is drawn along by a rope attached to a steam-engine, which moves at a very uniform rate, and its speed can be exactly ascertained

---

18 Figure 40 is taken by permission from an article by Mr. E. W. Dana, which appeared in *Nature* for June 5, 1902, the diagram being borrowed from a paper by Naval Const. D. W. Taylor, U.S., read before the (U.S.) Society of Naval Architects and Marine Engineers (1900).

## WAVES AND RIPPLES MADE BY SHIPS.

and automatically recorded. This moving carriage has a rod or lever depending from it, to which the model ship is attached. The pull on this rod is exactly registered on a moving strip of paper by very delicate recording mechanism. The experiment is conducted by placing the model at one end of the tank, and taking a run at known and constant speed to the other end. The experimentalist is thus able to discover the total resistance which it is necessary to overcome in pushing the model ship at a certain known speed through the water. The immersed surface of the model being measured and the necessary calculations made, he can then deduct from the total resistance the resistance due to skin friction, and the residue gives the resistance due to wave-making. Suppose, then, that the experiment has been performed with a model of a ship yet to be built, the run being taken at a "corresponding speed." The observations will give the wave-making resistance of the model, and from Mr. Froude's second law the wave-making resistance of the real ship is predicted. Adding to this the calculated skin-friction resistance of the real ship, we have the predetermined actual total ship-resistance at the stated speed. For the sake of giving precision to these ideas, it may be well to give an outline of the calculations for a real ship, as given in a pamphlet by Mr. Archibald Denny.[19]

The tank at the Leven shipyard, constructed by Messrs. Denny Bros. for their own experiments, is 300 feet long, 22 feet wide, and 10 feet deep, and contains 1500 tons of fresh water. At each end are two shallower parts which serve as docks for ballasting and trimming models. As an example of the use of the tank in predicting the power required to drive a ship of certain design through the water, Mr. A. Denny gives the following figures:

---

[19] "Practical Applications of Model Experiments to Merchant Ship Design," by Mr. Archibald Denny, Engineering Conference, Institution of Civil Engineers, May 25, 1897.

## WAVES AND RIPPLES

The ship to be built was 240 feet in length, and from the drawings a model was constructed 12 feet in length, or one-twentieth the size.

It was then required to predetermine the power required to drive the ship through the water at a speed of 13½ knots. A knot, be it remarked, is a speed or velocity of 1 nautical mile an hour, or 6080 feet per hour. It will be seen that this is not far from 100 feet per minute.

By Froude's first law, the corresponding speed for the 12-foot model is therefore—

$$13\tfrac{1}{2} \times \tfrac{6080}{60} \times \sqrt{\tfrac{12}{240}} = 306 \text{ feet per minute}$$

The model was accordingly dragged through the tank at a speed of nearly 5 feet per second, and, after deducting from the total observed pull the resistance due to the calculated skin friction of the model, it was found that the resistance to the motion of the model at this speed due to wave-making was 1.08 lb. Hence, by Froude's second law, the wave-making resistance of the ship was predetermined to be

$$13\tfrac{1}{2} \times 1.08 \times \left(\tfrac{240}{12}\right)^3 \times \tfrac{40}{39} = 8850 \text{ lbs.}$$

The last fraction $\tfrac{40}{39}$ is a correcting factor in passing from fresh water to salt water.

The surface of the proposed ship was 10,280 square feet, and the skin friction was known to be 1.01 lbs. per square foot at a speed of 13.5 knots. Hence the total skin resistance of the ship would be

$$10,280 \times 1.01 \times \tfrac{40}{39} = 10,620 \text{ lbs.}$$

Adding to this, the 8850 lbs. for wave-making resistance, we have a total resistance of 19,470 lbs. predetermined as the total pressure required to be overcome in moving the ship at a speed of 13.5 knots. Hence, since 1 horse-power is defined to be a power which overcomes a resistance of 33,000 lbs. moved 1 foot per minute, it is easy to see that 19,470 lbs. overcome at a rate of 13.5 knots represents a power of

## WAVES AND RIPPLES MADE BY SHIPS.

$$\frac{19,470 \times 13.5 \times 6080}{33,000 \times 60} = 810 \text{ horse-power}$$ but now, in the case of a screw-driven steamer, a part of the power is lost in merely churning up the water, and a part in internal frictional losses in the engine and screw-shaft.

It is not far from the truth to say that 50 per cent, of the applied engine-power is lost in useless water-churning. Hence, for the above steamer, an actual power of at least 1600 H.P. would have to be applied to the screw-shaft. To allow, however, for the loss of power in friction, and to allow a margin for emergencies, it would be usual to provide for such a steamer engines of at least 3000 *indicated* horse-power.

Each shipbuilder has, however, at call a mass of data which enable him, from actual measured mile trials, to determine the rates between the calculated driving horse-power and the indicated horse-power of the engines, and so enable him, in the light of experience, to provide in any new ship the exact amount of steam-power necessary to produce the required speed. As an instance of how accurately this can be done by the aid of the tank experiments, Mr. A. Denny gives an example drawn from experience in building the well-known paddle-steamers *Princess Josephine* and *Princess Henriette* for the Belgian Government Dover to Ostend fast mail-steamer service. The speed guaranteed before the boats were built was 20½ knots. The estimate was made for 21 knots, and the actual results of trials on the measured mile, when the ships were built, showed that each did 21.1 knots on prolonged and severe test.

The reader, therefore, cannot fail to see how important are these methods, laws, and researches of Mr. Froude.

The above-described process for testing models is being continually conducted in the case of all new battleships and cruisers for the British Navy, and also is pursued by the naval constructors of other nations. In connection with the extensive programme of battleship construction which has been carried out of late years, Sir William White, the late eminent Chief Director of Naval Construction, states that it is not too much to say that these methods of investigation and experiment have placed in the hands of the naval architect an instrument of immense power for guiding him safely and preventing costly mistakes. Sir William White has declared that it would have been impossible to proceed with the same certainty in battleship design, were it not for the aid afforded by these methods.

Mr. Froude was not content, however, with experiments made with models. He ascertained by actual trials the total force required to drive an actual ship through the water at various speeds, and obtained from other experiments valuable data which showed the proportion in which the total resistance offered to the ship was divided between the skin friction and the wave-making resistance.

Then he made experiments on a ship of 1157 tons, viz. H.M.S. *Greyhound*. This vessel was towed by another vessel of 3078 tons, viz. H.M.S. *Active*, by means of a tow-rope and a dynamometer, which enabled the exact "pull" on this hawser to be ascertained when the *Greyhound* was towed at certain speeds. The following are some of the results obtained:

| Speed in knots of H.M.S. Greyhound | Strain in tons on towing-rope. |
|---|---|
| 4 knots | 0.6 tons |
| 6 " | 1.4 tons |
| 8 " | 2.5 tons |
| 10 " | 4.7 tons |
| 12 " | 9.0 tons |

It will be seen that the total resistance increases very rapidly with the speed, varying in a higher ratio than the square of the speed.

In addition, the indicated horse-power of the engines of the *Greyhound* was taken when being self-driven at the above speeds, and it was found that only 45 per cent of the indicated horse-power of the engines was used in propelling the ship, the remaining 55 per cent, being wasted in engine and shaft friction and in useless churning of the water by the screw.

It is an important thing to know how this total resistance is divided between skin friction and wave-making resistance.

Mr. R. E. Froude has kindly furnished the author, through the intermediation of Sir William White, with some figures obtained from experiments at Haslar, showing the proportion of the whole ship-resistance which is due to skin friction for various classes of ships going at certain speeds.

|  | At full speed. | At 10 knots |
|---|---|---|
| Battleships | 55 per cent. | 79 per cent. |
| Cruisers | 55 " | 84 " |
| Torpedo-boat destroyers | 43 " | 80 " |

The above table gives the percentage which the skin friction forms of the total resistance, and the remainder is, of course, wave-making and eddy-resistance.

The curves shown in Fig. 41 (taken, by kind permission of the editor, from an article by Mr. E. H. Tennyson-D'Eyncourt, in *Cassier's Magazine* for November, 1901) give, in a diagrammatic form, an idea of the manner in which the two principal sources of ship-resistance vary with the speed.

It will be seen that when a ship is going at a relatively slow speed, the greater portion of the whole resistance is due to skin friction, but when going at a high speed, the greater portion of the resistance is due to wave-making. Hence the moral is that ships and boats intended to move at a high speed must be so fashioned as to reduce to a minimum the wave-making power. In general, the naval architect has to consider many other matters besides speed. In battleship design he has to consider stability, power of carrying guns and armour, and various other qualities. In passenger-steamers he has to take into consideration capacity for passengers and freight, also steadiness and sea-going qualities; and all these things limit and control the design. There is one class of vessel, however, in which everything is sacrificed to speed, and that is in

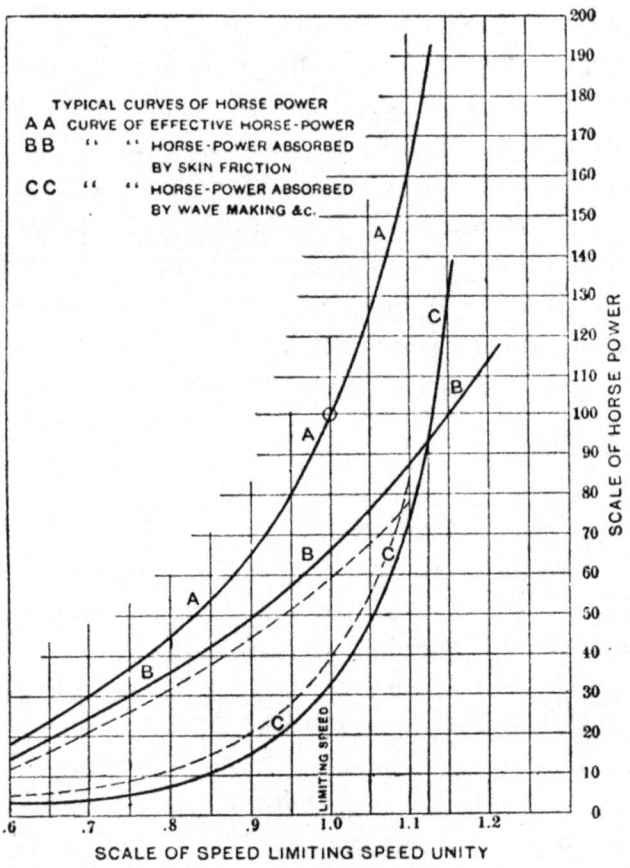

FIG. 41.—(Reproduced, by permission, from *Cassier's Magazine*.)

racing-yachts. Hence, in the design of a racing-yacht, the architect has most scope for considerations which bear chiefly upon the removal of all limitations to speed. A little examination, therefore, of the evolution of the modern racing-yacht shows how the principles we have endeavoured to explain have had full sway in determining the present form of such boats.

Attention has chiefly been directed to this matter in connection with the international yacht race for the possession of the America Cup.

In 1851 a yacht named the *America* crossed the Atlantic and made her appearance at Cowes to compete for a cup given by the Royal Yacht Squadron. Up to that time British yachts had been designed with full bluff bows and a tapering run aft. These boats were good sea-boats, but their wave and eddy making powers were considerable. The *America* was constructed with very fine lines and a sharp bow, and was a great advance on existing types of yacht. In the race which ensued the *America* won the cup, and carried it off to the United States.

Since that date there has been an intermittent but steady effort on the part of British yachtsmen to recover the trophy, so far, however, without success.

In a very interesting article in *Harmsworth's Magazine*, in 1901, Mr. E. Goodwin has traced the gradual evolution of the modern yacht, such as *Shamrock II.* or the *Columbia*, from the *America*.

No doubt the methods of "measurement" in force at the time, or the dimensions which determine whether the boat can enter for the Cup race or not, have had some influence in settling the shape. The reader, however, will see, on comparing the outlines of some of the competing yachts as shown in Fig. 42,[20] that there has been a gradual tendency to reduce the underwater surface as much as possible, and also to remove the wave-making tendency by overhanging the bows. The only rule now in force restricting the yacht size, for the Cup race is that it must not be more than 90 feet in length when measured on the water-line. In order that the yacht may have stability, and be able to carry a large sail-surface, it must have a certain depth of immersed hull. This is essential also to prevent the boat from making leeway when sailing with the wind abeam. But consistently with this object, the two great aims of the yacht-builder are, *first*, to reduce as much as possible the skin friction by making the yacht-surface smooth and highly polished. Thus modern racing-yachts are not always built of wood, but very often of some metal, such as bronze,

---

20 Reproduced here by the kind permission of the editor of *Harmsworth's Magazine*.

WAVES AND RIPPLES

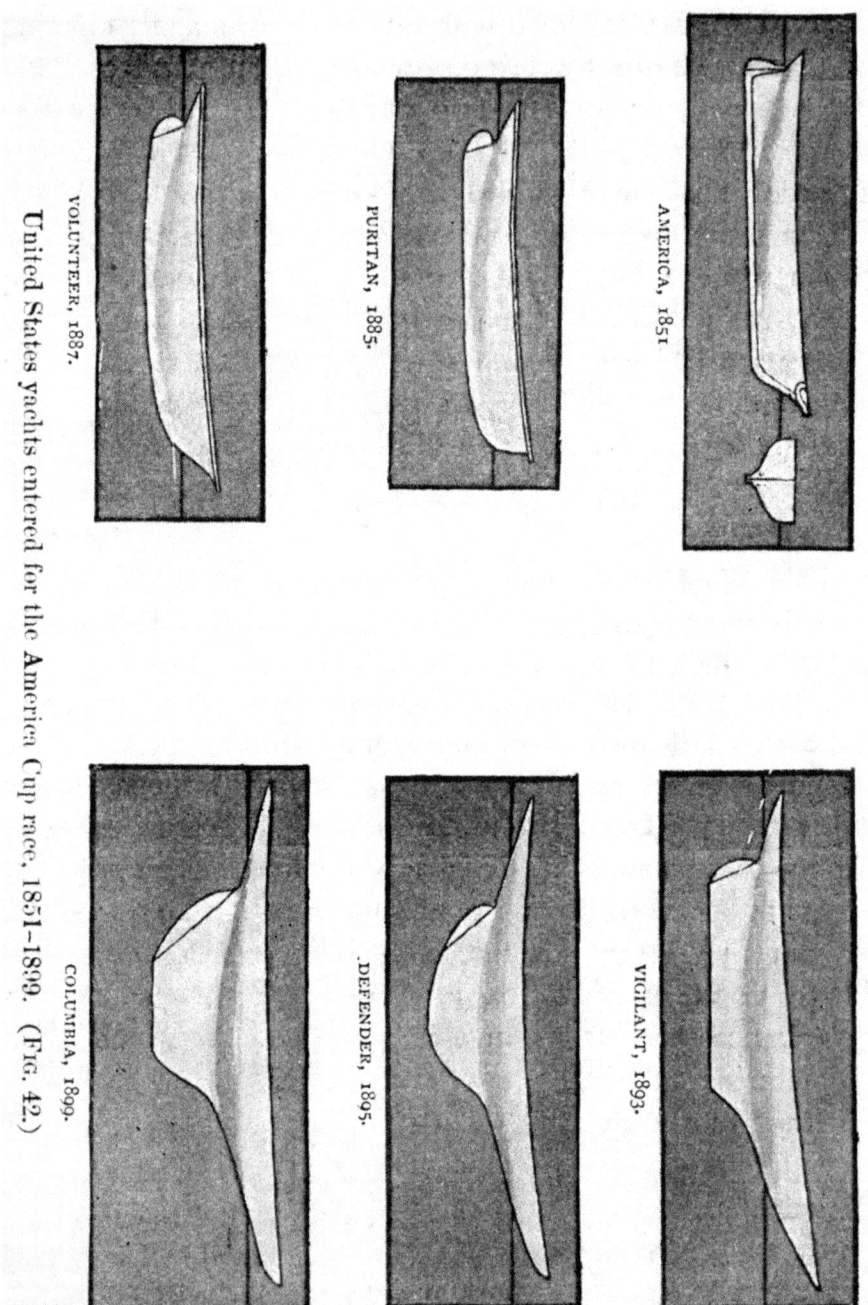

United States yachts entered for the America Cup race, 1851–1899. (Fig. 42.)

steel, or aluminium alloys, which admit of a very high polish. This hull-surface is burnished as much as possible before the

## WAVES AND RIPPLES MADE BY SHIPS.

race, to reduce to a minimum the skin friction. Then in the *second* place, the designer aims at fashioning the form of the bow of the yacht so as to reduce as much as possible its wave-making qualities. A fine type of modern yacht glides through the water with hardly any perceptible bow wave at moderate speeds.

Thus the following extract from the *Chicago Recorder* of September 4, 1901, respecting Sir Thomas Lipton's yacht, *Shamrock II.*, during her trials for the Cup race, shows how marked a feature this is in the case of a yacht of the best modern type:

"With her owner, designer, builder, manager, and sailmaker on board, the yacht Shamrock II. sailed her seventh trial race to-day off Sandy Hook. Although at times there was not more than a three-knot air, at no time did the yacht act sluggishly.

"She slipped through the water at an amazingly good rate under the influence of her great mainsail and light sails. The water was smooth, but even when pressed to a speed of 9 knots *the yacht made a very small wave at the bow*, and left an absolutely clean wake."

We may say, therefore, that the ideal form of yacht is one which would travel through the water without making any wave at all at bow or stern. This condition can, however, only be reached approximately, but the clear recognition of the principle has enabled yachts to be designed with vastly greater speed powers than in the old days of bluff bows and tapering bodies.

Before passing away from the subject of waves made by ships, it is desirable to refer a little more in detail to the complicated wave-system made by a ship in motion. This has been most carefully elucidated by Lord Kelvin, who, in this as in so many other matters, is our great teacher. Lord Kelvin has shown that if a small floating body is towed through the water at a uniform speed, it originates a system of waves, each one of which is of the form shown in Fig. 43. The whole system of waves formed is represented in Fig. 37, where the position of the ship or moving object is at the point marked A.

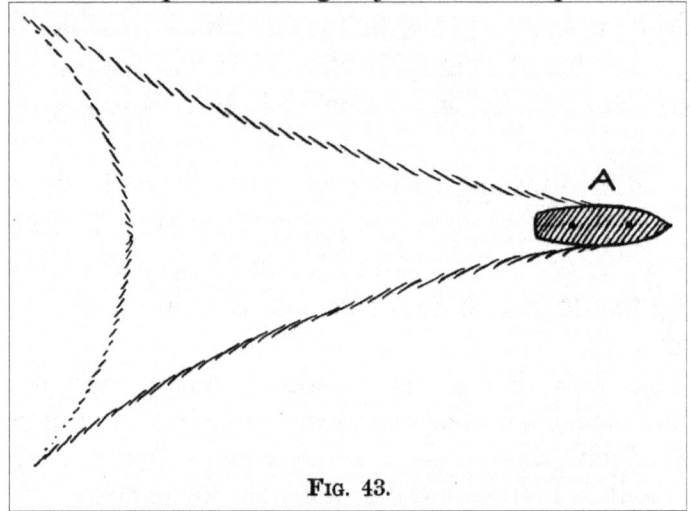

Fig. 43.

The key to a correct comprehension of this ship wave-system is to be found in the fact explained in Chapter I., that a group of water waves on an indefinitely extended water surface advances at half the speed of a single wave. It has already been shown that when a single wave-disturbance is made upon water it gradually develops itself into a group of waves. The single wave when created causes a disturbance on water which extends both forwards and backwards. As the wave moves forward the wave-disturbance is always growing in front and dying away behind, and the *wave-group* therefore moves forward, but the centre or limits of the group move with only half the velocity of a single wave.

Now consider the ship originally at B (see Fig. 36), and let us suppose the ship to make a small jerk forward. This operation is like plunging a stone into the water, and it starts a wave-system. But if the ship moves forward with a uniform speed, by the time the ship has reached the point A, the end of the wave-group will have reached a point C, such that C is halfway between B and A. The movement of the ship, however, originates a group of waves, and the velocity of a wave on water is dependent upon its wave-length, as already explained, so that the greater the wave-length the greater the velocity. Hence the conditions that determine the form of the wave-system round the ship are: (1) that the head of the procession goes forward with the speed of the ship; (2) that there is an end or limit to the transverse system of waves behind, which moves forward with half the speed of the ship; (3) the inclination of the wave at any point to the direction of motion of the ship must be such that its velocity, in its own direction, is consistent with the wave-length at that place. These general conditions determine the form of the wave-group as shown in Fig. 37; but the detailed predetermination of the exact form of the oblique arid rear wave cannot be made without the employment of mathematical reasoning of a somewhat advanced character.

For the purposes of the general reader it will be sufficient to note that this procession of ever-extending waves, which lengthens backwards behind a ship, requires energy to produce it. This energy must be supplied from the ship, and the wave-production constitutes therefore a cause of resistance to motion which is felt and has to be overcome in keeping the speed of the ship constant.

In close connection with this subject is the fine investigation made about the year 1834 by another eminent engineer, Mr. Scott Russell, on the motion of canal-boats. His researches were communicated to the Royal Society of Edinburgh. It has already been explained that when a wave is started in a canal, the wave-length being large compared with the depth of the canal, then the velocity of the long wave is the same as that attained by a stone in falling through air a distance equal to half the depth of the canal. Scott Russell made the interesting discovery that it is only when the speed of a canal-boat is *less* than that of a long wave in the canal that the boat leaves behind it a procession of waves. The position of the boat is then on the rearward side of the first wave. As already mentioned, the boat leaves behind it a trail of waves, and the rear of this procession travels forward at half the speed of the boat. If the speed of the boat is greater than that of the longest free wave in that canal, it cannot make any procession of waves, and then there would be no system of ever-lengthening waves behind it, but only one wave or hummock travelling along under the boat. Lord Kelvin describes, in his lecture on "Ship Waves,"[21] how this important discovery was in fact made by a horse. The horse belonged to one William Houston, and its daily duty was to drag a canal-boat on the Glasgow and Ardrossan Canal. On one occasion the horse took fright and galloped off, and Houston, being an observant man, noticed that when once the horse had attained a certain speed the tractive resistance evidently became lessened, and the boat was dragged along more easily and without wash behind it. Accordingly, he started a system of light canal-boats or fly -boats, as they were called each 60 feet long, and drawn by two horses at 7, 8, or 9 miles an hour. The horses were whipped up and made to gallop, and soon dragged the boat up on to the top of its own wave, whereupon it went along much more easily, and without a system of stern waves. Mr. Scott Russell instituted a searching investigation into this effect in 1837 at the bridge of Hermiston, on the Forth and Clyde Canal, at a place where there was a straight run of 1500 feet. The depth of the canal water was 4 to 5 feet, and the speed of the long wave was accordingly 12 feet per second, or 8 miles an hour.

SCOTT RUSSELL'S EXPERIMENTS ON CANAL-BOATS.

| Tractive force in pounds | Speed in miles per hour. |
|---|---|
| 112 | 6.19 |
| 261 | 7.57 |
| 275 | 8.52 |
| 250 | 9.04 |
| 269 | 10.48 |

---

[21] See Lord Kelvin's Popular Lectures, vol. iii., "Navigation," "Lecture on Ship Waves."

## WAVES AND RIPPLES MADE BY SHIPS.

Experiments were made, amongst others, with a boat called *Raith*, the weight of which was 10,239 lbs., or 5 tons. This boat was towed along the canal, and the "pull" on the tow-rope measured by means of an instrument called a dynamometer. It was found by Mr. Scott Russell that the pull or force required to drag the boat did not increase with the speed regularly, but fell off in a marked manner when the speed of the boat reached [†] miles per hour. This is shown by the following table:

For another boat weighing 12,579 lbs., or 6 tons, the results obtained in the same manner were as follows:

| Tractive force in pounds | Speed in miles per hour |
|---|---|
| 250 | 6.19 |
| 500 | 7.57 |
| 400 | 8.52 |
| 280 | 9.04 |

This last experiment shows, in a very remarkable manner, the way in which the force required to drag the boat falls off as the critical speed of 9 miles an hour is reached.

Here, then, we have the outlines of the proof first given by Mr. Scott Russell, that the tractive force undergoes a sudden diminution when the speed of the boat in a canal approximates to or just exceeds that of the long wave in that particular depth of water. If passenger traffic on canals had not been destroyed by the advent of railways, we should, no doubt, have seen extensive applications of the principle discovered so curiously by the aid of an alarmed horse, and so skilfully investigated by a celebrated engineer.

The whole theory of the trail of waves made by a canal-boat is only comprehensible if it is clearly seen that a water-surface wave has a certain velocity determined by its wave-length. If the wave-speed is small, the waves are short. As the speed increases the waves get longer. Or the matter may be put in another way. We may say that just as a pendulum has a

---

† Transcriber's note: No value for miles per hour was in the original.

certain rate of vibration depending on its length, so a water wave has a certain frequency, and therefore, a certain speed of propagation dependent upon the wave-length, or shortest distance from one wave-crest to the next. When a boat moves along a canal the waves it makes move with it, and the first wave of all moves with the speed of the boat. Hence the wave-length must accommodate itself to that speed. As the speed of the boat increases towards that of the free "long wave," the wave-length gets greater and greater, and when the boat-speed is equal to that acquired by a heavy body, say a stone in falling through half the depth of the canal, then there is only one wave, and the boat rides up on that one. The next wave is practically so far behind that it is non-existent, and the boat ceases to be followed by any trail of waves, or "wash."

# CHAPTER III.

# WAVES AND RIPPLES IN THE AIR.

LEAVING the consideration of waves and ripples on a water-surface, we pass on to discuss the subject of waves and ripples in the air. Nearly every one is aware, in a general way, that sound is due to a disturbance created in the atmosphere. Few, however, are fully acquainted with the nature of the movements in the air which excite our sense of hearing, and to which we owe, not only the pleasures of conversation and the enjoyment of all the sounds in nature, but those delights of music which are amongst the purest forms of pleasure we possess.

In the first place, it is necessary to demonstrate the fact that in a place where there is no air there can be no sound. Before you on the table is a brass plate covered with a glass dome. Under the dome is a piece of clockwork, which, when set in action, strikes a gong. This clockwork is suspended by silk strings from a frame to keep it out of contact with the plate. The plate is in connection, by a pipe, with an air-pump downstairs, and from the space under the dome we can at pleasure remove the air. Before so doing, however, the clockwork shall be set in motion, so that you will then see the hammer striking the gong, and you also hear the sound. If now we exhaust the air, the sound rapidly dies away, and when a fairly perfect vacuum has been made, whilst you see the hammer continuing to pound the bell, you notice that no sound at all reaches your ears. Turning a tap, I let in the air, and once more the ring of the bell peals forth. The experiment shows conclusively that sound is conveyed to us through the air, and that if we isolate a sounding body by removing the air around it, all transmission of sound is stopped. Even rarefying the air greatly weakens the sound, for it is noticed that an exploding pistol or cracker does not create the same intensity of sensation in the ear at the top of a very high mountain as it does in the valley below.

We have then to show, in the next place, that a substance which is emitting sound is in a rapid state of vibration, or to-and-fro movement. Taking a tuning-fork in my hand, I strike its prongs against the table, and you hear it faintly sounding. Your unassisted vision will not, however, enable you to see that the prongs are in rapid motion. If, however, I hold it against a pith-ball suspended by a silk fibre, you see by the violent bouncing of the ball that the prongs must be in energetic vibration.

Another experiment of the same kind, which you can yourselves repeat, is to elicit a sound from a small table-gong by striking it with the hammer. Then hold near the surface of the metal a small ball of wood or cork, to which a suspending thread has been tied. The ball will keep jumping from the gong-surface in a manner which will convince you that the latter is in a state of violent agitation. The mode and extent of this movement in a sound-emitting body must next be more thoroughly examined. Let me explain the means by which I shall make this analysis. On the prong of a tuning-fork, T (see Fig. 44), is fixed a small mirror, M, and a ray of light is reflected from an electric lantern on to this mirror. The ray is then reflected back again on to a sort of cubical box, C, the sides of which are covered with looking-glass, and finally it

## WAVES AND RIPPLES IN THE AIR.

falls upon the screen. The mirrors are so arranged that if the cubical mirror is at rest and the fork also, a bright spot of light is seen upon the screen. If the fork is set in vibration, then the spot of light moves up and down so rapidly that it forms a vertical bar or line of light upon the screen. The cubical mirror is carried upon an axis, and can be set in rotation. If the fork is at rest and the cubical mirror revolves, then the spot of light in arches horizontally across the screen, and when the motion of the mirror is sufficiently rapid it forms a horizontal and brilliant band of light. If, then, these two motions are performed at the same time, the tuning-fork being set in vibration and the cubical mirror in rotation, we find that the spot of light on the screen executes a wavy motion, and we see in consequence a sinuous bright line upon the wall.

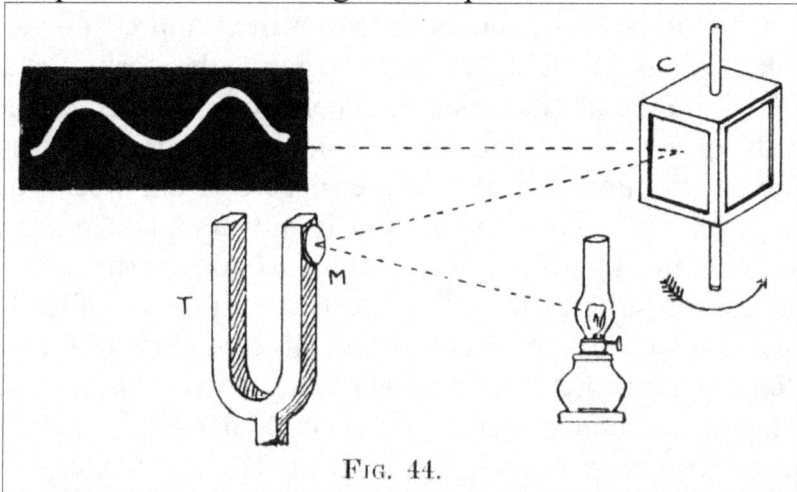

FIG. 44.

We have here two principles involved, which it may be better to explain a little more in detail. An impression made upon the eye lasts for about the tenth part of a second. Hence, if a luminous point or bright object moves sufficiently rapidly, we cease to be able to follow its movement, and we receive on our eyes merely the effect of a luminous line of light. Every boy sees this when he whirls round a lighted squib or stick with a flaming end. In the next place, notice that two independent movements at right angles combine into what is called a resultant motion. Thus the vertical up-and-down motion of the spot of light in our experiment, combined with its uniform horizontal movement, results in the production of a wavy motion. For the sake of those who wish to repeat the experiment, a few little hints may be given. The revolving cubical mirror is a somewhat expensive piece of apparatus, but found in every well-appointed physical laboratory. A cheap substitute, however, may be made by firmly sticking on to the sides of a wooden box pieces of thin looking-glass. The box is then to be suspended by a string. If the string is twisted, the box may be set spinning like a joint of meat roasting before the fire. An ordinary magic lantern may be used to provide a parallel beam of light. In lecture demonstrations it is necessary to employ the electric arc lamp, and to make use of an arrangement of lenses to create the required powerful parallel beam of light. Then as regards the fork. We are employing here a rather elaborate contrivance called an electrically driven tuning-fork, but for home demonstration it is sufficient to make use of a single piece of stout steel clock-spring, or any other flexible and highly tempered piece of steel. This must be fixed to a block of wood as a support, and to its end must be fastened with care a small piece of lead, to which is attached a fragment of thin silvered glass of the kind called a galvanometer mirror, which may be procured of any scientific instrument maker. The position of this vibrating spring must be such that, if the spring vibrates alone, it will reflect the ray of light on to one face of the cubical mirror, and thence on to a white wall, and create a vertical bar of light, which becomes a spot of light when the spring is at rest. It is possible to purchase very small concave mirrors about half an inch in diameter, made of glass silvered at the back. If one of these can be procured, then there is no need to employ an optical lantern; with an ordinary table-lamp, or even a candle as a source of light, it is easy to focus a bright spot of light upon the screen, which effects the desired purpose of making evident the motion of the spring.

Before we dismiss the experiment, let me say one or two more words about it. You notice when it is proceeding that the luminous wavy line is a regular and symmetrical one. This shows us that the motion of the prong of the fork is similarly regular. This kind of backwards-and-forwards motion is called an *harmonic motion*, or a *simple periodic motion*. It is very similar to the kind of movement executed by the piston of a steam-engine as it oscillates to and fro. The exact nature of the wavy line of light you see upon the screen can be delineated by a line drawn as follows: On a sheet of paper describe a circle, and divide its circumference into twelve equal parts (see Fig. 45). Through the centre and through each of these points on the circumference draw parallel lines. Divide up a length of the line drawn through the centre into twelve equal

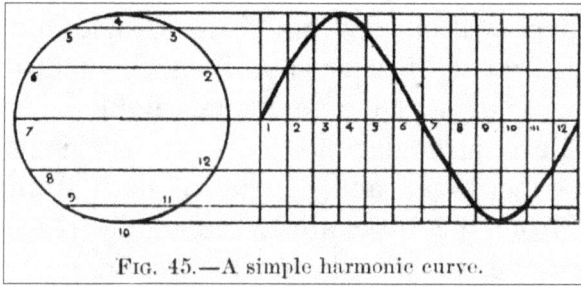

Fig. 45.—A simple harmonic curve.

parts, and number these divisions 1 to 12. Number also the points on the circumference of the circle. Through the twelve points on the horizontal line erect perpendiculars. Make a dot at the intersection of the perpendicular, or ordinate, as it is called, drawn through point 1 on the horizontal line, and the horizontal through point 1 on the circumference of the circle. Do this for all the twelve intersections, and then carefully draw a smooth curve through all these points. We obtain a wavy curve, which is called a *sine curve*, or *simple harmonic curve*, and is the same form of curve as that exhibited on the screen in the experiment with the tuning-fork and spot of light. The piece of the curve drawn as above is called *one wave-length* of the harmonic curve.

In our case the tuning-fork is making one hundred complete vibrations (to *and* fro) per second. Hence the periodic time, or time occupied by one complete wave, is the hundredth part of a second. To realize what this small interval of time means, it is sufficient to remember that the hundredth part of a second is to one second as the duration of this lecture (one hour) is to four days and nights.

The prongs of a sounding tuning-fork or the surface of a gong or a bell, when struck, are therefore in rapid motion. We can then proceed to an experiment fitted to indicate the difference between those motions in sounding bodies which create musical tones, and those which create mere noises or vocal sounds.

I have on the table before me a bent brass tube provided with a mouthpiece at one end, and the other end of the tube is covered over with a very thin piece of sheet indiarubber tied on like the cover of a jam-pot. To the outer surface of this indiarubber is cemented a very small, light silvered-glass mirror. The same arrangements are made as in the case of the previous experiment, and the ray of light from a lantern is reflected from the little mirror on to the revolving cubical mirror, and thence on to the screen. Setting the cubical mirror in rotation, we have a line of bright light upon the screen. If, then, my assistant sings or speaks into the mouthpiece, the motion of the indiarubber sets in vibration the little attached mirror. This mirror is not attached to the centre of the membrane, but a little to one side. Hence you can easily understand that when the indiarubber is bulged in or out, the attached mirror is more or less tilted, and the spot of light is displaced up or down on the screen. In this manner the movements of the spot imitate those of the diaphragm. Hence the form of the bright line on the screen is an indication of the kind of movement the diaphragm is making. Let us then, in the first place, sing into the tube whilst the cubical mirror is uniformly rotated. If my assistant sounds a full pure note, you will see that the straight line of light instantly casts itself into a wavy form, which is not, however, quite of the same shape as in the case of the tuning-fork. Here the zigzag line resembles the outline of saw-teeth (see Frontispiece).

If he varies the loudness of his sound, you see the height of the teeth alter, being greater the louder his note. If he changes the tone, singing a bass or a treble note, you observe that, corresponding to a high or treble note, the waves are short, and corresponding to a deep or bass note, the waves are long. Accordingly, the shape of the line of light upon the screen gives us exact information as to the nature of the movement of the indiarubber diaphragm, viz. whether it is moving in and out, slowly or quickly, much or little.

Again, suppose, instead of singing into the tube, my assistant speaks a few words. If, for instance, he repeats in a loud tone the simple but familiar narrative of "Old Mother Hubbard," you will see that, corresponding to each word of the sentence, the line of light upon the screen bends itself into a peculiar irregular form, and each particular word is as it were written in lines of fire upon the wall.

Notice how certain sounds, such as *b* and *p* and also *t* are represented by very high notches or teeth in this line of light. These sounds are called *explosive consonants*, and if you examine the manner in which they are made by your mouth, you will notice that it consists in closing the mouth by the lips or tongue placed between the teeth, and then suddenly withdrawing the obstruction so as to allow the air from the lungs to rush forcibly out. Hence the air outside, and in this case the diaphragm, receives a sudden blow, which is represented by this tall tooth or notch in the luminous band. The experiment teaches us that whereas *musical tones* are caused by certain very regular and uniform vibrations of the sounding body, *vocal sounds* and *noises* are caused by very irregular movements. Also that loud sounds are created by large motions, and feeble ones by small motions. Again, that the difference between tones in music is a difference in the rate of vibration of the sounding body. We may infer also that the difference between the quality of sounds is connected with the *form* of the wave-motion made by them.

Having established these facts, we must, in the next place, proceed to notice a little more 'closely the nature of an air wave. It will be necessary to remind you of certain qualities possessed not only by the air we breathe, but by all gases as well. Here is a cylinder with a closely fitting piston, and a tap at the bottom of the tube. If I close the tap and try to force down the piston, I feel some resistance, which increases as the piston is pushed forward. If the pressure is removed, the piston flies back to its old position, as if there were a spring underneath it. The air in the tube is an elastic substance, and it resists compression. At constant temperature the volume into which the air is squeezed is inversely as the pressure applied.

The air, therefore, possesses *elasticity of bulk*, as it is called, and it resists being made to occupy a smaller volume. Again, the air possesses *inertia*, and when it is set in motion it continues to move like any other heavy body, after the moving force is withdrawn. We have, therefore, present in it the two essential qualities for the production of a wave-motion, as explained in the first lecture. The air *resists* compression in virtue of elasticity, and when it is allowed to expand again back, it *persists* in motion in virtue of inertia.

Let us consider next the process of production of a very simple sound, such as an explosion. Suppose a small quantity of gun-cotton to be detonated. It causes a sound, and therefore an air wave. The process by which this wave is made is as follows: The explosion of the gun-cotton suddenly creates a large quantity of gas, which administers to the air a very violent outward push or blow. In consequence of the inertia of the air, it cannot respond everywhere instantly to this force.

## WAVES AND RIPPLES IN THE AIR.

Hence a certain spherical layer of air is compressed into a smaller volume. This layer, however, almost immediately expands again, and in so doing it compresses the next outer layer of air and rarefies itself. Then, again, the second layer in expanding compresses a third, and so on.

Accordingly, a state of compression is handed on from layer to layer, and each state of compression is followed by one of rarefaction. The individual air-particles are caused to move to and fro in the direction of the radii of the sphere of which the source of explosion is the centre. Hence we have what is called a spherical longitudinal wave produced.

Each air-particle swings backwards and forwards in the line of propagation of the wave. The actual motion of each air-particle is exceedingly small.

The speed with which this zone of compression travels outwards, is called the velocity of the sound wave, and the extent to which each air-particle moves backwards and forwards is called the amplitude of the wave.

Suppose, in the next place, that instead of a merely transitory sound like an explosion, we have a continuous musical sound, we have to inquire what then will be the description of air-movement executed. The experiments shown already will have convinced you that, in the case of a musical sound, each air-particle must repeat the same kind of motion again and again.

The precise nature of the displacement can be best illustrated by the use of two models. Before you is placed a frame to which are slung a series of golf-balls suspended by threads (see Fig. 4, Chapter I.). Between each pair of balls there is a spiral brass spring, which elastically resists both compression and extension. You will see that the row of balls and springs, therefore, has similar properties to the air. In virtue of the springs it resists compression and expansion, and in virtue of the mass or inertia of the balls any ball, if displaced and allowed to move back, overshoots its position of equilibrium because it persists in motion. The row of balls, therefore, resists extension and compression in consequence of the elasticity of the springs, and each ball persists in movement in consequence of the inertia of the ball.

If we then administer a little pat to the first ball, you will see a wave-motion run along the line of balls. Each ball in turn moves to and fro a little way, and its movement is handed on to its neighbours. We have here an example of a longitudinal wave-motion which resembles that of the air when it is traversed by a sound wave.

Another model which is of a more elaborate character shows us the sort of motion made in a tube when a sound wave due to a continuous musical sound is passing along it. It consists of a glass disc which is blackened, and has the paint removed along certain excentric circular lines. This disc is made to revolve in front of a wide slit in a piece of metal. By means of an optical lantern we project on to the screen an image of the slit, which you see is crossed by certain bright bars of light, crowded together at some places and more spaced apart at others.

When the disc revolves, these bars of light each move to and fro successively, and the result is that the crowded place moves along, or is displaced.

A wave of compression is propagated along the slit, and the localities where the bars of light are compressed or expanded continually change their place. If we imagine the air in a tube to be divided into slices, represented by these bars of light, the motion of the model exactly represents the motion of the air in the tube when it is traversed by a series of sound waves. The distance from one place of greatest compression to the next is called the wave-length of the sound wave. Hence, although a sound such as that of an explosion may consist in the propagation of a single layer of compression, the production of a continuous musical note involves the transference of a series of equidistant compressional zones, or waves.

These models will have assisted you, I trust, to form a clear idea of the nature of a sound wave in air. It is something very different, in fact, from a wave on the surface of water, but it is characterized by the same general qualities of wave-motion. It is a state of longitudinal periodic motion in a row of particles, which is handed on from one to another. Each particle of air oscillates in the line of propagation of the wave, and moves a little way backwards and forwards on either side of its undisturbed position.

It will be seen, therefore, that a solitary sound wave is a state of air-compression which travels along in the otherwise stationary air. The air is squeezed more tightly together in a certain region, and successive layers of air take up this condition. In the case of water-surface waves the wave is a region of elevation at which the water is raised above the general or average level, and this elevated region is transferred from place to place on otherwise stationary water. In the case of an air- wave train we have similar regions of compression following each other at distances, it may be, of a fraction of an inch or of several feet.

Thus in the case of ordinary speech or song, the waves are from 2 to 8 feet in length, that is, from one compressed region to the next. In the case of a whistle, the wave-length may be 1 or 2 inches, whilst the deepest note of an organ produces a sound of which the wave-length is about 32 feet.

As in every other instance of wave-motion, air waves may differ from each other in three respects. First, in wave-length; secondly, in amplitude; and thirdly, in wave-form. The first determines what we call the tone, i.e. whether the sound is high or low, treble or bass; the second determines the intensity of the sound, whether faint or loud; and the third determines its quality, or, as the Germans expressively call it, the sound-colour (Klangfarbe).

We recognize at once a difference between the sound of a vowel, say ah, sung by different persons to the same note of the piano and with the same loudness. There is a personal element, an individuality, about voices which at once arrests our attention, apart altogether from the tone or loudness. This sound-quality is determined by the form of the wave-motion, that is, by the nature of the movement of the air-particle during its little excursion to and fro in which it takes part in producing a zone of compression or rarefaction in the air and so forms a sound wave.

We have next to discuss the speed with which this air-compression is propagated through the air. Every one knows that it is not instantaneous. We see the flash of a gun at a distance, and a second or so afterwards we hear the bang. We notice that the thunder is heard often long after the lightning flash is seen. It would take too long to describe the experiments which have been made to determine precisely the speed of sound waves. Suffice it to say that all the best experiments show that the velocity of a sound wave in air, at the temperature of melting ice, or at $0°$ C. = $32°$ Fahr., is very nearly 1087 feet per second, or 33,136 centimetres per second. This is equivalent to 741 miles per hour, or more than ten times the speed of an express train. At this rate a sound wave would take 4 hours to cross the Atlantic Ocean, 16 hours to go half round the world or to the antipodes, and some 2 minutes to cross from Dover to Calais.

An opportunity of observing this speed of sound waves on a gigantic scale occurred about 20 years ago on the occasion of a great volcanic eruption near Java. If you open the map of Asia and look for Java and Sumatra in the Asiatic Archipelago, you will easily find the Sunda Strait, and on a good map you will see a small island marked called Krakatoa. This island possesses, or rather did possess, a volcano which, until the year 1883, had not been known to be in eruption. In that year, however, it again burst into activity, and after pre-

## WAVES AND RIPPLES IN THE AIR.

liminary warnings a final stupendous outburst occurred on August 27, 1883. The roar of this volcanic explosion was probably the loudest noise ever heard upon this earth. The pent-up volcanic gases and vapours burst forth from some subterranean prison with such appalling power that they created an air wave which not only encircled the earth, but reverberated to and fro seven times before it finally faded away. The zone of compressed air forming the mighty air wave as it passed from point to point on the earth's surface, caused an increase of atmospheric pressure which left its record on all the self-registering barometers, and thus enabled its steps to be traced. A diligent examination of these records, as collected in a celebrated Report of the Royal Society upon the Eruption of Krakatoa, showed exactly the manner in which this great air wave expanded. Starting from Krakatoa at 10 a.m. on the 27th of August, 1883, the air wave sped outwards in a circle of ever-increasing diameter until, by 7 p.m. on the same day, or 9 hours later, it formed a girdle embracing the whole world. This stupendous circular air wave, 24,000 miles in circumference, then contracted again, and in 9 hours more had condensed itself at a point in the northern region of South America, which is the antipodes of Krakatoa. It then rebounded, and, expanding once more, just like a water wave reflected from the side of a circular trough, returned on its own steps, so that 36 hours afterwards it had again reached the point from whence it set out. Again and again it performed the same double journey, but each time weaker than before, until, after seven times, the echoes of this mighty air wave had completely died away. This is no fancy picture, but a sober record of fact obtained from the infallible records of self-registering air-pressure-measuring instruments. But we have evidence that the actual sound of the explosion was heard, 4 hours after it happened, on the other side of the Indian Ocean, by human ears, and we have in this an instance of the measurement of the velocity of sound on the largest scale on which it was ever made.

There are many curious and interesting facts connected with the transmission of a sound wave through air, affecting the distance at which sounds can be heard. The speed of sound in air is much influenced by the temperature of the air and by wind.

The speed of sound increases with the temperature. For every degree Fahrenheit above the melting-point of ice (32° Fahr.) the speed is increased by one foot per second. A more accurate rule is as follows: Take the temperature of the air in degrees Centigrade, and add to this number 273. In other words, obtain the value of 273 + t° where t° is the temperature of the air. Then the velocity of sound in feet per second at this temperature is equal to the value of the expression

$$1090\sqrt{\frac{273+t°}{273}}$$

There is one point in connection with the velocity of propagation of a sound wave which should not be left without elucidation. It has been explained that the velocity of a wave in any medium is numerically given by the number obtained by dividing the square root of the elasticity of the medium by the square root of its density. The number representing the elasticity of a gas is numerically the same as that representing its absolute pressure per square unit of surface. The volume elasticity of the air may therefore be measured by the absolute pressure it exerts on a unit of area such as 1 square foot. At the earth's surface the pressure of the air at 0° C. is equal to about 2116.4 lbs. per square foot. The absolute unit of force in mechanics is that force which communicates a velocity of 1 foot per second to a mass of 1 lb. after acting upon it for 1 second. If we allow a mass of 1 lb. to fall from rest under the action of gravity at the earth's surface, it acquires after 1 second a velocity of 32.2 feet per second. Hence the force usually called "a pressure of 1 lb." is equal to 32.2 absolute units of force. Accordingly, the atmospheric pressure at the earth's surface is 2116.4 × 32.2 = 68,148 absolute units of force in that system of measurement in which the foot, pound, and second are the fundamental units.

The absolute density of the air is the mass of 1 cubic foot: 13 cubic feet of air at the freezing-point, and when the barometer stands at 30 inches, weigh nearly 1 lb. More exactly, 1 cubic foot of air under these conditions weighs 0.080728 lb. avoirdupois. If, then, we divide the number representing the absolute pressure of the air by the number representing the absolute density of air, we obtain the quotient 844,168; and if we take the square root of this, we obtain the number 912.6.

The above calculation was made first by Newton; and he was unable to explain how it was that the velocity of the air wave, calculated in the above manner from the general formula for wave-speed, gave a value for the velocity, viz. 912.6, which was so much less than the observed velocity of sound, viz. 1090 feet per second at 0° C. The true explanation of this difference was first given by the celebrated French mathematician Laplace. He pointed out that in air, as in all other gases, the elasticity, when it is compressed slowly, is less than that when it is compressed quickly. A gas, when compressed, is heated, and if we give this heat time to escape, the gas resists the compression less than if the heat stays in it. Hence air is a little more resilient to a very sudden compression than to a slow one. Laplace showed that the ratio of the elasticity under sudden compression was to that under slow compression in the same ratio as the quantities of heat required to raise a unit mass of air 1 C. under constant pressure and under constant volume. This ratio is called "the ratio of the two specific heats," and is a number close to 1.41. Hence the velocity, as calculated above, must be corrected by multiplying the number 844,168 by the number 1.41, and then taking the square root of the product. When this calculation is made, we obtain, as a result, the number 1091, which is exactly the observed value of the velocity of sound in feet per second at 0° C. and under atmospheric pressure. The velocity of sound is much affected by wind or movement of the air. Sound travels faster with the wind than against it. Hence the presence of wind distorts the shape of the sound wave by making portions of it travel faster or slower than the rest.

These two facts explain how it happens that loud sounds are sometimes heard at great distances from the source, but not heard at places close by.

Consider the case of a loud sound made near the surface of the earth. If the air were all at rest, and everywhere at the same temperature, the sound waves should spread out in hemispherical form. But if, as is generally the case, the temperature near the ground is higher than it is up above, then the part of the wave near the earth travels more quickly than that in the higher regions of the air. It follows that the sound wave will have its direction altered, and instead of proceeding near the earth in a direction parallel to the ground, it will be elevated, so as to strike in an upward direction. Again, it may be brought down by meeting with a current of air which blows against the lower portion and so retards that to a greater extent than it does the upper part. So it comes to pass that a sound wave may, as it were, "play leap-frog" over a certain district, being lifted up and then let down again; and persons in that region will not hear the sound, although others further off will do so. A very striking instance of this occurred on the occasion of the funeral procession of our late beloved Queen Victoria of blessed memory. The body was conveyed across the Solent on February 1, 1901, between lines of battleships which fired salutes with big guns. Arrangements were made to determine the greatest distance the sound of these guns was heard. In a very interesting article in *Knowledge* for June, 1901, Dr. C. Davison has collected the results of observation from eighty-four places, some of which are indicated in the map (see Fig. 47), taken, by kind permission of the editor of

## WAVES AND RIPPLES IN THE AIR.

*Knowledge*, from that journal. Observations were received from places as far distant as Alderton (Suffolk), 139 miles from the Solent. At several places the sound of the guns was loud enough to make windows shake. This occurred at Longfield (56 miles), Sutton (58 miles), and Richmond Hill (61 miles). But whilst there is clear evidence that the sound of the guns was heard even at Peterborough (125 miles), most curious to say, the sound was hardly heard at all in the neighbourhood of the Solent. The nearest place from which any record was received was Horley, in Surrey (50 miles). Hence it appears evident that the sound was lifted up soon after leaving the Solent, and passed right over the heads of observers near, travelling in the higher air for a considerable distance, probably 40 or 50 miles, and was then deflected down again, and reached observers on the earth's surface at much greater distances. An examination of the wind-charts for that day makes it tolerably clear that this was due to the manner in

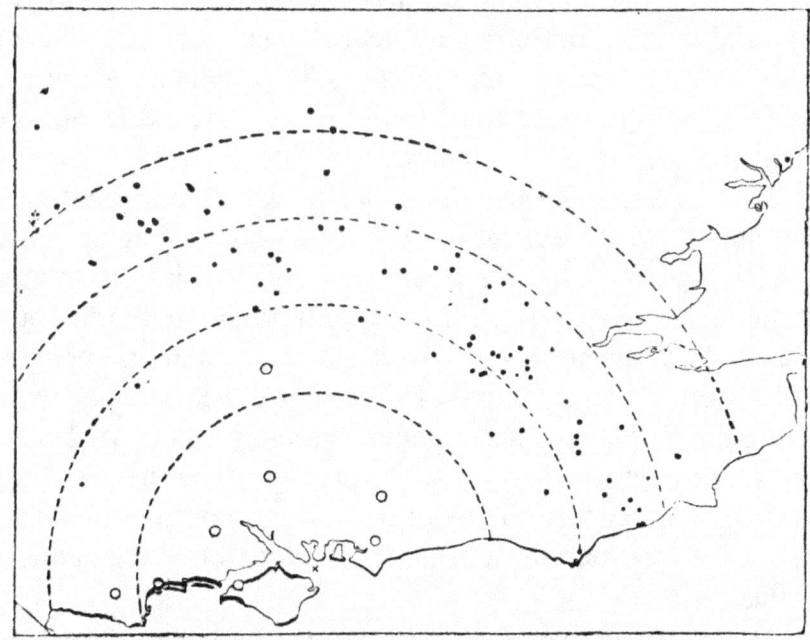

Fig. 47 (reproduced by permission of proprietors of *Knowledge*).—Map of South of England, showing places (black dots) at which sound of funeral guns was heard, February 1, 1901.

which the wind was blowing at the time. Dr. Davison, *loc. cit.*, says

"Now, on February 1, the wind at places to the west of Spithead was generally light, and from the west or nearly so, though near Lyndhurst there was a fresh breeze from about W.N.W. or N.W. At Portsmouth, again, the wind is described as from the shore. On the other hand, many of my correspondents at great distances from Spithead state that the wind, when sensible, was southerly in direction. Thus the sound-rays were first of all refracted by contrary winds over the heads of observers between 10 and 45 miles, and were afterwards brought down again by favourable upper currents, so that the reports were clearly audible beyond 50 miles and up to 140 miles from Spithead, and were so loud at a distance of 84 miles that labourers in the fields put down their spades and listened."

The same explanation has been given of the extraordinary differences that are found at various times in the distance at which lighthouse fog-horns are heard by ships at sea. There is in this case, however, another possible explanation, due to what is called interference of sound waves, the explanation of which will be given presently. The late Professor Tyndall, who was an authority on this subject, was of opinion that in some states of the atmosphere there existed what he called "acoustic opacity," the air being non-uniform in temperature and moisture; and through this very irregular medium, sound waves, when passing, lost a great deal of their intensity by internal reflection, or eclipses, just as light is stopped when passing through a non-homogeneous medium like crushed ice or glass. At each surface a little of the light is wasted by irregular reflection, and so the medium, though composed of fragments of a transparent substance, is more or less opaque in the mass.

On the subject of sound-signals as coast-warnings, some exceedingly interesting information has recently been supplied by Mr. E. Price-Edwards (see *Journal of the Society of Arts*, vol. 50, p. 315, 1902). The Lighthouse Boards of different countries provide the means for making loud warning sounds at various lighthouses, as a substitute for the light when fog comes on. The distance at which these sounds can be heard, and the distance-traversing power of various kinds of sounds, have been the subject of elaborate investigations.

The instrument which has been found to be the most effective in producing very powerful sound waves is called a siren. It consists of a tube or horn, having at the bottom a fixed disc with slits in it. Outside this disc is another movable one which revolves against the first, and which also has slits in it. When the second disc revolves, the passage way into the horn is opened and closed intermittently and suddenly, as the slits in the discs coincide or not. Air or steam under a pressure of 10 to 40 lbs. on the square inch is blown into the horn, and the rapid interruption of this blast by the revolving slits causes it to be cut up into puffs which, when sufficiently frequent, give rise to a very loud sound. The air under pressure is admitted to a back chamber and awaits an opportunity to escape, and this is given to it when the revolving disc moves into such a position that the slits in the fixed and moving disc come opposite each other. In comparative trials of different sound-producing instruments, nothing has yet been found to surpass this siren as a producer of penetrating sounds.

It has been found very important that the frequency of the note given by the siren should coincide with the fundamental tone of the trumpet or horn. As will be explained in the next lecture, every column of air in a tube has a particular natural time-period of oscillation. Suppose, for instance, that for a certain length of trumpet-tube this is $\frac{1}{100}$ of a second. Then the siren with that trumpet will be most effective if the interruptions of the air-blast are 100 per second.

Lord Rayleigh has also shown that the shape of the mouth of the trumpet is important, and that this should not be circular as usual, but elliptical or oval, the shortest diameter of the ellipse being one quarter of the longest one. Also that the mouth should occupy such a position that the longer axis is vertical. Moreover, he considers that the short axis of the oval should not exceed half the wave-length of the sound being emitted. With a trumpet-mouth of such a shape, the sound is prevented to some extent from being projected up and down, but diffused better laterally a result which is desired in coast sound-signals.

The information accumulated as regards the distances at which sounds can be heard is very briefly as follows:

First as regards wind. The direction of the wind has a most remarkable influence on the distance at which a given loud sound can be heard. In one instance, the noise of a siren was heard 20 miles in calm weather; whereas, with an opposing wind, it was not heard more than 1¼ mile away.

It has been found that for calm weather a low-pitched note is better in carrying power than a high note, but in rough weather the opposite is the case.

One thing that has been noticed by all who have experimented with this subject is the curious occurrence of "areas of silence." That is to say, a certain siren will be well heard close to its position. Then a little farther off the sound will be lost, but on going farther away still it is heard again.

Many theories have been advanced to account for this, but none are completely satisfactory. It is, however, a well-established effect, and one with which it behoves all mariners to be acquainted.

One curious fact is the very great power that can be absorbed in creating a loud siren note. Thus in one case, a siren giving a high note was found to absorb as much as 600 horse-power when the note was sounded continuously. The most striking and in one sense the most disappointing thing about these loud sounds is the small distance which they travel in certain states of the wind. As a general result, it has been found that the most effective sound for coast-warnings is one having a frequency of 100, or a wave-length of about 10 feet. When dealing with the subject of waves in general, it was pointed out that the velocity of a wave depended upon the elasticity and the density of the medium in which it was being propagated. In the case of a sound wave in air or any other gas, the speed of wave-transmission is proportional to the square root of the elasticity of the gas, and inversely proportional to the square root of the density.

At the same temperature the elasticity of a gas may be taken to be the same as its pressure. Hence, at the same pressure, the speed of sound-wave transmission through different gases varies inversely as the square root of their densities. An example will make this clear. If we take the density of hydrogen gas to be unity (= 1), then the density of oxygen is 16. The ratio of the densities is therefore 1 to 16, and the square roots of the densities are as $\sqrt{1}$ to $\sqrt{16}$, or as 1 to 4. Accordingly, the velocity of sound waves in hydrogen gas is to that in oxygen gas as 1 is to ¼. In other words, sound travels four times faster in hydrogen than it does in oxygen at the same temperature and pressure. The following table shows the velocity of sound in different gases at the melting-point of ice (=0 C.) and atmospheric pressure (= 760 mm. barometer).

| Gas | Velocity |
|---|---|
| Hydrogen | 4163 feet per second |
| Carbonic Oxide | 1106 feet per second |
| Air | 1090 feet per second |
| Oxygen | 1041 feet per second |
| Carbonic Acid | 856 feet per second |

Accordingly, we see that the lighter the gas the faster sound travels in it, pressure and temperature being the same. If the atmosphere we breathe consisted of hydrogen instead of a mixture of oxygen, nitrogen, and many other gases, a clap of thunder would follow a flash of lightning much more quickly than it does in our present air, supposing the storms to be at the same distance. Under present circumstances, if 20 seconds elapse between the flash and the peal, it indicates that the storm is about 4 miles away, but if the atmosphere were of hydrogen, for a storm at the same distance the thunder would follow the lightning in about 5 seconds.

Furnished with these facts about the propagation of air waves, it is now possible to point out some interesting consequences. It will be in your recollection that in the first chapter it was pointed out that a wave on water could be reflected by a hard surface, and that it could be refracted, or bent, when it passed from a region where it was moving quickly to one where it was moving more slowly. It will be necessary now to prove experimentally that the same things can be done with sound, in order that a body of proof may be built up in your minds convincing you that the external cause of sound-sensation must be a wave-motion in the air.

In the first place, I must describe to you, somewhat in detail, the nature of the arrangements we shall employ for producing and detecting the sound waves which will be used in these experiments.

It would not do to rely upon the ear as a detector because you cannot all be so placed as to hear the sounds which will be produced, and we shall, therefore, employ a peculiar kind of flame, called a *sensitive flame*, to act as a detector.

If ordinary coal-gas stored in a gasometer is burnt at a small jet under considerable pressure, we are able to produce a tall flame about 18 to 24 inches in height. The jet used is one with a steatite top and small pin-hole gas exit about $\frac{1}{25}$ inch in diameter. The pressure of gas must be equal to about 10 inches of water, and it cannot be drawn straight off the house gas-pipes, but must be supplied from a special gasometer or gasbag under a pressure sufficient to make a flame 18 inches or so in height. If the pressure is too great, the flame roars; if the pressure is slightly reduced, the flame can be made to burn quietly and form a tall reed-like flame (A, Fig. 48). This flame, when properly adjusted, is curiously sensitive to shrill, chirping sounds. You may shout or talk loudly near it, and it takes no notice of your voice, but if you chirrup or whistle in a shrill tone, or clink your keys or a few coins in your hand, the flame at once shortens itself to about 6 or 7 inches in height, and becomes possessed of a peculiarly ragged edge, whilst at the same time it roars (B, Fig. 48). When in adjustment, the clink of a couple of coins in the hand will affect this sensitive flame on the other side of the room.[22]

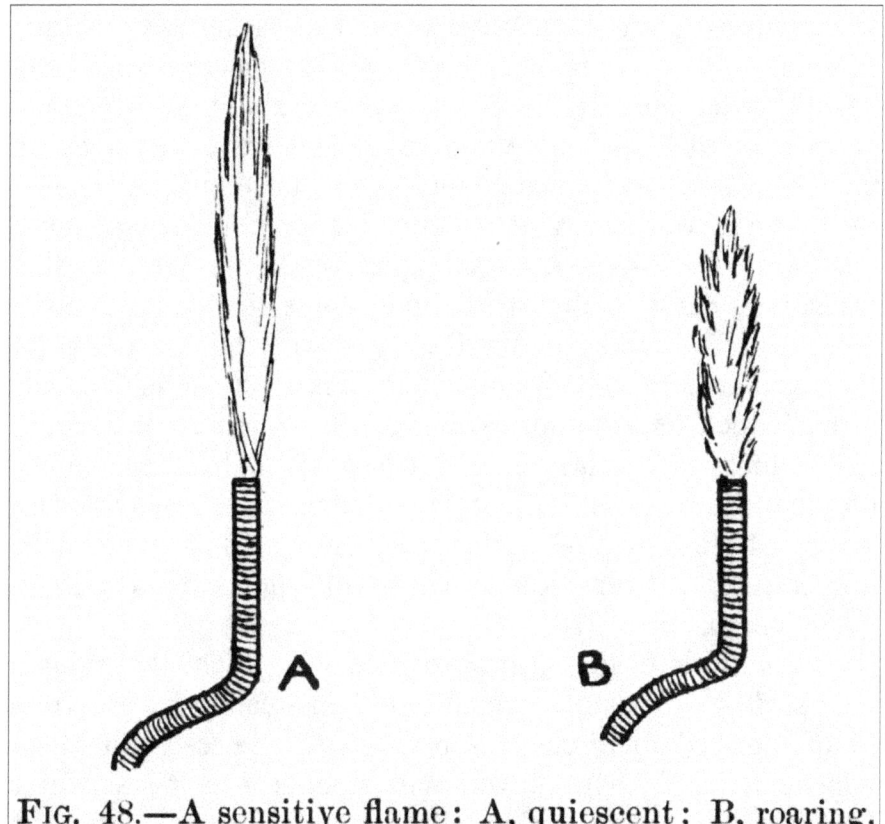

FIG. 48.—A sensitive flame: A, quiescent; B, roaring.

The flame is also very sensitive to a shrill whistle or bird-call. It will be clear to you, from previous explanations, that the flame responds, therefore, to very short air waves forming high notes. The particular flame I shall now use responds with great readiness to air waves of 1 inch to ½ inch in length.

---

22 See Professor W. F. Barrett, *Nature*, 1877, vol. 1C, p. 12.

It may be well to explain that the sensitive portion of the flame is the root, just where it emerges from the burner, and it is the action of the sound wave in throwing this portion of the flame into vibration which is the cause of its curious behaviour.

If you think what the action must be, you will easily see that the operation of the sound wave is to throw the particles of the gas, just as they escape from the hole in the jet, into vibration in a direction transverse or at right angles to the direction of their movement in the flame. The gas molecules are, when unacted upon by the sound wave, rushing out of the jet, in an upward direction. When the sound wave impinges on them they are, so to speak, caught, and caused to rock to and fro in a direction across the flame. The combination of these two motions results in a spreading action on the flame, so that instead of being a thin lance-like shape, it becomes more blunt, stumpy, and ragged at the sides. The flame acts, therefore, as a detector of certain sounds. It is a very sensitive kind of ear which listens and responds to the slightest whisper if only uttered in certain tones, but is deaf to all other sounds. Its great use to us is that it acknowledges the presence of air waves of short wave-length, and shows at once when it is immersed in a stream of air waves or ripples of very short wave-length.

In addition to this, I am provided with a whistle giving a very shrill or high note, which is blown steadily by a current of air supplied under constant pressure from a reservoir. If the whistle is set in action, you will at once see the sensitive flame dip down and acknowledge the presence of the airwaves sent out by the whistle.

The air waves sent out by this whistle proceed, of course, in all directions, but for our present purpose we require to create what I may call a *beam of sound*. You all know the action of a magnifying-glass, or lens, upon a ray of light. What boy is there who has not, at some time or other, amused himself by concentrating the rays of the sun by a burning-glass, and by bringing them to a focus set light to a piece of paper, or burnt his own or companion's hand? In this case we use a piece of glass called a lens, which is thicker in the middle than at the edges, to converge parallel rays of light to a point or focus. We also use such a lens in our optical lantern to render the diverging rays from an electric lamp parallel, and so make a parallel beam of light. I shall defer for a moment an explanation of this action, and simply say here that it is possible to construct a *sound-lens*, which operates in the same manner on rays of sound. I have had such a sound-lens constructed for our present experiments, and it is made as follows:

It is possible to buy small balloons made of very thin material called *collodion*, this latter consisting of gun-cotton dissolved in ether and alcohol, and then poured out on a glass plate and allowed to dry. If one of these balloons is purchased, it is possible with great dexterity to cut from it two spherical segments or saucer-shaped pieces. These have then to be cemented with *siccotine* to a wooden ring having two small pipes opening into it (see Fig. 49). By means of these pipes we can inflate the lens-shaped bag so formed with a heavy gas called carbonic acid gas, made by pouring strong acid upon marble or chalk. The result of these operations, all

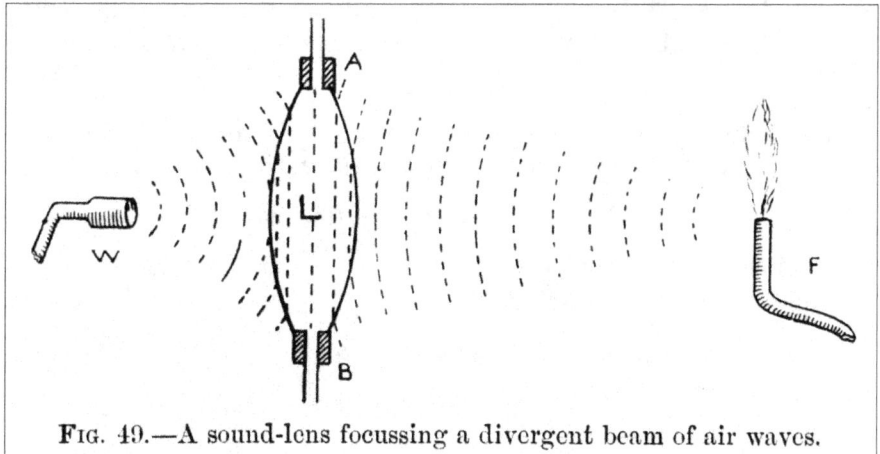

Fig. 49.—A sound-lens focussing a divergent beam of air waves.

## WAVES AND RIPPLES

of which require considerable skill of hand, is to furnish us with a sound-lens consisting of a collodion film in the shape of a magnifying-glass, or double convex lens, filled with carbonic acid gas heavier than the air.

The sound-lens so made is fixed up against a hole in a glass screen of the same size as the lens, and on one side of the lens is placed the whistle, and on the other side the sensitive flame. These have to be adjusted so that the whistle W, the centre of the lens L, and the jet of the flame F are in one straight horizontal line perpendicular to the glass plate.

The distance of the whistle from the lens has then to be adjusted so as to produce on the other side a nearly parallel beam of sound. In other words, the whistle must be placed in the focus of the lens. A rule for doing this is as follows: If the balloon from which the segments of collodion were cut was nearly spherical, and had a diameter of 8 inches, then the whistle must be placed at slightly less than 8 inches from the side of the lens next to it.[23] The exact distance, however, will have to be found by trial, but it is somewhere near the point so determined. The sensitive flame should be about 4 or 5 feet away from the lens on the other side of the screen.

These arrangements having been made and the whistle set in action, it will be found that the flame responds vigorously when it is placed on the axis-line of the lens, but if moved a few inches to right or left of this line, it will cease to flare. This shows us that we have formed a beam of sound, and with

---

23 This follows from the ordinary formula for the focal length f of a biconvex lens, each surface having a radius of curvature equal to r. For then it can be shown that $f = \frac{r}{2} \cdot \frac{1}{\mu - 1}$ where μ is <the index of refracture of the lens material. As shown later on, the acoustic index of refraction of carbonic acid, when that of air is taken as unity, is 1.273. Hence, $\mu - 1 = 0.273$, and $\frac{1}{\mu - 1} = 3\frac{2}{3}$. Hence, $f = 2r\frac{11}{12}$, or f is slightly less than twice the radius of curvature of the spherical segment forming the sound-lens.

some little care it is possible to make this a nearly parallel beam, so that when plunged in this stream of air waves the flame dips, but by removing it just outside the stream of sound it no longer flares. I have found it not difficult, when using a sound-lens 6 or 7 inches in diameter, to make a beam of sound from a whistle some 10 inches wide at about 4 feet from the lens.

Supposing the sound-lens and sensitive flame so adjusted, it is then necessary for our purpose to provide a sound-prism, made in the following manner: A zinc box is made in wedge form, and the two inclined sides are cut out, and these windows are covered with thin collodion film. The box has two pipes connected with it, by means of which it can be filled with carbonic acid gas.

Provided with this apparatus, it is now possible to show you a series of experiments which will leave no doubt in your minds that the external agency which creates in us the sensation of sound is a wave-motion in the air we breathe. Let me, in the first place, show you that a sound-beam can be reflected. We adjust our sensitive flame and set the whistle in action, and create, as described, by the lens, a beam of sound. At a little distance, say a couple of feet, outside the parallel beam we place the sensitive flame, and, being sheltered from the direct action of the whistle, it remains perfectly quiescent. Taking a sheet of glass in my hand, I hold it at an angle of 45 in the sound-beam, and you see the flame at once roars. The beam has been reflected on to the flame, but a very small angular movement of the glass is sufficient to reflect the sound-ray past the flame without touching it, and the flame then exhibits no agitation.

A few experiments of this kind with the flame in various positions are sufficient to show that the sound-beam is reflected by the glass in accordance with the law of reflection of wave-motion, viz. that the angle of incidence is equal to the angle of reflection. We can in the same way reflect the sound-beam by a wooden board, a piece of cardboard, a looking-glass, or a sheet of metal. We can reflect it from a wet duster, but not very well from a dry handkerchief. If we place the flame in the direct beam, it is easy to show that all the above good reflectors of sound are opaque to a sound-ray, and cast an acoustic shadow. In fact, I can prevent the flame from roaring by merely interposing my hand in front of it. A wet duster is found to be opaque to these sound waves, but a dry linen handkerchief is fairly transparent.

The collodion film used in making the lens and prism is also exceedingly transparent to these short air waves. We may then go one step further, and show that these air waves are capable of refraction. It will be in your remembrance that, in speaking of water ripples, it was shown by experiment that, when water ripples passed over a boundary between two regions, in one of which they travelled more quickly than in the other, a bending of the direction of ripple-motion took place. We can show precisely the same thing with these air waves.

The collodion prism has been filled with a heavy gas called carbonic acid. This gas is about half as heavy again as air, and it is this heavy and poisonous gas which, by accumulating in old wells or brewers' vats or in coal-mines after an explosion, causes the death of any man or living animal immersed in it.

It has already been explained that the velocity of sound waves in different gases varies inversely as the square root of their density. Hence the speed of a sound wave in carbonic acid gas will be less than that in air in the ratio of the square roots of the densities of these gases. The density of carbonic acid gas is to that of air as 1.552 is to 1. The square root of 1.552 is 1.246, or nearly 1¼. Accordingly, the speed of a sound wave in carbonic acid gas is to the speed in air as 4 is to 5. A sound wave in air will therefore travel 5 feet or 5

## WAVES AND RIPPLES IN THE AIR.

inches in the same time that it travels 4 feet or 4 inches in carbonic acid gas.

Let us now consider what must happen if a sound wave falls obliquely upon the face of our carbonic acid prism.

Let ABC be the prism (see Fig. 50) represented in plan, and let *ab*, *ab*, *ab*, be a train of sound waves advancing against the face AC. As soon as the left end *b* of the

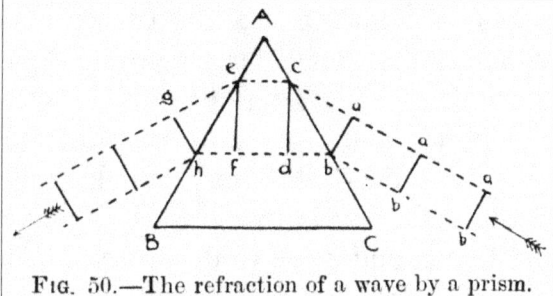

FIG. 50.—The refraction of a wave by a prism.

wave *ab* touches the face AC, and enters the carbonic acid gas, its speed will begin to be retarded, and in the time taken by the right end *a* to move in air from *a* to *c*, the left end will have moved in carbonic acid gas, by a less distance, *bd*, the distances *ca* and *db*, being in the ratio of 5 to 4. Hence it is clear that the wave-front *ab* will be swung round, and when the wave has wholly entered the prism, its direction of motion will have been bent round to the left.

The same thing will happen at emergence. The right end, *e*, of the wave *ef* gets out into the air whilst the left end, *f*, is still in carbonic acid. Accordingly, in the time taken for the end *f* to move to *k*, the end *e* will have moved a greater distance, in the ratio of 5 to 4, to *g*, and therefore we have again a bending round of the wave-direction. It is evident, therefore, that this unequal retarding of the two sides of the wave will result in a refraction, or bending, of the wave-direction, and that whereas the sound-ray was proceeding, before entering the prism, in the direction of the arrow on the right hand, it is altered, after passing through the prism, so as to be travelling in the direction of the arrow on the left-hand side. The double bending of the sound-ray is therefore caused by, and is evidence of the fact that, the sound wave travels more slowly in carbonic acid gas than it does in air.[24]

Let us, then, bring these statements to the test of experiment. We again start in action the whistle W, and place the sensitive flame in the line of the lens-axis, and notice how violently the flame flares (see Fig. 51). The flame is now at a distance of 4 feet from the lens. I move the flame 1 foot to the left hand, and it is now outside the beam of sound, and remains quiescent. The prism P, previously filled with carbonic acid gas, is then inserted between the sound-lens and the flame, and close to the former. When properly placed, the sensitive flame F immediately dips and roars. It will be abundantly evident. The refraction of a sound ray. to you that this can only arise because the prism has bent round the

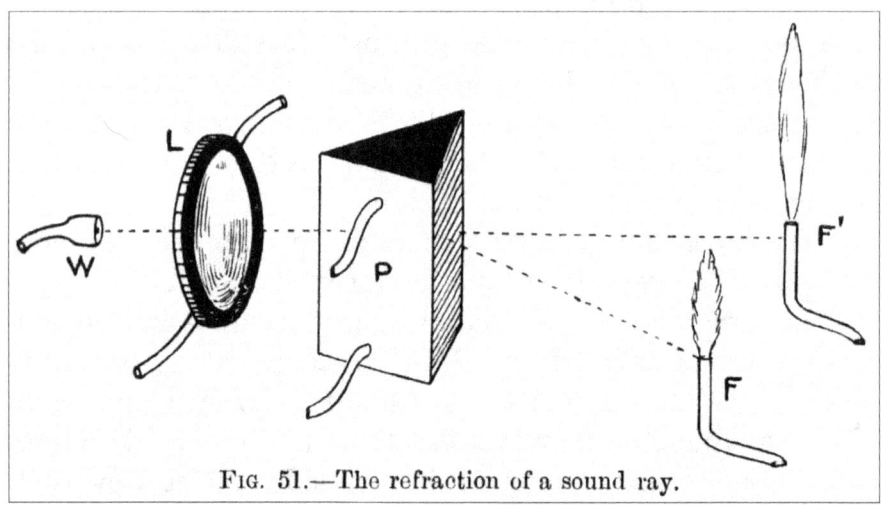

FIG. 51.—The refraction of a sound ray.

---

24 We can, in fact, discover the ratio of the velocities from the amount of bending the ray experiences and the angle BAG of the prism, called its refracting angle. It can be shown that if we denote this refracting angle by the letter A, and the deflection or total bending of the ray by the letter D, then the ratio of the velocity of the wave in air to its velocity in carbonic acid gas (called the *acoustic refractive index*), being denoted by the Greek letter $\mu$; we have 
$$\mu = \frac{\sin\left(\frac{A+D}{2}\right)}{\sin\left(\frac{A}{2}\right)}$$

sound-beam, and deflected it on to the flame. But if the beam is bent round, then it follows that if the flame is now moved back to the central position F', the prism remaining in front of the lens, that the flame will not now roar, and this we find to be the case. If, however, the prism is then removed, the flame at once bursts into a roar.

This experiment proves to demonstration that we can refract waves of sound just as we can refract ripples on water.

Having regard to what we have now seen, I do not think you will have any difficulty in seeing how it is that the biconvex sound-lens, filled with carbonic acid gas, is able to render divergent sound-rays parallel; in other words, can convert a spherical sound wave into a plane sound wave.

Consider what the effect really must be. Let the sound-lens be represented in section by AB (see Fig. 49), and let W be the whistle sending out spherical sound waves, represented by the dotted lines.

When the spherical wave meets the lens, the central portion of the wave passes into a retarding medium, whilst the right and left wings of the wave are still in air. Hence, as before, the wings gain on the centre. Again, at emergence the wings emerge before the centre of the wave, and hence again the wings gain on the centre. After complete emergence the spherical wave-surface has been flattened out and made into a plane wave. Hence the sound-rays diverging from the whistle are rendered parallel or even convergent, provided that the whistle is properly placed with regard to the lens.

You will see, therefore, that we can use a gas denser than the air, contained in a transparent bag or vessel of collodion, as the means of changing the form and direction of sound waves. We can make lenses and prisms of carbonic acid gas which act on rays of sound just as do lenses and prisms of glass on rays of light. There is, however, one great difference between the operation of a carbonic acid prism on rays of sound, and that of a glass or other prism on rays of light. In the lectures on æther waves it will be made clear to you that what we call light really consists in waves in a medium known as the æther.

But when such light waves are propagated through a transparent material like glass, the speed of transmission depends on the wave-length, just as in the case of water waves. But as regards sound waves there is no difference between the velocity of propagation or speed with which waves of different wave-lengths move. Hence a bass note travels just as fast as a treble note, and the sound waves from a flute have a speed of the same value as that from a trumpet or bassoon. If it were not so, it would be impossible for us to hear music or song at a distance, because the notes would arrive all in the wrong order, and the most familiar melody would be unrecognizable. It follows from this that air waves, no matter what their wave-length, are equally refracted on passing from one medium to another of different density. We shall see later on that this is not the case with waves of light and æther waves generally.

In the case of most transparent substances the æther waves which constitute light are transmitted with different velocities, the longer waves moving faster than the shorter ones. Hence we have the familiar result of the decomposition of a ray of white light into its different constituents by a glass prism. We cannot, however, perform a similar experiment on a complex series of waves of sound by means of a carbonic acid prism. In other words, a sound-prism refracts, but does not disperse sound waves of various wave-lengths.

One thing, however, should be pointed out before dismissing this experiment, and that is that to show successfully the experiment with the prism, the length of the sound waves used must be small compared with the dimensions of the prism. The reason for this is that otherwise there would be too much bending of the waves round the obstacle. When a train of waves, no matter whether waves in air or waves in water,

## WAVES AND RIPPLES IN THE AIR.

meets with an impervious body, there is always a certain bending of the waves round it, which is technically called *diffraction*. We may see this effect on a large scale when sea waves, rolling in, pass by some large rock standing up like an island out of the water. The waves meet it, pass round it, and, so to speak, embrace it and continue on the other side. If there is to be any calm water on the leeward side, the island must be large compared with the length of the waves. The same thing holds good with regard to air waves.

In order that an object may form an acoustic or sound-shadow, it is necessary that the construction shall be large compared with the length of the wave.

Thus the hand held in front of the mouth does not much obstruct the waves of the speaking voice, because these waves are about 2 to 4 feet long. But as you have seen when using sound waves only 1 inch long, the hand, will form a very well-marked sound-shadow, as shown by its effect when held between a whistle and a sensitive flame.

In order to complete our proof that the agency which affects our ears as sound is really due to air waves, it is necessary to be able to show that we can produce interference with air waves, as in the case of waves on water. The nature of the effect called *interference* by which one wave is made to annihilate another has been already fully explained. I will now endeavour to exhibit to you the interference of two sound-wave trains in an experiment due to Lord Rayleigh, the apparatus for which he has kindly lent to me.

It consists, as you see, of a stand, to which is fixed a jet, from which we form a tall sensitive flame. Behind the flame is placed a sheet of glass, which is held vertically, but can be slid towards or from the flame. At a little distance we place a bird-call, or sort of whistle, which produces, when blown with air, a note so shrill as to be inaudible to human ears.

The air-vibrations so generated are at the rate of 33,000 per second, which is beyond the limit of audition. Hence, even when blown strongly, you hear no sound from this appliance.

It produces, however, as you can see, a very violent effect upon the sensitive flame. Hence this flame hears a note which we cannot hear, and it suggests that perhaps some animals or insects may have a range of hearing quite beyond the limits fixed for our human ears.

Such being the case, you will see that if the glass plate is placed behind the flame at a certain distance, the flame at once stops flaring and becomes quiescent. If, however, the plate is moved to or from the flame by a very small distance equal to about the one-twelfth part of an inch, the tall flame at once drops in height and begins to flare. If we move the plate steadily backwards by equal small distances, we find the flame alternately quiescent and waving.

The explanation of this effect is that it is due to the interference between the direct and reflected sound-rays. The waves of air are turned back when they meet the glass in such a manner that the crests of the arriving waves are made to coincide with the hollows of the reflected waves, or, to speak more correctly, the zones of condensation of one are coincident with the places of rarefaction of the other. When the glass is adjusted so that this happens, all air- wave motion just in front of it is destroyed, and hence the sensitive detecting flame remains quiescent. If, however, the glass is moved nearer to or further from the flame, then the condensations of the reflected wave may be made to fall in the same places as the condensations of the arriving wave, and in that case the disturbance is doubled, and not destroyed.

A little model may be made which will help the reader to grasp this point. Cut out a piece of paper in the form shown in Fig. 52 to represent a wave. Bend back the paper on itself at the dotted line *ab*, and let one half represent the arriving wave, and the other the reflecting wave. It will be seen that in this case the crests of the incoming wave are obliterated by the hollows of the returning wave. If, however, the paper is bent back at cd, then the crests of the reflected and incident waves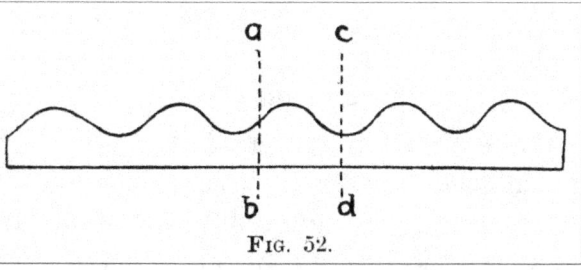

FIG. 52.

conspire, and there is no interference.

Whenever we can produce *interference* in this manner between two sets of sound-rays, or light-rays, or rays of any other kind, we have the strongest possible proof that we are concerned with a *wave-motion*; because in no other way that we can understand is it possible that a destruction of sound by sound can take place by, so to speak, superimposing two sound-rays, or a destruction of light by bringing together two rays of light.

We may, then, conclude our discussion of this part of our subject by examining the manner in which vibrating bodies communicate a different form of wave to the air. As already explained, we are by our ears enabled to appreciate the fact that the air is thrown into a wave-motion, and that this wave-motion may consist of waves of great or small wave-length, and great or small amplitude. But we are able to do something more we are able to detect a difference between the form of two waves, so that if represented by a wavy line of light, as you have seen, the nature of the outline of that line impresses itself upon our consciousness. Nothing is more remarkable than the extraordinary delicacy of the ear in this respect. Amongst all our scores of friends and acquaintances we recognize each by a *quality* of voice which we speak of as harsh, melodious, sympathetic, rasping, penetrating, or clear. This is not altogether a matter of enunciation or vocalization, for if different persons pronounce correctly the same vowel-sound, we can detect a great difference between their voices. We have, then, to ask wherein this difference consists when considered with respect simply to what goes on outside of us in the air.

Great light was thrown on this by the invention and perfection of the phonograph and telephone, and also a more recent and wonderful invention, variously called the microphonograph or telegraphone. You have all heard a phonograph speak, or sing, or reproduce music. In its original form the Edison phonograph consisted of a cylinder covered with tinfoil, against which pressed lightly a steel point attached to the centre of a metal disc. In its modern form, as improved by Edison, Bell, Tainter, and others, it is a far more perfect instrument for recording and reproducing sound. It now consists of a cylinder covered with a composition similar to very hard soap. This cylinder is carried on a metal drum, and caused to revolve by clockwork slowly and very uniformly. A metal arm carries an elastic metal disc called a receiving diaphragm, and to the back of this is attached a very delicate cutting-tool like a small chisel. By means of a screw the chisel and diaphragm are made to travel along the cylinder, and if no vibration is given to the disc the tool cuts a spiral on the recording cylinder, which is a clean groove with smooth bottom ploughed out of the soft composition. If, however, we speak or sing to the diaphragm, the air waves cause it to vibrate, and this makes the tool cut a furrow, the bottom of which is irregular, the undulations corresponding exactly to the movements of the diaphragm. Thus, if we could look at the section of the furrow, we should see it undulating like a miniature switchback railway, each up-and-down corresponding with one vibration of the diaphragm. In this manner we store up a record of air waves on the hard-soap cylinder. In the next place, to reproduce the sound, another diaphragm with a trumpet mouthpiece has at its back a little pointed lever or set of levers, one extremity resting upon the bottom of the irregular furrow.

## WAVES AND RIPPLES IN THE AIR.

Then, if the cylinder is so set that this reproducing diaphragm travels over the record cut by the receiving diaphragm, we have a motion communicated to it which is the exact facsimile of that which produced the furrow. Accordingly, the reproducing diaphragm gives back to the air impulses which reproduce the same wave-trains, and therefore the same speech or song, as that which created the record.

We may in this manner record any human utterance and receive it again, word-perfect, months or years after it was made.[25]

The action of the phonograph leads us to inquire how a disc of metal or other elastic material responds to aerial vibrations which fall upon it, and I shall conclude this lecture by showing you one experiment of a kind to illustrate this point, which, though not very easy to perform, is certainly one of the most attractive that can be shown.

There is on the table a brass tube, of a shape some-what like a square-shouldered funnel, and over the smaller end is loosely slipped a wide indiarubber tube with a mouthpiece. It is essential that the indiarubber tube shall not fit tightly, but shall be supported so that an air space exists all round between it and the brass funnel tube. The latter may be carried on a wooden stand. The wider end of the funnel must have a diameter of about 2½ inches, and the lip must be quite smooth. The interior of the funnel should be blackened. A soap solution has then to be prepared as for blowing soap-bubbles. A good formula for making this solution is given by Professor Vernon Boys, in his book, "Soap Bubbles and the

---

25 On the occasion when this lecture was given at the Royal Institution, a large phonograph, kindly lent by the Edison-Bell Phonograph Company, Ltd., of Charing Cross Road, London, was employed to reproduce a short address on Natural History to the young people present which had been spoken to the instrument ten days previously by Lord Avebury, at the request of the author. The address was heard perfectly by the five or six hundred persons comprising the audience.

Forces which mould them," and is as follows: Fill a clean stoppered bottle three-quarters full of soft water. Add one-fortieth part of its weight of oleate of soda, which will probably float on the water. Leave it until it is dissolved. Then nearly fill up the bottle with Price's glycerine, and shake well. Leave the bottle stoppered for a week in a dark place. Then syphon off the clear liquid from the scum at the top. Add one or two drops of strong ammonia to every pint of the liquid. Do not warm or filter the liquid, and keep it carefully from exposure to the air. Do not expose the liquid to the air more than necessary; but in blowing a bubble pour out a little of the liquid into a saucer.

In default of this good solution a substitute may be found by dissolving bits of clear yellow soap in soft water; but this soapy water does not yield films which last so long as those made with the Plateau solution above described.

By dipping the wide end of the funnel tube into some of the soap solution placed in a saucer, it is easy to cover the end with a flat soap film which will last a considerable time. This tube has then to be fixed in front of an electric arc or limelight lantern, so that a powerful parallel beam of light can be directed on to the film by a small flat mirror or looking-glass. A lens is also placed so as to focus an image of the film on to a screen. In finding the right position for the lens, it is a great help to place a piece of white card with some bold black letters upon it over the brass funnel in the place which will be occupied with the soapy film, and to focus this so as to obtain a sharp image of the letters on the screen. When the soap film is then substituted for the card, we should have on the screen a reflection of the film surface, which at first will appear as a patch of white light upon the screen. If we allow the film to stand for a few seconds, it begins to get thinner at the upper part than at the bottom, and the image on the screen will exhibit gorgeous bands of red and green, called interference colours, which are due, like the colours on a soap-bubble, to the interference of the rays of light reflected from the inner and outer surfaces of the film, If the experiment is skilfully performed, the appearance on the screen will then be very beautiful. We shall have a patch of light which exhibits bands of colours, becoming more intense the longer the film stands, and towards the end having somewhat the appearance of an unusually lovely sunset.

Just before this condition of the film is reached, if we sing gently into the mouthpiece of the indiarubber tube, the soap film will be thrown into vibration. The image on the screen will exhibit a set of regularly arranged concentric stationary ripples, which will alter in appearance with every change in the note sung. The experiment requires some care and practice to perform it properly, and should not be attempted in public without many rehearsals; but when well shown it is a most effective and interesting experiment. We see, therefore, that so delicate an object as a stretched soap-film can take up the vibrations of the air and be itself thrown into vibration. The reason is that the soap-film, as already explained in the first lecture, resists stretching, and behaves like a sheet of elastic indiarubber. Hence, as each air wave falls upon it, the film is alternately pushed out and pulled in, but being held at the edges, it can only accommodate itself by stretching. We have, therefore, set up in the film a set of stationary waves similar to those set up on a rope fixed at one end when the loose end is regularly jerked up and down by the hand. The experiment shows us clearly the way in which an elastic disc is set in vibration when compressional waves fall upon it, and in the next lecture we shall proceed to discuss the vibrations of this kind which give rise to musical effects.

# CHAPTER IV.
## SOUND AND MUSIC.

OUR discussion of waves and ripples in the air would be very incomplete if we left it without any further reference to the difference between those motions in the air which constitute noise or sound, and th6se to which we owe the pleasure-producing effects of musical tones. I propose, therefore, to devote our time to-day to a brief exposition of the properties and modes of production of those air-vibrations which give rise to the class of sensations we call music. Sufficient has already been said to make it clear to you that one essential difference between sound or noise and music, as far as regards the events taking place outside of our own organism, is that, in the first case, we have a more or less irregular motion in the air, and, in the second, a rhythmical movement, constituting a train of air waves. The greater pleasure we experience from the latter is, no doubt, partly due to their rhythmic character. We derive satisfaction from all regularly repeated muscular movements, such as those involved in dancing, skating, and rowing, and the agreeable sensation we enjoy in their performance is partly due to their periodic or cyclical character.

In the same way, our ears are satisfied by the uniformly repeated and sustained vibrations proceeding from an organ-pipe or tuning-fork in action, but we are irritated and annoyed by the sensations set up when irregular vibrations of the air due to the bray of a donkey or the screech of a parrot fall upon them. Before, however, we can advance further in an analysis of the nature of musical sounds, two things must be clearly explained. The first of these is the meaning of the term *natural period of vibration*, and the second is the nature of the effect called *resonance*. You see before you three small brass balls suspended by strings. One string is 1 foot long, the second 4 feet, and the third 9 feet. These suspended balls are called *simple pendulums*. Taking in my hands the balls attached to the 1-foot and the 4-foot strings, I withdraw them a little way from their positions of rest and let them go. They vibrate like pendulums, but, as you see, the 1-foot pendulum makes two swings in the time that the 4-foot makes one swing. Repeating the experiment with the 1-foot and the 9-foot pendulum, we find that the short one now makes three swings in the time the long one makes one swing. The inference immediately follows that these pendulums, whose respective lengths are 1, 4, and 9 feet, make their swings from side to side in times which are respectively in the ratio of 1, 2, and 3.

Again, if we withdraw any of the pendulums from its position of rest and let it swing, we shall find that in any stated period of time, say 1 minute, it executes a certain definite number of oscillations which is peculiar to itself. You might imagine that, by withdrawing it more or less from its position of rest, and making it swing over a larger or smaller distance, you could make these swings per minute more or less as you please. But you would find, on trying the experiment, that this is not the case, and that, provided the arc of vibration is not too great, the time of one complete swing to and fro is the same whether the swing be large or small.

In scientific language this is called the *isochronism of the pendulum*, and is said to have been discovered by Galileo in the Cathedral at Pisa, when watching the swings of a chan-

## SOUND AND MUSIC.

delier die away, whilst counting their number by the beats of his pulse. This periodic time of vibration, which is independent of the amplitude of vibration, provided the latter is small, is called the natural time of vibration of the pendulum, or its *free periodic time*.

In the case of the simple pendulum the free periodic time is proportional to the square root of the length of the pendulum. Accordingly, a short pendulum makes more swings per minute than a long one, and this rate of swinging is quite independent of the weight of the bob. We can, of course, take hold of the bob with our hand and force it to vibrate in any period we please, and thus produce a *forced vibration*; but a *free* vibration, or one which is unforced, has a natural time-period of its own.

In order that any body may vibrate when displaced and then set free, two conditions must exist. In the first place, there must be a controlling force tending to make the substance return to its original position when displaced.

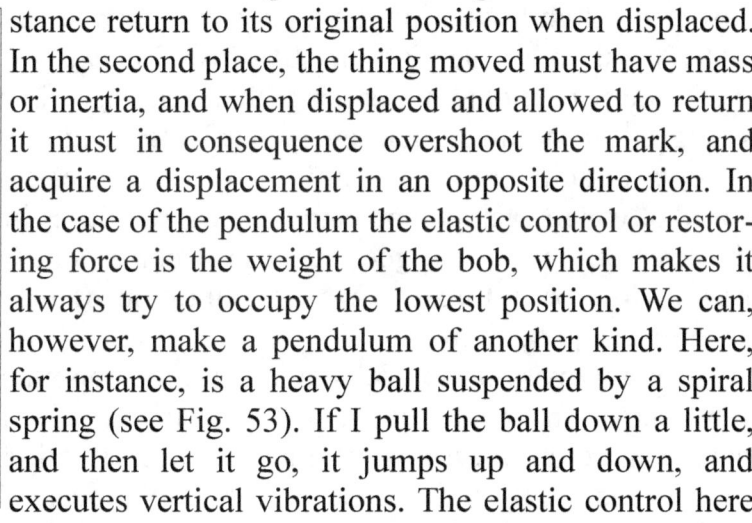

Fig. 53.

In the second place, the thing moved must have mass or inertia, and when displaced and allowed to return it must in consequence overshoot the mark, and acquire a displacement in an opposite direction. In the case of the pendulum the elastic control or restoring force is the weight of the bob, which makes it always try to occupy the lowest position. We can, however, make a pendulum of another kind. Here, for instance, is a heavy ball suspended by a spiral spring (see Fig. 53). If I pull the ball down a little, and then let it go, it jumps up and down, and executes vertical vibrations. The elastic control here is the spring which resists extension. In this instance, also, there is a natural free time of vibration, independent of the extent of the motion, but dependent upon the weight of the ball and the stiffness of the spring.

A good illustration of the above principles may be found in the construction of a clock or a watch. A clock contains a pendulum which vibrates in a certain fixed time. The arrangements we call the "works" of a clock are only a contrivance for counting the swings, and recording them by the "hands" of the clock. Owing, however, to the friction of the "works," the Pendulum would soon come to rest, and hence we have a mainspring or "weights" which apply a little push to the pendulum at each swing, and keep it going. In a watch there is no pendulum, but there is a "balance-wheel and hair-spring," or a wheel which has a spiral spring attached to it, so that it can swing backwards and forwards through a small angle. The so-called "escapement" is a means by which the swings are counted, and a little impulse given to the wheel to keep it swinging. The watch "keeps time" if this hair-spring is of the right degree of stiffness, and the balance-wheel of the right weight and size. Thus a clock can be made to go faster or slower by slightly altering the length of its pendulum, and the watch by slightly changing the stiffness of its hair-spring.

It may be noted in passing that our legs, in walking, swing like pendulums, and every particular length of leg has its own natural time of vibration, so that there is a certain speed at which each person can walk which causes him or her the least amount of fatigue, because it corresponds with the natural free or unforced period of vibration of the leg considered as a pendulum.

We now pass on to notice another very important matter. If we have any pendulum, or mass suspended by a spring, having therefore a certain natural period of vibration, we can set it in motion by administering to it small repeated blows or pushes. If the interval between these impulses corresponds with the natural time-period of oscillation, it will be found that quickly a very large swing is accumulated or produced. If, on the other hand, the interval between the blows does not correspond with the natural time of vibration, then their effect

## SOUND AND MUSIC.

in producing vibration is comparatively small. This may be illustrated with great ease by means of the ball suspended by a spring. Suppose that by means of an indiarubber puffball I make a little puff of air against the suspended ball. The small impulse produces hardly any visible effect. Let this puff be repeated at intervals of time equal to that of the natural free period of vibration of the suspended ball. Then we find that, in the course of a very few puffs, we have caused a very considerable vibration or swing to take place in the heavy ball. If, however, the puffs of air come irregularly, they produce very little effect in setting the ball in motion. In the same manner a pendulum, consisting of a heavy block of wood, may be set swinging over a considerable range by a very few properly timed taps of the finger. We may notice another instance of the effect of accumulated impulses when walking over a plank laid across a ditch. If we tread in time with the natural vibration-period of the flexible plank, we shall find that very soon we produce oscillations of a dangerously large extent. Whereas, if we are careful to make the time of our steps or movement disagree with that of the plank, this will not be the case.

It is for this reason that soldiers crossing a suspension bridge are often made to break step, lest the steady tramp of armed men should happen to set up a perilous state of vibration in the bridge. It is not untruthful to say that a boy with a pea-shooter could in time break down Charing Cross Railway Bridge over the Thames. If we suppose a pea shot against one of the sections of this iron bridge, there is no doubt that it would produce an infinitesimal displacement of the bridge. Also there is no question that the bridge, being an elastic and heavy structure, has a natural free time of vibration. Hence, if pea after pea were shot at the same place at intervals of time exactly agreeing with the free time-period of vibration of the bridge, the effects would be cumulative, and would in time increase to an amount which would endanger the structure.

Impracticable and undesirable as it might be to carry out the experiment, it is nevertheless certainly true, that a boy with a pea-shooter, given sufficient patience and sufficient peas, could in time break down an iron girder bridge by the accumulation of properly timed but infinitely small blows.

The author had an instance of this before him not long ago. He was at a place where very large masts were being erected. One of these masts, about 50 feet long, was resting on two great blocks of wood placed under each end. This mast was a fine beam of timber, square in section, and each side about 2 feet wide. The mast, therefore, lay like a bridge on its terminal supports. Standing or jumping on the middle of this great beam produced hardly any visible deflection. The writer, however, placed his hand on the centre of the log and pressed it gently. Repeating this pressure at intervals, discovery was soon made of the natural time-period of vibration, and by repeating the pressures at the right moment it was found that large oscillations could be accumulated. If he had ventured to proceed far with this operation, it is certain that, with properly timed impulses, it would have been possible, by merely applying the pressure of one hand, to break in half this great wooden mast.

We have constant occasion in mechanical work to notice that whereas one pull or push of great vigour will not create some desired displacement of an object, a number of very small hits, or properly timed pushes or pulls, will achieve the requisite result. We might summarize the foregoing facts by saying that it is a maxim in dealing with bodies capable of any kind of free vibration that impulses, however small, will create oscillations of any required magnitude, if only applied at intervals equal to the natural free period of vibration of the body in question.

We can illustrate these principles by a few experiments which have special reference to musical instruments. If we fasten one end of a rope to a fixed support, we find we can

## SOUND AND MUSIC.

produce a wave or pulse in the rope by jerking the free end up and down with the hand. The speed with which a pulse or wave travels along a rope depends upon its weight per unit of length, or, say, on the number of pounds it weighs per yard, and on the tension or pull on the rope. The tighter the rope, the quicker it travels; and for the same tension the heavier the rope, the slower it travels.

It is not difficult to show that the speed with which the pulse travels is measured by the square root of the quotient of the tension of the rope by its weight per unit of length, or, as it may be called, the density of the rope.

We have already explained that, in a medium such as air, a wave of compression is propagated at a speed which is measured by the square root of the quotient of the air-pressure, or elasticity, by its density. In exactly the same way the hump that is formed on a rope by giving one end of it a jerk, runs along at a speed which is measured by the square root of the quotient of the stretching force, or tension, by the density. The propagation of a pulse or wave along a string is most easily shown for lecture purposes by filling a long indiarubber tube with sand, and then hanging it up by one end. The tube so loaded has a large weight per unit of length, and accordingly, if we give one end a jerk a hump is created which travels along rather slowly, and of which the movement can easily be watched. We may sometimes see a canal-boat driver give a jerk of this kind to the end of his horse-rope, to make it clear some obstacle such as a post or bush.

If we do this with a rope fixed at one end, we shall notice that when the hump reaches the end it is reflected and returns upon itself. If we represent by the letter $l$ the length of the rope, and by $t$ the time required to travel the double distance there and back from the free end, then the quotient of $2l$ by $t$ is obviously the velocity of the wave. But we have stated that this velocity is equal to the square root of the tension of the rope (call it $e$) by the weight per unit of length, say $m$. Hence clearly—$\dfrac{2l}{t} = \sqrt{\dfrac{e}{m}}$; or $t = 2l \cdot \sqrt{\dfrac{m}{e}}$

Supposing, then, that the jerks of the free end are given at intervals of time equal to t, or to the time required for the pulse to run along and back again, we shall find the rope thrown into so-called *stationary waves*. If, however, the jerks come twice as quickly, then the rope can accommodate itself to them by dividing itself into two sections, each of which is in separate vibration; and similarly it can divide itself into three, four, five, or six, or more sections in stationary vibration. The rope, therefore, has not only one, but many natural free periods of vibration, and it can adapt itself to many different frequencies of jerking, provided these are integer multiples of its fundamental frequency.

The above statements may be very easily verified by the use of a large tuning-fork and a string. Let a light cord or silk string be attached to one prong of a large tuning-fork which is maintained in motion electrically as presently to be explained. The other end of the cord passes over a pulley, and has a little weight attached to it. Let the tuning-fork be set in vibration, and various weights attached to the opposite end of the cord.

It is possible to find a weight which applies such a tension to the cord that its time of free vibration, as a whole, agrees with that of the fork. The cord is then thrown into stationary vibration. This is best seen by throwing the shadow of the cord upon a white screen, when it will appear as a grey spindle-shaped shadow. The central point A of the spindle is called a ventral point, or anti-node, and the stationary points N are called the nodes (see Fig. 54). Next let the tension of the string be reduced by removing some of the weight attached to the end. When the proper adjustment is made, the cord will vibrate in two segments, and have a node at the centre. Each segment vibrates in time with the tuning-fork, but the time of vibration of the whole cord is double that of

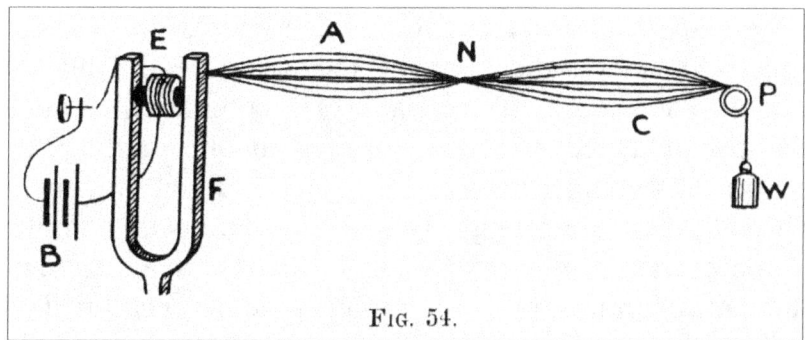

Fig. 54.

the fork. Similarly, by adjusting the tension, we may make the cord vibrate in three, four, or more sections, constituting what are called the harmonics of the string.

The string, therefore, in any particular state as regards tension and length, has a fundamental period in which it vibrates as a whole, but it can also divide itself into sections, each of which makes two, three, four, or more times as many vibrations per second.

In the case of a violin or piano string, we have an example of the same action. In playing the violin, the effective length of the string is altered by placing the finger upon it at a certain point, and then setting the string in vibration by passing along it a bow of horsehair covered with rosin. The string is set in vibration as a whole, and also in sections, and it therefore yields the so-called fundamental tone, accompanied by the *harmonics* or *over-tones*. Every violinist knows how much the tone is affected by the point at which the bow is placed across the string, and the reason is that the point where the bow touches the string must always be a ventral point, or anti-node, and it therefore determines the harmonics which shall occur.

Another good illustration of the action of properly intermittent small impulses in creating vibrations may be found in the following experiment with two electrically controlled tuning-forks: A large tuning-fork, F (see Fig. 54), has fixed between its prongs an electro-magnet, E, or piece of iron surrounded with silk-covered wire. When an electric current from a battery, B, traverses the wire it causes the iron to be magnetized, and it then attracts the prongs and pulls them together. The circuit of the battery is completed through a little springy piece of metal attached to one of the prongs which makes contact with a fixed screw. The arrangement is such that when the prongs fly apart the circuit is completed and the current flows, and then the current magnetizes the iron, and this in turn pulls the prongs together, and breaks the circuit. The fork, therefore, maintains itself in vibration when once it has been started. It is called an electrically driven tuning-fork. Here are two such forks, in every way identical. One of the forks is self-driven, but the current through its own electromagnet is made to pass also through the electro-magnet of the other fork, which is, therefore, not self-driven, but controlled by the first. If, then, the first fork is started, the electro-magnet of the second fork is traversed by intermittent electric currents having the same frequency as the first fork, and the electro magnet of the second fork administers, therefore, small pulls to the prongs of the second fork, these pulls corresponding to the periodic time of the first fork. If, as at present, the forks are identical, and I start the first one, or the driving fork, in action it will, in a few seconds, cause the second fork to begin to sound. Let me, however, affix a small piece of wax to the second fork. I have now altered its proper period of vibration by slightly weighting the prongs. You now see that the first fork is unable to set the second fork in action. The electro-magnet is operating as before, but its impulses do not come at the right time, and hence the second fork does not begin to move.

If we weight the two forks equally with wax, we can again tune them in sympathy, and then once again they will control each other.

## SOUND AND MUSIC.

All these cases, in which one set of small impulses at proper intervals of time create a large vibration in the body on which they act, are said to be instances of *resonance*. A more perfect illustration of acoustic resonance may be brought before you now. Before me, on the table, is a tall glass cylindrical jar, and I have in my hand a tuning-fork, the prongs of which make 256 vibrations per second when struck (see Fig. 55). If the fork is started in action, you at a distance will hear but little sound. The prongs of the fork move through the air, but they do not set it in very great oscillatory movement. Let us calculate, however, the wave-length of the waves given out by the fork. From the fundamental formula, *wave-velocity* = *wave-length* x *frequency*; and knowing that the velocity of sound at the present temperature of the air is about 1126 feet per second, we see at once that the length of the air wave produced by this fork must be nearly 4.4 feet, because 4.4 x 256 = 1126.4. Hence the quarter wave-length is nearly 1.1 foot, or, say, 1 foot 1 inch. I hold the fork over this tall jar, and pour water into the jar until the space between the water-surface and the top of the jar is a little over 1 foot, and at that moment the sound of the fork becomes much louder. The column of air in the jar is 1.1 foot in length and this resounds to the fork. You will have no difficulty in seeing the reason for this in the light of previous explanations. The air column has a certain natural rate of vibration, which is such that its fundamental note has a wave-length four times the length of the column of air. In the case of the rope fixed at one end and jerked up and down at the other so as to make stationary vibrations, the length of the rope is one quarter of the wave-length of its sta-

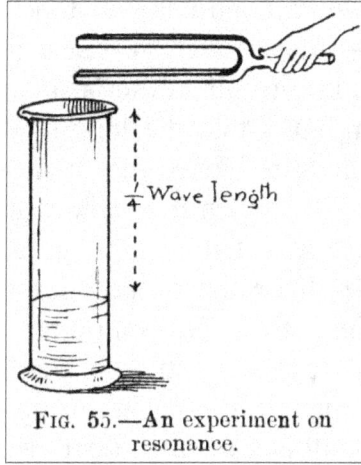

Fig. 55.—An experiment on resonance.

tionary wave. This is easily seen if we remember that the fixed end must be a node, and the end moved up and down must be an anti-node, or ventral segment, and the distance between a *node* and an *anti-node* is one quarter of a wave-length. Accordingly the vibrating column of air in the jar also has a fundamental mode of vibration, such that the length of the column is one quarter of a wave-length. Hence the vibrating prongs of the 256-period tuning-fork, when held over the 1.1 foot long column of air, are able to set the air in great vibratory movement, for the impulses from the prongs come at exactly the right time. Accordingly, the loud sound you hear when the fork is held over the jar proceeds, not so much from the fork as from the column of air in the jar. The prongs of the fork give little blows to the column of air, and these being at intervals equal to the natural time-period of vibration of the air in the jar, the latter is soon set in violent vibration.

We can, in the next place, pass on now to discuss some matters connected with the theory of music. When regular air-vibrations or wave-trains fall upon the ear they produce the sensation of a musical tone, provided that their frequency lies between about 40 per second and about 4000. The lowest note in an organ usually is one having 32 vibrations per second, and the highest note in the orchestra is that of a piccolo flute, giving 4752 vibrations per second. We can appreciate as sound vibrations lying between 16 and 32,000, but the greater portion of these high frequencies have no musical character, and would be described as whistles or squeaks.

When one note has twice the frequency of another it is called the *octave* of the first. Thus our range of musical tones is comprised within about seven octaves, or within the limits of the notes whose frequencies are 40, 80, 160, 320, 640, 1280, 2560, and 5120.

These musical notes are distinguished, as every one knows, by certain letters or signs on a *clef*. Thus the note called the middle C of a piano has a frequency of 248, and is denoted by the sign

The octave is divided into certain musical intervals by notes, the frequencies of which have a certain ratio to that of the fundamental note. This ratio is determined by what is called the scale, or gamut. Thus, in the major diatonic natural scale, if we denote the fundamental note by C, called *do* or *ut* in singing, and its frequency by n, then the other notes in the natural scale are denoted by the letters, and have frequencies as below.

| *do* | *re* | *mi* | *fa* | *sol* | *la* | *si* | *do'* |
|------|------|------|------|-------|------|------|-------|
| C | D | E | F | G | A | B | C¹ |
| $n$ | $\frac{9}{8}n$ | $\frac{5}{4}n$ | $\frac{4}{3}n$ | $\frac{3}{2}n$ | $\frac{5}{3}n$ | $\frac{15}{8}n$ | $2n$ |

Hence if the note C has 248 vibrations per second, then the note D will have 9 × 248 ÷ 8 = 279 vibrations per second. On looking at the above scale of the eight notes forming an octave, it will be seen that there are three kinds of ratios of frequencies of the various notes.

1. The ratio of C to D, or F to G, or A to B, which is that of 8 to 9.
2. The ratio of D to E, and G to A, which is that of 9 to 10.
3. The ratio of E to F, or B to C¹ which is that of 15 to 16.

The first two of these intervals or ratios are both called a *tone*, and the third is called a *semitone*. The two tones, however, are not exactly the same, but their ratio to one another is that of $\frac{8}{9}$ or $\frac{9}{10}$, or of 80 to 81. This interval is called a *comma*, and can be distinguished by a good musical ear.

Several of these intervals or ratios of frequencies have received names. Thus the interval C to E, = 4:5, is called a *major third*, and the interval E to G, = 5:6, is called a *minor third*; the interval C to G, = 2:3, is called a *fifth*, and that of C to $C^1$, = 1:2, is called an *octave*. For the purposes of music it has been found necessary to introduce other notes between the seven notes of the octave. If a note is introduced which has a frequency greater than any one of the seven in the ratio of 25 to 24, that is called a *sharpened* note; thus the note of which the frequency is $\frac{3}{2}n \times \frac{25}{24}$ would be called *G sharp*, and written G♯. In the same way, if the frequency of any note is lowered in the ratio of 24 to 25, it is said to be flattened. Then the note whose frequency is $\frac{3}{2}n \times \frac{24}{25}$ If would be called *G flat*, and written G♭.

It is obvious that if we were to introduce flats and sharps to all the eight notes we should have twenty-four notes in the octave, and the various intervals would become too numerous and confusing for memory or performance. Hence in keyed instruments the difficulty has been over-come by employing a *scale of equal temperament*, made as follows: The interval of an octave is divided into twelve parts by introducing eleven notes, the ratio of the frequency of each note to its neighbours on either side being the same, and equal to the ratio 1 to 1.05946.

The scale thus formed is called the *chromatic scale*, and by this means a number of the flats and sharps become identical; thus, for in stance, C♯ and D♭ become the same note. The octave has therefore twelve notes, which are the seven white keys, and the five black ones of the octave of the key-board of a piano or organ.

Every one not entirely destitute of a musical ear is aware that certain of these musical intervals, such as the fifth, the octave, or the major third, produce an agreeable impression on the ear when the notes forming them are sounded together. On the other hand, some intervals, such as the seventh, are not pleasant. The former we call *concords*, and the latter *discords*. The question then arises—What is the reason for this difference in the effect of the air-vibrations on the ear? This leads us to consider the nature of simple and complex air vibrations or waves. Let us consider, in the first place, the effect of sending out into the air two sets of air waves of slightly different wave lengths. These waves both travel at the same rate, hence we shall not affect the combined effects of the waves upon the air if we consider both sets of waves to stand still. For the sake of simplicity, we will consider that the wave-length of one train is 20 inches, and that of the other is 21. Moreover, let the two wave-trains be so placed relatively to one another that they both start from one point in the same phase of movement; that is, let their zero points, or their humps or hollows, coincide. Then if we draw two wavy lines (see Fig. 56) to represent these two trains, it will be evident that, since the wave-length of one is 1 inch longer than that of the other that is, a distance equal to twenty wave-lengths one wave-train will have gained a whole wave-length upon the other, and in a distance equal to ten wave-lengths, one wave train will have gained half a wave-length upon the other. If we therefore imagine the two wave-trains superimposed, we shall find, on looking along the line of propagation, an alternate doubling or destruction of wave-effect at regular intervals. In other words, the effect of superimposing two trains of waves of slightly different wave-lengths is to produce a resultant wave-train in which the wave-amplitude increases up to a certain point, and then dies away again nearly to nothing, as shown in the lowest of the three wave-lines in Fig. 56.

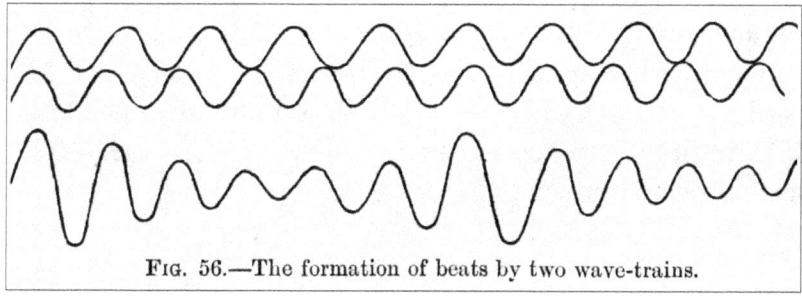

Fig. 56.—The formation of beats by two wave-trains.

We must, then, determine how far apart these points of maximum wave-amplitude or points of no wave effect lie. If the wave-length of one train is, as stated, 20 inches, then a length of ten wave-lengths is 200 inches, and this must be, therefore, the distance from a place of maximum combined wave-effect to a place of zero wave-effect. Accordingly, the distance between two places where the two wave-trains help one another must be 400 inches, and this must also be the distance between two adjacent places of wave-destruction. If, therefore, we look along the wavy line representing the resultant wave, every 400 inches we shall find a maximum wave-amplitude, and every 400 inches a place where the waves have destroyed each other. We may call this distance a *wave-train length*, and it is obviously equal to the product of the constituent wave-lengths divided by the difference of the two constituent wave-lengths.

It follows from this that if we suppose the two wave-trains to move forward with equal speed, the number of maximum points or zero points which will pass any place in the unit of time will be equal to the *difference*, between the frequencies of the constituents. Let us now reduce this to an experiment. Here are two organ-pipes exactly tuned to unison, and when both are sounded together we have two identical wave-trains sent out into the air. We can, however, slightly lengthen one of the pipes, and so put them out of tune. When this is done you can no longer hear the smooth sound, but a sort of waxing and waning in the sound, and this alternate increase and diminution in loudness is called *a beat*. We can easily take count of the number of beats per second, and by the reasoning given above we see that the number of beats per second must be equal to the difference between the frequencies of the two sets of waves. Thus if one organ-pipe is giving 100 vibrations per second to the air, and the other 102, we hear two beats per second.

Now, up to a certain point we can count these beats, but when they come quicker than about 10 per second, we cease to be able to hear them separately. When they come at the rate of about 30 per second they communicate to the combined sound a peculiar rasping and unpleasant effect which we call a discord. If they come much more quickly than 70 per second we cease to be conscious of their presence by any discordant effect in the sound.

The theory was first put forward by the famous physicist, Von Helmholtz, that the reason certain musical intervals are not agreeable to the trained ear is because the difference between the frequencies of the constituent fundamental tones *or the harmonics present in them* give rise to beats, approximately of 30 to 40 per second.

In order to simplify our explanations we will deal with two cases only, viz. that of the *octave* interval and that of the *seventh*. The first is a perfect concord, and the second, at least on stringed instruments, is a discord. It has already been explained that when a string vibrates it does so not only as a whole, but also in sections, giving out a fundamental note with superposed harmonics. Suppose we consider the octave of notes lying between the frequencies 204 and 528, which correspond to the notes C and $C^1$ forming the middle octave on a piano. The frequencies and differences of the eight tones in this octave are as follows:—

| Frequencies of the Notes of the Middle Octave of a Piano. ||||||
|---|---|---|---|---|---|
| Notes. | Frequency. | Difference. | Notes. | Frequency. | Difference. |
| C | 264 | | G | 396 | |
| | | 33 | | | 44 |
| D | 297 | | A | 440 | |
| | | 33 | | | 55 |
| E | 330 | | B | 495 | |
| | | 22 | | | 33 |
| F | 352 | | $C^1$ | 528 | |
| | | 44 | | | |

It will thus be seen that the differences between the frequencies of adjacent notes are such as to make beats between them which have a number per second so near to the limits of 30 to 40 that adjacent notes sounded together are discords.

Suppose, however, we sound the *seventh*, viz. *C* and *B*, together. The frequencies are 264 and 495, and the difference is 231. Since, then, the difference between the frequencies lies far beyond the limit of 30 to 40 per second, how comes it that in this case we have a discord? To answer this question we must consider the harmonics present with the fundamentals. Write down each frequency multiplied respectively by the numbers 1, 2, 3, 4, etc.—

|  | C. | B. |
|---|---|---|
| Fundamental | 264 | 495 |
| First harmonic | 528 | 990 |
| Second ,, | 792 | 1475 |
| Third ,, | 1056 | 1980 |
| Fourth ,, | 1320 | 2475 |
| Fifth ,, | 1584 | 2970 |

On looking at these numbers we see that although the difference between the frequencies of the two fundamentals is too great to produce the disagreeable number of beats, yet the difference between the frequencies of the fundamental of note B (495) and the first harmonic of note C (528) is exactly 33, which is, therefore, the required number. Accordingly, the discordant character of the seventh interval played on a piano is not due to the beats between the primary tones, but to beats arising between the first harmonic of one and the fundamental of the other. It will be a useful exercise to the reader to select any other interval, and write down the primary frequencies and the overtone frequencies, or harmonics, and then determine whether between any pairs disagreeable beats can occur.

The presence of harmonics or overtones is, therefore, a source of discord in some cases, but nevertheless these overtones communicate a certain character to the sound.

Helmholtz's chief conclusions as regards the cause of concord and discord in musical tones were as follows:

## SOUND AND MUSIC.

1. Musical sounds which are pure, that is, have no harmonics mixed up with them, are soft and agreeable, but without brilliancy. Of this kind are the tones emitted by tuning-forks gently struck or open organ- pipes not blown violently.
2. The presence of harmonics up to the sixth communicates force and brilliancy and character to the tone. Of this kind are the notes of the piano and organ-pipes more strongly blown.
3. If only the uneven harmonics, viz. the first, third, fifth, etc., are present, the sound acquires a certain nasal character.
4. If the higher harmonics are strong, then the sound acquires great penetrating force, as in the case of brass instruments, trumpet, trombone, clarionet, etc.
5. The causes of discord are beats having a frequency of 30 to 40 or so, taking place between the two primary tones or the harmonics of either note.

The pleasure derived from the sound of a musical instrument is dependent, to a large extent, on the existence of the desirable harmonics in each tone, or on the exclusion of undesirable ones.

In the next place, let us consider a little the means at our disposal for creating and enforcing the class of air-waves which give rise to the sensations of musical tones. Broadly speaking, there are three chief forms of musical air-wave-making appliance, viz. those which depend on the vibrations of columns of air, on strings, and on plates respectively.

One of the oldest and simplest forms of musical instrument is that represented by the pan-pipes, still used as an orchestral accompaniment in the case of the ever-popular peripatetic theatrical display called Punch and Judy.

If we take a metal or wooden pipe closed at the bottom, and blow gently across the open end, we obtain a musical note. The air in the pipe is set in vibration, and the tone we obtain depends on the length of the column of air, which is the same as the length of the pipe. The manner in which this air-vibration is started is as follows: On blowing across the open end of the pipe closed at the bottom a partial vacuum is made in it. That this is so, can be seen in any scent spray-producer, in which two glass tubes are fixed at right angles to each other. One tube dips into the scent, and through the other a puff of air is sent across the open mouth of the first. The liquid is sucked up the vertical tube by reason of the partial vacuum made above it. If we employ a pipe closed at the bottom and blow across the open end, the first effect of the exhaustion is that the jet of air is partly sucked down into the closed tube, and thus compresses the air in it. This air then rebounds, and again a partial vacuum is made in the tube. So the result is an alternate compression and expansion of the air in the closed tube. The column of air is alternately stretched and squeezed, and a state of stationary vibration is set up in the air in the tube; just as in the case of a rope fixed at one end and jerked up and down at the other end. The natural time-period of vibration of the column of air in the tube controls the behaviour of the jet of air blown across its mouth, the energy of the jet of air being drawn upon to keep the column of air in the tube in a state of oscillation. Thus a flutter is excited in the air in the tube, which is maintained as long as there is a blast of air across its mouth, and this communicates to the air outside a wave-motion. We have, therefore, a musical note produced, the wave-length of which is four times the length of the closed tube across the mouth of which we are blowing. Accordingly, a very simple musical instrument such as the pan-pipes consists of a row of tubes closed at the bottom, the tubes being of different lengths. A current of air from the mouth is blown across the tubes taken in a certain order, and we can obtain a simple melody by that process of selection.

An organ-pipe is only a more perfect means for doing the same thing. Organ-pipes may be either open or closed pipes. Also they have either a reed or a flute at one end for the purpose of establishing air-vibrations when a current of air is blown into the pipe. The form of organ-pipe most easy to understand is the closed flute pipe. This consists of a wooden tube closed at the upper end, and at the lower end having a foot-tube and mouthpiece as shown in section in Fig. 57. When a gentle current of air is blown in at the foot-tube, it impinges on the sharp edge or chamfer of the mouthpiece, and it acts just as when blown across the open end of a simple closed pipe. That is to say, it sets up a state of alternate compression and expansion of the air in the pipe. At the closed end, period-changes in density in the air are established, but no great movement takes place. At the open end or mouth there are no great changes of density, but the air is alternately moving in and out at the mouthpiece. The steady blast of air against the chamfer, therefore, sets up a state of steady oscillation of the air in the pipe, the air being squeezed up and extended alternately so that there is first a state of compression, and then a state of partial rarefaction in the air at the closed end of the pipe. In this case, also, the wave-motion communicated to the surrounding air has a wave-length equal to four times the length of the pipe.

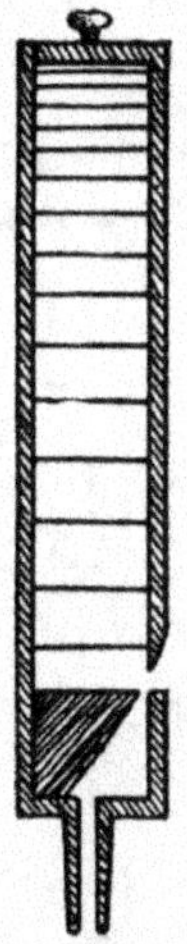

Fig. 57. — A closed organ-pipe.

If we open the upper end of the pipe, it at once emits a note which has a wave-length equal to double the length of the pipe. Hence the note emitted by an open-ended organ-pipe is an octave higher than that given out by a closed organ-pipe of the same length.

The action of an open organ-pipe is not quite so easy to comprehend as that of a closed pipe. The difficulty is to see how stationary air waves can be set up in a pipe which is open at both ends. The easiest way to comprehend the matter is as follows: When the blast of air against the lip of the pipe begins to partially exhaust the air in it, the rarefaction so begun does not commence everywhere in the pipe at once. It starts from the mouthpiece end, and is propagated along the pipe at a rate equal to the velocity of sound. The air at the open ends of the pipe moves in to supply this reduced pressure, and, in so doing, overshoots the mark, and the result is a region of compression is formed in the central portions of the pipe (see Fig. 58). The next instant this compressed air expands again, and moves out at the two open ends of the pipe. We have thus established in the pipe an oscillatory state which, at the central region of the pipe, consists in an alternate compression and expansion or rarefaction of the air, whilst at the open end and mouthpiece end there is an alternate rushing in and rushing out of the air. Hence in the centre of the pipe we have little or no movement of the air, but rapid alternations of pressure, or, which is the same thing, density; and at the two ends little or no change in density, but rapid movement of the air in and out of the pipe.

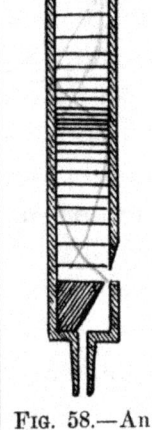

FIG. 58.—An open organ-pipe.

An analogy between the vibration of the air in a closed and open organ-pipe might be found in considering the vibration of an elastic rod first, when clamped at one end, and secondly, when clamped at the two ends. The deflection of the rod at any point may be considered to represent change of air-pressure, and the fixed point or points the open end of the pipe at which there can be no change of density, because there it is in close communication with the open air outside the pipe. It is at once evident that the length of the open organ-pipe, when sounding its fundamental tone, is one-half of the length of the air wave it produces. Accordingly, from the formula, *wave-velocity = frequency x wave-length*, we see that,

## SOUND AND MUSIC.

since the velocity of sound at ordinary temperature is about 1120 feet per second, an approximate rule for obtaining the frequency of the vibrations given out by an open organ-pipe is as follows:

*Frequency = 1120 divided by twice the length of pipe.*

We say *approximate*, because, as a matter of fact, for a reason rather too complicated to explain here, the wavelength of the air-vibrations is equal to rather more than double the length of the pipe. In fact, what we may call the effective length of the pipe is equal to its real end-to-end length increased by a fraction of its diameter, which is very nearly four-fifths.

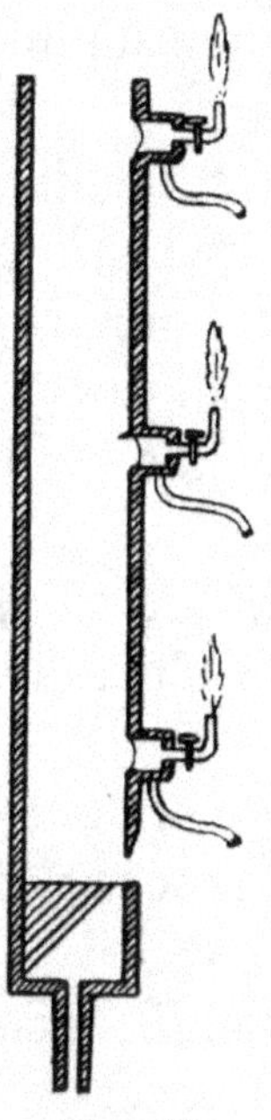

We can confirm by experiments the statements made as to the condition of the air in a sounding organ-pipe. Here is a pipe with three little holes bored in it at the top, middle, and bottom (see Fig. 59). Each of these is covered with a thin indiarubber membrane, and this, again, by a little box which has a gas-pipe leading to it and a gas-jet connected with it. If we lead gas into the box and light the jet, we have a little flame, as you see. If, then, the indiarubber membrane is pressed in and out, it will cause the gas-flame to flicker. Such an arrangement is called a *manometric flame*, because it serves to detect or measure changes of pressure in the pipe. The flicker of the flame when the organ-pipe is sounded is, however, so rapid that we cannot follow it unless we look at the image in a cubical revolving mirror of the kind already used. If we sound the organ-pipe gently and look at the bands of light corresponding to the three flames, we see that the flames at the top and bottom of the pipe are nearly steady, but that the one at the middle of the pipe is flickering rapidly, the band of light being changed to a saw-tooth-like form (see Fig. 60).

FIG. 59.

153

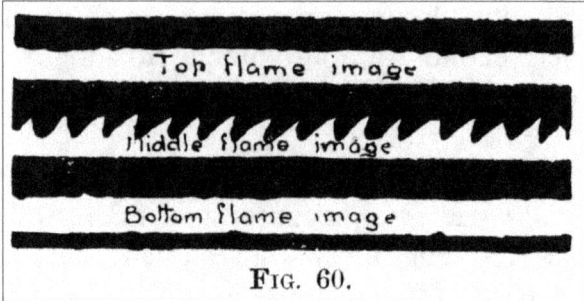

Fig. 60.

This shows us that rapid changes of pressure are taking place at the centre of the pipe.

Again, if we prepare a little tambourine (by stretching parchment-paper over a wooden ring), and lower it by a string into 'the sounding organ-pipe, we shall find that grains of sand scattered over this tambourine jump about rapidly when the membrane is held near the top or the bottom of the pipe, but are quiescent when it is at the middle.

This shows us that there is violent movement of the air at the ends, but not in the centre, thus confirming the deductions of theory.

It should be noted that if the pipe is over-blown or sounded too strongly, harmonics will make their appearance, and the simple state of affairs will no longer exist.

The celebrated mathematician, Daniel Bernouilli, discovered that an organ-pipe can be made to yield a succession of musical notes by properly varying the pressure of the current of air blown into it. If the pipe is an open one, then, if we call the frequency of the primary note 1, obtained when the pipe is gently blown, if we blow more strongly, the pipe yields notes which are the harmonics of the fundamental one, that is to say, have frequencies represented by 2, 3, 4, 5, etc., as the blast of air increases in force.

Thus, if the pipe is one about 2 feet in length, it will yield a note near to the middle C on a piano. If more strongly blown, it gives a note, $C^1$, an octave higher, having double the frequency. If more strongly blown still, it yields a note which

## SOUND AND MUSIC.

is the fifth, $G^1$, above the last, and has three times the frequency of the primary tone; and so on.

If the pipe is closed at the top, then over-blowing the pipe makes it yield the odd harmonics, or the tones which are related in frequency to the primary tone in the ratio of 1, 3, 5, etc. Hence, if a stopped pipe gives a note, C, its first overtone is the fifth above the octave, or $G^1$.

It is usual, in adjusting the air-pressure of an organ-bellows, to allow such a pressure as that some of the over-tones, or harmonics, shall exist. The presence of these harmonics in a note gives brilliancy to it, whereas an absolutely pure or simple musical tone, though not disagreeable to the ear, is not fully satisfying. Any one with a good ear can detect these harmonics or overtones in a single note sounded on a piano or organ due to the subdivision of the vibrating string or air-column into sections separated by nodes.

It will be seen that the acoustic action of the organ-pipe depends essentially upon some operation tending at the commencement to make an expansion of the air in the pipe at one end, and subsequently to cause an increase of air-pressure in it.

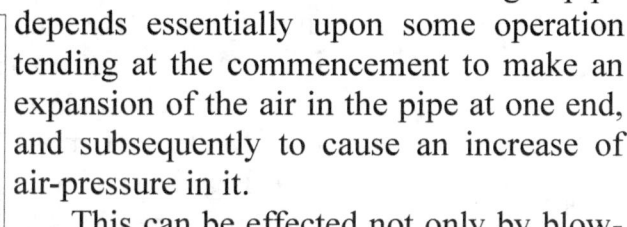

Fig. 61.

This can be effected not only by blowing into the pipe, but in another way, by introducing a hot body into a pipe open at both ends. We can show here as an illustration of this an interesting experiment due to Lord Rayleigh. A long cast-iron water-pipe about 4 inches in diameter and 8 feet long is suspended from the ceiling. About 1 foot up the tube from the lower end a piece of iron-wire gauze is fixed (see Fig. 61). By means of a gas-burner introduced into the tube, we heat the gauze red hot, and on withdrawing the lamp the tube suddenly emits a deep organ-like note for a few moments. The heated metal creates an up-draught in the tube at the lower end, and, as in the case of the open organ-pipe, causes also an in-suction of air at the upper end. The column of air is thus set vibrating with a point of alternate condensation and rarefaction in the centre, and in-draughts and out- rushes of air at the ends.

Indeed, this rush of air into and out of the pipe at the lower end during the time it is sounding its note is so violent that if the hands are placed just below the bottom end of the tube they will feel chilled, as if placed near an electric fan, by the blast of air. Closing the bottom end of the pipe with a sheet of metal at once "stops the air-movement, and with it the musical note.

In another form the experiment has long been known under the name of a *singing flame*. A small jet of burning hydrogen gas is introduced into a glass tube about 3 feet in length. The jet must consist of a long narrow brass tube, and the proper position for the jet must be found by trial (see Fig. 62). When this is done, however, the tube emits a clear musical note, due to the tube acting as an open organ-pipe. If the flame is examined in a revolving mirror when the tube is singing, it will be found to be in vibration in sympathy with the movement of air in the tube. The tube often refuses to start singing, but may be made to do it by giving it a little tap. The actions taking place in the tube are something as follows: When the flame is introduced, it heats and rarefies the air around it. This causes an in-rush of air both at the top and bottom of the tube. A state of steady oscillation is then established, in which the

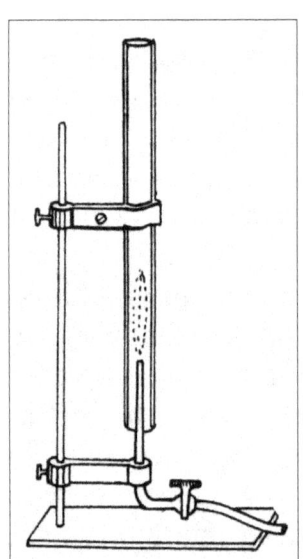

FIG. 62.—Singing flame.

air at the centre undergoes periodical expansions and compressions, and the pressure of the air round the flame changes in the same manner. The flame is therefore alternately expanded and contracted. When it expands, it heats the air more. When it is compressed, it heats it less. This variation of the flame causes air to be sucked in or expelled from both open ends of the tube, and establishes the state of steady vibration in accordance with the length of the tube. The flame and the air-column act and react on each other, and establish a state of stationary aerial oscillation in accordance with the natural time-period of the column of air. The tube can be made to give out not only its fundamental note, but a series of harmonics, or overtones, with frequencies 2, 3, 4, 5, etc., times the fundamental note, by varying the position of the flame, which must always be just under the place where a node, or place of alternate condensation and rarefaction, occurs.

We may, in the next place, with advantage briefly examine the principles of construction of one musical instrument, and allude to some recent improvements. One of the most interesting of all the musical appliances devised by human ingenuity is the violin, comprising as it does in its construction an art, a science, and a tradition. In principle the violin is nothing but a wooden box, along the top of which are stretched four strings, which are strained over a piece of wood called a bridge. These strings have their effective length altered in playing by placing the finger of the performer at some place on them, and they are set in vibration by drawing over them a well-rosined bow made of horse-hair. The vibrating string communicates its vibrations to the surface of the box or body by means of the bridge, and this again to the air in the interior. The body thus serves two purposes. It acts as a resonating-chamber, and also it affords a large surface of contact with the surrounding air, whereby a greater mass of air is set simultaneously in wave-motion. The four strings are normally tuned in *fifths*, so that the fundamental note of each is an interval of a fifth above the next.

The performer varies the note given by each string by shortening its vibrating length by pressing the finger upon it. The skilled violinist has also great control over the tone, and can determine the harmonics, or overtones, which shall accompany the fundamental by altering the point on the string at which the bow is applied, and lightly touching it at some other point.

The great art in the construction of the violin rests in the manufacture of the wooden body. Its form, materials, and minute details of construction have been the subject of countless experiments in past ages, and until quite recently no essential improvement was made in the instrument as completed by the masters of violin construction three centuries ago. In classical form the violin consists of a wooden box of characteristic shape, composed of a back, belly, and six ribs. These are shaped out of thin wood, the belly being made of pine, and maple used for the rest. A neck or handle is affixed to one end, and a tail-piece, to which the gut-strings are fastened, to the other.

The strings are strained over a thin piece of wood which rests on two feet on the belly. One of these feet rests over a block of wood in the interior of the box called the sound-post, and this forms a rigid centre; the other foot stands on the resonant part of the belly. The belly is strengthened in addition by a bar of wood, which is glued to it just under the place where the active foot of the bridge rests. The ribs or sides of the box are bent inwards at the centre to enable the playing-bow to get at the strings more easily. The selection of the wood and its varnishing is the most important part of the construction. The wood must be elastic, and its elasticity has to be preserved by the use of an appropriate hard varnish, or else it will not take up the vibrations imparted by the strings. The

## SOUND AND MUSIC.

old makers used wood which was only just sufficiently seasoned, and applied their varnish at once.

An essential adjunct is a good bow, which is of more importance than generally supposed. Something may be got out of a poor violin by a good player, but no one can play with a bad bow.

The process of eliciting a musical tone from the violin is as follows: The player, holding the instrument in the left hand, and with its tail end pressed against the left shoulder, places a finger of the left hand lightly on some point on a string, and sweeps the bow gently across the string so as to set it in vibration, yielding its fundamental note, accompanied by the lower harmonics. The purity and strength of the note depend essentially upon the skill with which this touch of the bow is made, creating and sustaining the same kind of vibration on the string through-out its sweep. The string then presses intermittently on the bridge, and this again turns, so to speak, round one foot as round a pivot, and presses intermittently on the elastic wooden belly. The belly takes up these vibrations, and the air in the interior is thrown into sympathetic vibration by resonance. The sound escapes by the $f$-holes in the belly. The extraordinary thing about the violin is that the shape of the box permits it to take up vibrations lying between all the range of musical tones. The air-cavity does not merely resonate to one note, but to hundreds of different rates of vibration.

The peculiar charm of the violin is the quality of the sound which a skilled player can elicit from it. That wonderful pleading, sympathetic, voice-like tone, which conveys so much emotional meaning to the trained musical ear, is due to the proper admixture of the harmonics, or overtones, with the fundamental notes. The string vibrates not merely as a whole, but in sections. Hence the place at which the bow touches must always be an anti-node, or ventral point, and the smallest change in this position greatly affects the quality of the tone.

Quite recently an entirely new departure has been made in violin construction by Mr. Augustus Stroh, a well-known inventor. He has abolished the wooden body and bridge, and substituted for them an aluminium trumpet-shaped tube as the resonant chamber, ending in a circular corrugated aluminium disc, on the centre of which rests an aluminium lever pivoted at one point. The strings are strained over this lever, and held on a light tube, which does duty as a point of attachment of all parts of the instrument. The strings are the same, and the manipulation of the instrument identical with that of the ordinary violin. The vibrations of the strings are communicated by the pivoted lever over which they pass to the corrugated aluminium disc, and by this to the air lying in the trumpet-tube. This tube points straight away from the player, and directs the air waves to the audience in front. The tone of the new violin is declared by connoisseurs to be remarkably full, mellow, and resonant. The notes have a richness and power which satisfies the ear, and is generally only to be found in the handiwork of the classical constructors of the ordinary form of violin. One great advantage in the Stroh violin is that every one can be made perfectly of the same excellence. The aluminium discs are stamped out by a steel die, and are therefore all identical. The element of chance or personal skill in making has been eliminated by a scientific and mechanical construction. Thus the musician becomes possessed of an instrument in which scientific construction predominates over individual art or tradition in manufacture, yet at the same time the musical effects which skill in playing can produce are not at all diminished.

Whilst our attention has so far been fixed on the external operations in the air which constitute a train of music-making waves, it seems only appropriate to make, in conclusion, a brief reference to the apparatus which we possess in our ears

# SOUND AND MUSIC.

for appreciating these subtle changes in air-pressure with certainty and pleasure. The ear itself is a marvellous appliance for detecting the existence of waves and ripples in the air, and it embodies in itself many of the principles which have been explained to-day.

The organ of hearing is a sort of house with three chambers in it, or, rather, two rooms and an entrance hall, with the front door always open. This entrance passage of the ear is a short tube which communicates at one end with the open air, being there provided with a sound-deflecting screen in the shape of an external ornamental shell, commonly called the ear. In many animals this external appendage is capable of being turned into different positions, to assist in determining the direction in which the sound wave is coming. The entrance tube of the ear is closed at the bottom by a delicate membrane called the tympanum, or drum. Against this drumhead the air waves impinge, and it is pressed in and out by the changes of air-pressure. This drum separates the outer end from a chamber called the middle ear, and the middle ear communicates, by a sort of back staircase, or tube called the Eustachian tube, with the cavity at the back of the mouth (see Fig. 63).

Behind the middle ear, and buried in the bony structure of

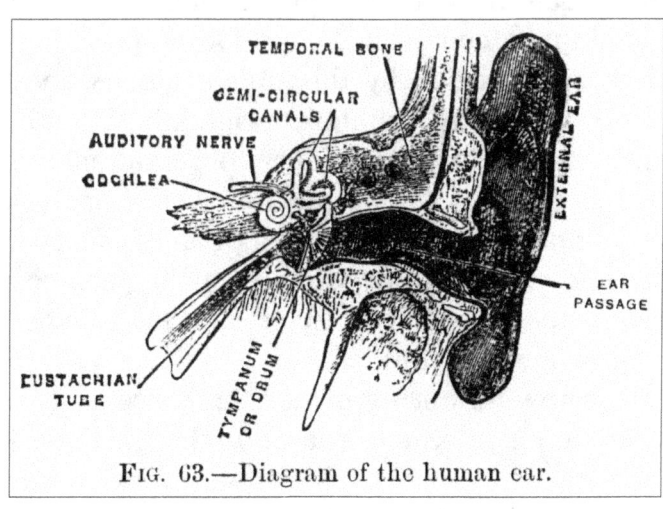

Fig. 63.—Diagram of the human ear.

the skull, is a third, more secret chamber, called the inner ear. This is separated from the middle ear by two little windows, which are also covered with delicate membranes. In the middle ear there is a chain of three small bones linked with one another, which are connected at one end with the tympanum, or drum, and at the other end with the so-called oval window of the inner ear. Helmholtz has shown that this little chain of bones forms a system of levers, by means of which the movements of the tympanum are diminished in extent, but increased in force in the ratio of 2 to 3.

The internal ear is the real seat of audition, and it comprises the parts called the labyrinth, the semicircular canals, and the cochlea. These are cavities lined with delicate membranes and filled with fluid. In the cochlea there is an organ called Corti's organ, which is a veritable harp of ten thousand strings. This consists of innumerable nerve-fibres, which are an extension of the auditory nerve. The details of the organic structure are far too complicated for description here. Suffice it to say that air waves, beating against the tympanum, propagate vibrations along the chain of bones into the fluids in the inner ear, and finally expend themselves on these nerve-fibres, which are the real organs of sound-sensation.

Helmholtz put forward the ingenious hypothesis that each fibre in the organ of Corti was tuned, so to speak, to a different note, and that a composite sound falling upon the ear was analyzed or disentangled by this organ into its constituents. Although this theory, as Helmholtz originally stated it, has not altogether been upheld by subsequent observation, it is certain that the ear possesses this wonderful power of analysis. It can be shown by mathematical reasoning of an advanced kind that any musical sound, no matter what its quality, can be resolved into the sum of a number of selected pure sounds such as those given by a tuning-fork.

Consider now for one moment the physical state of the air in a concert-room in which a large orchestra is performing.

## SOUND AND MUSIC.

The air is traversed by a chaos of waves of various wavelengths. The deep notes of the violincello, organ, and trumpets are producing waves 10 to 20 feet in wave-length, which may be best described as billows in the air. The violin-strings and middle notes of the piano, harp, or flute are yielding air waves from 6 or 8 feet to a few inches long, whilst the higher notes of violins and flutes are air ripples some 3 or 4 inches in length.

If we could see the particles of the air in the concert-room, and fasten our attention upon any one of them, we should see it executing a most complicated motion under the combined action of these air-wave-producing instruments. We should be fascinated by the amazing dance of molecules to and fro and from side to side, as the medley of waves of compression or rarefaction embraced them and drove them hither and thither in their resistless grasp.

The tympana of our ears are therefore undergoing motions of a like complicated kind, and this complex movement is transmitted through the chain of bones in the middle ear to the inner ear, or true organ of sensation. But there, by some wondrous mechanism not at all yet fully understood, an analysis takes place of these entangled motions.

The well-trained ear separates between the effect due to each kind of musical instrument, and even detects a want of tuning in any one of them. It resolves each sound into its harmonics, appreciates their relative intensity, is satisfied or dissatisfied with the admixture. In the inner chamber of the ear physical movements are in some wholly inscrutable manner translated into sensations of sound, and the confused aggregation of waves and ripples in the air, beating against the tympanic membrane there, takes effect in producing impulses which travel up the auditory nerve and expend their energy finally in the creation of sensations of melody and tune, which arouse emotions, revive memories, and stir sometimes the deepest feelings of our minds.

# CHAPTER V.

# ELECTRIC OSCILLATIONS AND ELECTRIC WAVES.

IN the previous chapters your attention has been directed to the subject of waves on water and waves in air, and we shall now proceed to discuss some of the more difficult matters connected with the production of waves in the æther. We shall find that this portion of our subject makes more demands upon our powers of comprehension, since much that we have to consider is not directly the object of sense perception, and the inferences which we have to make from observed facts are less simple and easy to follow. Nevertheless, I trust that if you have been able to grasp clearly the nature of a surface-wave on water and of a compressional wave in air, you will not readily allow yourselves to be discouraged from encountering a new class of ideas, but will be able to advance still further, and gain a more or less clear conception of the nature of an electric wave in the æther.

In the first place, we must consider the medium in which these waves are created. We can see with our eyes a water-surface, and we are able to understand without much difficulty that the surface can be thrown into humps and hollows, or become wrinkled, and also that these elevations and depressions can change their position, thus creating a surface wave which moves forward. The movement of the water wave is, therefore, only the result of a local elevation of the surface which travels along or takes place progressively at different places on the surface. Then, again, in the case of an air wave, although we cannot see the air, we are able, with some little assistance from experiments, to present to ourselves a clear mental picture of a progressive movement through the air of a region of compression, that is to say, a certain slice, layer, or zone of the air is more compressed than the neighbouring portions, and this region of compression changes its place progressively. It has been carefully explained that the production of a wave of any kind implies, therefore, two things first, a medium or material in which the wave exists; and, secondly, some kind of periodic change or movement which is experienced by the various portions of this medium at different places successively.

If, therefore, we are given any medium, say water or air, and asked to explain the production of a wave in it, we have first to consider what kind of changes can take place in it, or on it, which can appear progressively at different parts. In the case of the water-surface, some parts may be heaped up higher than the rest, and the heaping up may occur at successive places in such fashion that when it disappears at one place it reappears at a contiguous or neighbouring place. In the case of air, some portion may be compressed more than the rest, and the place of compression may move forward, so that as the compression is released in one place it makes its appearance in an adjacent one. In the first case, we have a wave of elevation on water; in the second case, a wave of compression in the air.

In the next place, let me carry you with me one step more. Here is a glass bulb from which the greater part of the air has been removed. We say, therefore, that there is a vacuum in the bulb. It is impossible for us to remove absolutely every trace of air from the bulb, and so produce what would be called a *perfect vacuum*; but we can imagine it to be accomplished, and we can picture to ourselves the glass bulb absolutely deprived of every trace of air or other material substance. The question then arises Is the bulb really empty, or is there still *something* in its interior?

The same inquiry may be put in another way. The air we breathe forms an atmosphere which surrounds our earth as a garment, but it decreases rapidly in density as we ascend. At a height of about 50 miles above the earth there is reason to believe the air is exceedingly rarefied and, except for the presence of meteoric dust, the space between the sun and the earth, and between the stars and the earth, is in all probability a highly perfect vacuum, in the sense that it is empty of generally diffused matter. The question then arises Is interstellar space absolutely and completely empty? We know perfectly well that rays of light come to us from the sun and stars through this empty space, and a fact of capital importance is, that these rays of light, swift-footed though they are, take time to travel. It was long ago suspected that this was the case, and the celebrated Galileo made the first experimental attempt to determine the velocity of light. No real knowledge on the subject was gained, however, until after he had made his discovery that the planet Jupiter is accompanied by four moons (a fifth moon has been discovered since), and that these rotate round the planet in definite periods of time, constituting, therefore, the "hands" of a perfect celestial clock. The sunlight, falling on the great globe which forms the body of the planet Jupiter, casts behind it a conical shadow; and the little moons, in their rotation, are plunged into this shadow cone at intervals, and then for a time become invisible, or eclipsed.

As soon, however, as these eclipses of Jupiter's moons began to be regularly observed, it was found that the intervals of time between two eclipses of any one moon were not equal, but exhibited a progressive variation in magnitude, and were longer by about 16 minutes and 26 seconds at one time of the year than at the other. The astronomer Roemer, in the year 1675, correctly concluded that this difference must be due to the fact that rays of light take time to traverse the earth's orbit, and not to any want of regularity in the operation of this celestial timepiece. Hence, although the eclipses do happen at equal intervals of time, our information about them is delayed by the time taken for the ray of light to travel over the variable distance between Jupiter and our earth. These observations, critically considered, led, therefore, to the conclusion that the speed of light rays is about 186,500 miles a second. By means which it would take too long to describe here, experimental measurements of the velocity of light have been made many times since by various investigators by methods which do not involve astronomical observations, and the result has been to confirm the above value, and to give us a very exact knowledge of the speed with which rays of light travel through space. It is as shown in the table below:

| The Velocity of Light. | Miles per second. |
|---|---|
| From observations on Jupiter's satellites (Roemer) ... | 186,500 |
| ,, experimental measurements by Foucault (1862) ... | 185,177 |
| ,, ,, ,, ,, Cornu (1874) ... | 185,487 |
| ,, ,, ,, ,, ,, (1878) ... | 186,413 |
| ,, ,, ,, ,, Michelson (1879) ... | 186,364 |
| ,, ,, ,, ,, ,, (1882) ... | 186,328 |
| ,, ,, ,, ,, Newcomb (1882) ... | 186,333 |

When anything takes time to travel from one place to another, it can only be one of two things. It must either be an actual object which is transferred bodily from place to place, like a letter sent by post or a bullet fired from a gun, or else it must be a wave-motion created in a medium of some kind which fills all space. The illustrious Newton suggested an hypothesis or supposition as to the nature of light, viz. that it consists of small corpuscles shot out violently from every luminous body. It is a wonderful testimony to Newton's exalted powers of thought, that the most recent investigations show that hot and luminous bodies, such as the sun and a lamp, are in fact projecting small bodies called corpuscles into space, but there is abundant proof that these are not the cause of light. Subsequently to the date of Newton's speculations on the nature of light, the alternative hypothesis was developed, viz. that it consists in a wave-motion in a universally diffused medium called the æther. A great gulf, however, separates mere conjecture and speculation from that accumulation of rigid proof which scientific investigation demands, and hence, although this conception of an æther had arisen as an hypothesis in the minds of Huyghens, Descartes, and many other philosophers, it was not accepted by Newton, and the general assent of scientific investigators to the hypothesis of a universal æther was long deferred. The philosopher to whom we owe the crucial demonstration of the validity of, and indeed necessity for, this assumption was Dr. Thomas Young, the first Professor of Natural Philosophy in the Royal Institution of London. Young was a man whose exalted intellectual powers were not properly appreciated by the world until after his decease. His researches in physical optics alone are, however, epoch-making in character. He it was who first gave a proof that under some circumstances it is possible for two rays of light to destroy each other, and thus produce darkness. Briefly described, the experiment is as follows: If a beam of light of one colour, say red, proceeding from a single source of light, falls upon a screen in which are two small holes very near together, we shall obtain from these holes two streams of light originating, as it were, from closely contiguous sources. If we then hold a white screen not far from these holes, and receive on it the light proceeding from them, we shall find that the screen is marked with alternate bands of red light and black bands. If we cover up one of the small holes, the black bands vanish and the screen is uniformly illuminated. Young pointed out that this effect was due to *interference*, and that the difference of the distances from any black band to the two holes was an exact odd multiple of a certain small distance called the wave-length of the light. If light is a substance, no possible explanation can be given which will enable us to account for the combination of two rays of light producing darkness at their meeting-point. If, on the other hand, rays of light consist of waves of some kind in a medium, then, as we have seen in the case of water ripples and air waves, it is quite possible for two wave-trains to annihilate each other's effect at a certain point, if a hollow of one wave-train reaches that place coincidently with a hump belonging to the other.

Accordingly, the experiment of producing *interference* between two sets of light rays so that they destroy each other is a strong argument in favour of the view that light must consist in some kind of wave-motion existing in a medium susceptible of supporting it, filling all space, and existing in all transparent bodies. This medium we call the *luminiferous æther.*

The term "æther," or "ether," has been in use for many centuries to express the idea of something more rare, tenuous, or refined than ordinary matter.

The classical writers employed it to describe the space above the higher regions of the atmosphere, which was, as they supposed, occupied by a medium less palpable or material than even air itself. Thus Milton, speaking of the downfall of the enemy of mankind ("Paradise Lost," Book I. line 44), says

"... Him the Almighty Power
Hurled headlong, flaming, from the æthereal sky
With hideous ruin and combustion down."

But although poets and philosophers had made free use of the notion of an æther, or even assumed the existence of several æthers, the conception did not become a serious scientific hypothesis until it was experimentally shown by Young that the phenomena of optics imperatively demand the assumption of such a medium in space which is not ordinary matter, but

## ELECTRIC OSCILLATIONS AND ELECTRIC WAVES.

possesses qualities of a special kind, enabling it to have created in it waves which are propagated with the enormous velocity of nearly one thousand million feet a second. The proofs which have accumulated as to the validity of this hypothesis to explain optical effects show that this medium or æther must exist, not only in free space, but also in the interior of every solid, liquid, or gaseous body, although its properties in the interior of transparent bodies are certainly very different from those which it possesses taken by itself. This æther fills every so-called vacuum, and we cannot pump it out from any vessel as we can the air. It occupies, likewise, all celestial space, and suns and stars float, so to speak, in an illimitable ocean of æther. We cannot remove it from any enclosed place, because it passes quite easily through all material solid bodies, and it is for the same reason intangible, and it is not possessed of weight. Hence we cannot touch it, see it, smell it, taste it, or in any way directly appreciate it by our senses, except in so far as that waves in it of a certain kind affect our eyes as light.

The fact that there is such a space-filling æther is, therefore, only to be deduced by reasoning from experiments and observations, but it is not directly the object of our sense-perceptions in the same way that water or air can be. Nevertheless, there is abundant proof that it is not merely a convenient scientific fiction, but is as much an actuality as ordinary gross, tangible, and ponderable substances. It is, so to speak, matter of a higher order, and occupies a rank in the hierarchy of created things which places it above the materials we can see and touch.

The question we have next to discuss is What are the fundamental properties of this æther? and what are the terms in which we must describe its qualities? In order to answer these questions, we must direct attention to some electrical effects, since it has been shown that most of the electrical phenomena, like those of optics, point to the necessity for the assumption of a similar universal medium, different from ordinary matter. Abundant proof has been gathered in, that the electromagnetic medium and the luminiferous æther are one and the same.

We are met at the very outset of our electrical studies by the term *electric current*. Most of us know that the operation of electric telegraphs and telephones, electric lamps and electric railways, depend upon this employment of an agency called an electric current.

The question then arises—What is an electric current? and the answer to this question is not easy to give in a few words. We can, however, begin by explaining what an electric current can do, and how its presence can be recognized. Before me on the table is a spiral of copper wire, and in this wire, by special means, I can create what we call an electric current. I shall ask you to notice that when this is done two effects are immediately produced. In the first place, the wire becomes *hot*, and, secondly, it becomes *magnetic*. The fact that it is hot is evident, because it is now nearly red hot, and is visibly incandescent in the dark. If we dip the wire in iron filings, you will see that these cling to the wire and are taken up by it, just as when an ordinary steel magnet is substituted for the wire. The copper wire, when traversed by the current, also attracts a compass needle, and we thus demonstrate in another way its magnetic quality.

Whenever, therefore, we find these two states of heat and magnetism present together in and round a wire, we may take it as an indication that it forms part of a circuit through which an electric current is flowing. An electric current is a physical state or condition which can only exist in or all along a closed path which is called an electric circuit. This electric circuit may consist of a metallic wire, or, as we generally call it, a conductor, or, as we shall see, it may also in part consist of what is usually called a non-conductor.

It is necessary, in the next place, to point out that an electric current has a directive quality. It belongs to that category of things like forces and movements, which have direction as well as magnitude. It is not completely defined by the answer to the question—How much? We must also ask—In what direction? The direction of an electric current is settled by holding a small compass needle near to the conductor or wire in which the current exists. The little magnet will set itself with its north pole in one direction or in the opposite, across the wire. That is to say, the axis of the compass needle places itself at right angles to that of the wire. The direction of the electric current is decided in accordance with the following conventional rule: Imagine yourself placed with your arms extended straight out like a cross, and that the wire conveying the current is placed before your face in a vertical position. Imagine, also, that the position in which the compass needle naturally sets when held between you and the wire is such that its North pole is on your right-hand side. Then the current would be said to move *upwards* in the wire. A current which is always in one and the same direction in a wire is called a *continuous*, *direct*, or *one-way* current.

A current which periodically changes its direction so that it is first in one direction and then in the other is called an *alternating* or *two-way* current.

I can now show you two experiments, the employment of which will enable us always to decide whether a current in a wire is a one-way or a two-way current. In the first experiment you see a copper wire stretched between the poles of a powerful horseshoe magnet. When a one-way current is sent through the wire, it is pulled either up or down, like a fiddle or harp string being plucked by the finger. If, however, we send a two-way current through the wire, it moves alternately up and down, and vibrates just like a harp-string when plucked and left to itself.

The next experiment gives us, however, a more convenient method of ascertaining the presence in a wire of an alternating or two-way electric current. If two wire circuits are laid parallel to each other, and we send through one of these an electric current, then, in accordance with Faraday's most notable discovery, we find that the beginning or the ending of the one-way current in the first wire gives rise at the moment to a transitory current in the second wire. If, however, we pass through the first wire, which we call the primary circuit, a two-way current, then, since this is, so to speak, continually beginning and ending, we have a similar alternating or two-way electric current produced in the secondary circuit.

This fact may be most neatly and forcibly illustrated by the employment of the following pieces of apparatus: An insulated wire is wound many times round a great bundle of iron wire, thus forming what is called an electro-magnet. Through this wire is passed a strong alternating electric current which reverses its direction 160 times a second.

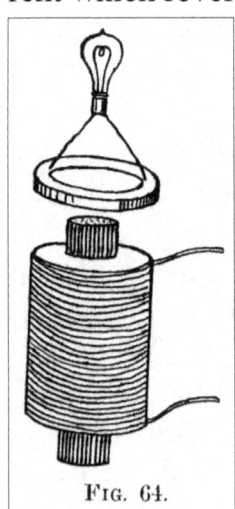

FIG. 64.

Over the top of the electro-magnet we hold another coil of insulated wire, the ends of which are connected to a small electric glow lamp (see Fig. 64). When held near to the pole of the electro-magnet, we find the little lamp in the secondary coil lights up brilliantly, because there is created in that circuit a secondary or induced alternating electric current by the action of the other current in the primary or electro-magnet circuit. Thus we see that one alternating electric current can, so to speak, give birth to another in a second circuit held parallel to the first. In like manner this secondary current can give rise to a third or tertiary current, and the third to a fourth, and so on indefinitely.

## ELECTRIC OSCILLATIONS AND ELECTRIC WAVES.

We can always make use of this test to ascertain and prove the existence of an alternating current in any electric circuit. If we provide a coil of insulated wire, having its ends connected to a small incandescent lamp, and hold this lamp coil or secondary circuit near to and parallel with any other circuit in which we suspect the existence of an alternating electric current, and if the lamp in the secondary circuit lights up, then we can say with certainty that there is an alternating or two-way electric current in the first circuit. Having, then, indicated briefly the effects which are produced by an electric current when it exists in a conducting circuit, and the way in which we can determine its presence and direction, we must pass on to discuss some other facts connected with its production.

It is a maxim in philosophy that every effect must have a cause; hence we must assign a name to the cause of the effect we call electric current. This cause we call *electromotive force*.

Electromotive force may be created in many ways, and time will not permit us to refer to these in detail, but it must be taken that electrical machines, batteries, and dynamos are all of them appliances for creating electromotive force, or, as it is sometimes called, electric pressure, just as various kinds of force-pumps are contrivances for creating pressure in fluids. We find that electromotive force acts differently on various substances when they are subjected to its operation. In some substances electromotive force produces a continuous electric current, and in these cases the material is called a *conductor*. In other cases electromotive force creates what is called *electric strain*, or electric displacement, and these substances are generally called *non-conductors*. The difference between conductors and non-conductors can be illustrated by a mechanical analogy. Consider, for instance, a force-pump consisting of a cylinder with a tightly fitted piston; suppose the bottom of the pump-tube to be closed by a pipe having in it a tap. If we open the tap and apply pressure to the piston, we can force out of the pipe a current of air which continues to flow as long as the piston is being pressed down. In this case the pressure on the piston corresponds to an electromotive force, and the current of air flowing out corresponds with the electric current in the electrical circuit.

Supposing, however, that we shut the tap and then attempt to force down the piston, we find at once an elastic resistance to motion. The piston can be pressed down a little way, compressing the air and thus creating a strain; but if the pressure is removed the piston flies up again, on account of the compressional elasticity of the air. In this operation we have a mechanical illustration of the action of electromotive force on a material such as glass, or air which is called a nonconductor, or sometimes a dielectric. In these bodies electromotive force produces an electric strain, just as the mechanical force produces in the air enclosed in the cylinder a mechanical strain. When the tap at the bottom of the cylinder is closed, we can, by applying pressure, force down the piston a little way, but that movement cannot be continued, because we are building up an opposing pressure due to the elasticity of the air.

It is possible to show you an electrical experiment which has a close analogy with the above simple mechanical experiment. Here is a glass tube which has platinum wires sealed into the two ends, and the tube is partly exhausted of its air. Such a tube is called a *vacuum tube*, and when an electrical current is passed through this rarefied air, it causes it to become luminous, and, as you see when the room is darkened, the tube is filled with a reddish light. A tube, therefore, of this kind is very convenient in some experiments, because we can, in effect, see the electric current passing through it. If I connect one end of this tube with the earth, and the other with the terminal of an electrical machine, and if then the handle of the electrical machine is turned, the tube will continue to glow as long as the electrical machine is rotated. The electrical machine must be regarded as a pump which is forcing something called electricity through the vacuum tube, and as long as the pressure is continued the current flows.

This corresponds with the case in which the tap at the bottom of the force pump was open and a continuous current of air could be forced out of it by pressing down the piston. Supposing, however, that I insert between the vacuum tube and the electrical machine a plate of glass, which is covered over with tinfoil on the two sides; such an arrangement constitutes what is called a condenser, or Leyden pane. We now repeat the experiment, and begin to turn the handle of the electrical machine. You will notice that the vacuum tube glows as before, and is filled with a reddish light for a short time, but as we continue to turn the handle this dies away, and after a few moments there is no further evidence of an electric current passing through the vacuum tube.

You will understand, therefore, that an electric current cannot be caused to flow for an indefinite time in one direction through a glass plate, although, by the application of electromotive force, it does evidently, as you see, pass through it for a short time. This is analogous to the operation of the force-pump when the tap at the bottom is closed. We then find that we can move the piston down a little way, compressing or straining the enclosed air, but that its motion is soon stopped by an opposing resistance. We therefore say that in the glass plate we have created an *electric strain* by the action of the electromotive force, just as we describe the effect of the mechanical pressure on the air by saying that we have created a compression in it.

But there is an additional resemblance between the electrically strained glass and the mechanically compressed air. When any elastic object has been strained, and is suddenly released, it regains its position of equilibrium by a series of oscillations or vibrations. Thus, for instance, if we take a strip of steel and fix one end of it in a vice, and pull the other end on one side and then release it, the steel regains its position of equilibrium only after having executed a series of diminishing swings to and fro.

In the same way, if we place some mercury or water in a glass tube bent in the shape of the letter **U**, and displace the liquid by blowing into the tube, then, on releasing the pressure suddenly, the liquid will regain its position of equilibrium by a series of oscillations which die gradually away. You will not have any difficulty in seeing that this is really due to the inertia of the material, whether it be steel or mercury or water which is displaced. In an exactly similar manner, we find that when we have produced an electric strain in a sheet of glass by the application of electromotive force, and if we then remove the electromotive force and connect the two tinfoil or metal surfaces by means of a piece of wire, the electric strain in the glass disappears with a series of electric oscillations; that is to say, the electric strain in the glass does not disappear or die away gradually, but it is alternately reversed, at each reversal the strain becoming less and less in magnitude. The result of this oscillatory strain in the glass is to produce in the connecting wire an alternating electric current.

A very familiar and simple piece of electric apparatus is that known as a Leyden jar (see Fig. 65). A Leyden jar consists of a glass vessel, the outside and inside surfaces of which are respectively covered with tinfoil. If we apply to these two surfaces an electro-motive force, we produce what is called an electric charge in the jar, which in reality consists in a state of electric strain in the walls of the vessel.

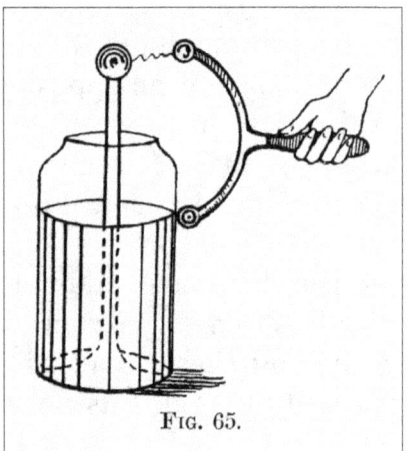

FIG. 65.

## ELECTRIC OSCILLATIONS AND ELECTRIC WAVES.

When the jar is charged, if we connect together, by means of a thick wire, the outside and the inside tinfoil surfaces, we have a bright spark produced at the moment of making contact, and we have a rapidly alternating electric current produced in the connecting wire. If this connecting wire has a low resistance in other words, is a very good conductor then this electric spark consists, not in a discharge of electricity uniformly in one direction, but of a series of rapidly succeeding sparks which are really discharges of electricity or electric currents passing through the air alternately in opposite directions. This can be demonstrated by taking a photograph of the electric spark on a rapidly revolving photographic plate or strip. You are probably all familiar with the sensitive photographic film which is employed in hand cameras, such as the kodak. If a strip of this sensitive film is bound round the edge of a wheel, and if the wheel is set in very rapid rotation, and if we throw on the film, by means of a lens, an image of an oscillatory electric spark, it will be clear to you that, if the spark is continuous, it will produce upon the moving photographic film an image which will be of the nature of a broad band. If, however, the electric spark is intermittent, then this photographic image will be cut up into a series of bars or patches, each one of which will correspond to a separate image of one constituent of the oscillatory spark.

Photographs of oscillatory electric sparks have in this way been taken by many observers, and have afforded a demonstration that the electric discharge of a Leyden jar, when taken through a wire of low resistance, is not a continuous movement of electricity in one direction, but a rapidly alternating electric current through the wire, forming the oscillatory spark, and corresponding with an equally rapid alternating electric strain in the glass, both strain and current dying gradually away.

Although this operation takes a long time to describe, yet, nevertheless, an oscillatory spark consisting of 20 or 30 electric oscillations may all be over in the $\frac{1}{10000}$ or even $\frac{1}{100000}$ second. In the photograph now thrown upon the screen (see Fig. 66) you see the image of an oscillatory electric spark, each oscillation of which lasted $\frac{1}{7000}$ second. We can, however, give a still further proof that the discharge of a Leyden jar or electric condenser is, under some circumstances, oscillatory, in the following manner: –

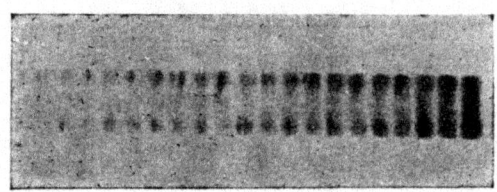

FIG. 66.—A photograph of an oscillatory electric spark (Hemsalech).

You have already seen that an alternating or two-way electric current existing in one circuit can produce another alternating or two-way electric current in a neighbouring circuit. Before me, on the table, is an arrangement by which a battery of six Leyden jars, L, is continually being charged and discharged through a thick wire which is wound a dozen times round a square wooden frame, P (see Fig. 67). In proximity to this wooden frame there is another wooden frame, S, also having on it a dozen or two turns of insulated wire; the circuit of this last conductor is completed by a small incandescent lamp, G. You will notice that when the Leyden jars are charged and discharged rapidly through the primary conductor, the little glow-lamp of the secondary circuit lights up brilliantly, and, in virtue of what has already been explained, you will see that this experiment is a proof that the discharge of the Leyden jars through the primary circuit must consist in an alternating or two-way current; in other words, it must be oscillatory.

# ELECTRIC OSCILLATIONS AND ELECTRIC WAVES.

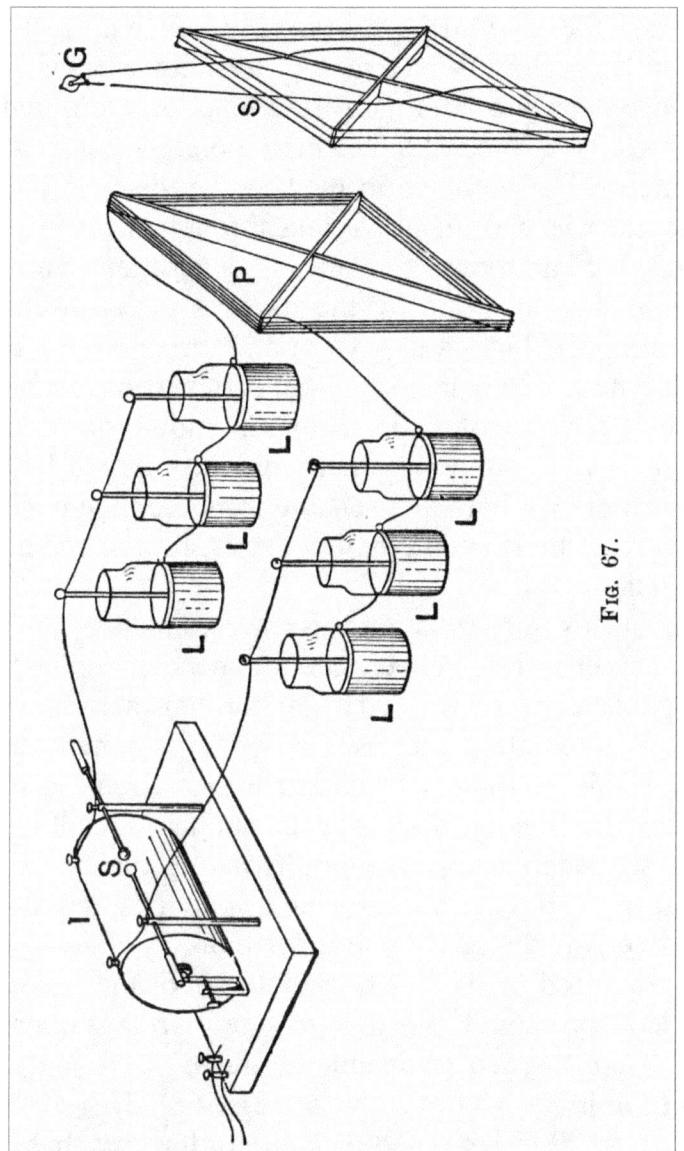

Fig. 67.

A still further proof may be given that the discharge of a Leyden jar or condenser, when taking place through a low-resistance circuit, is oscillatory in the following manner:—

We employ the vacuum tube that we brought to your notice a few moments ago. When an electric current is sent always in the same direction through such a tube, it is well known that the two ends of the tube are not alike in appearance. The tube, as you have seen, is filled with a luminous glow; but this glow is interrupted, forming what is called a dark space near one terminal of the tube, this terminal being that which is termed the negative pole. Accordingly, this unsymmetrical appearance in the light in the tube is a proof that the electric current is passing through it always in one direction. We can, however, vary the experiment, and instead of illuminating the tube by means of a direct-discharge or induction coil, which is always in one direction, we are able to illuminate it by means of a rapid series of discharges from a Leyden jar. You will then see that the glow-light in the tube is symmetrical the tube, in other words, is alike at both ends; and this shows us that the discharge from the tube under these circumstances must be alternating that is, first in one direction and then in the other.

Whilst this apparatus is in use, we can show you with it two other very pretty experiments dependent upon the fact that the discharge of a Leyden jar through a low-resistance circuit is alternating or oscillatory. A moment ago we employed this oscillatory discharge in one circuit to induce a secondary oscillatory discharge in another metallic circuit, and this secondary oscillatory or alternating current was made manifest by its power to illuminate a little incandescent lamp. If, however, we place a large glass bulb, P, which has been partly exhausted of its air, in the interior of the primary discharge coil, you will see that this primary oscillatory discharge of the Leyden jar is able to create in the glass bulb a brilliant luminous ring of light (see Fig. 68). This is called an *electrodeless discharge*, and it is due to the fact that the rapidly oscillatory current existing in the wire wrapped round the bulb creates a similar oscillatory discharge in the rarefied air in the interior of the bulb, this being a conductor, and thus renders it luminous along a certain line.

# ELECTRIC OSCILLATIONS AND ELECTRIC WAVES.

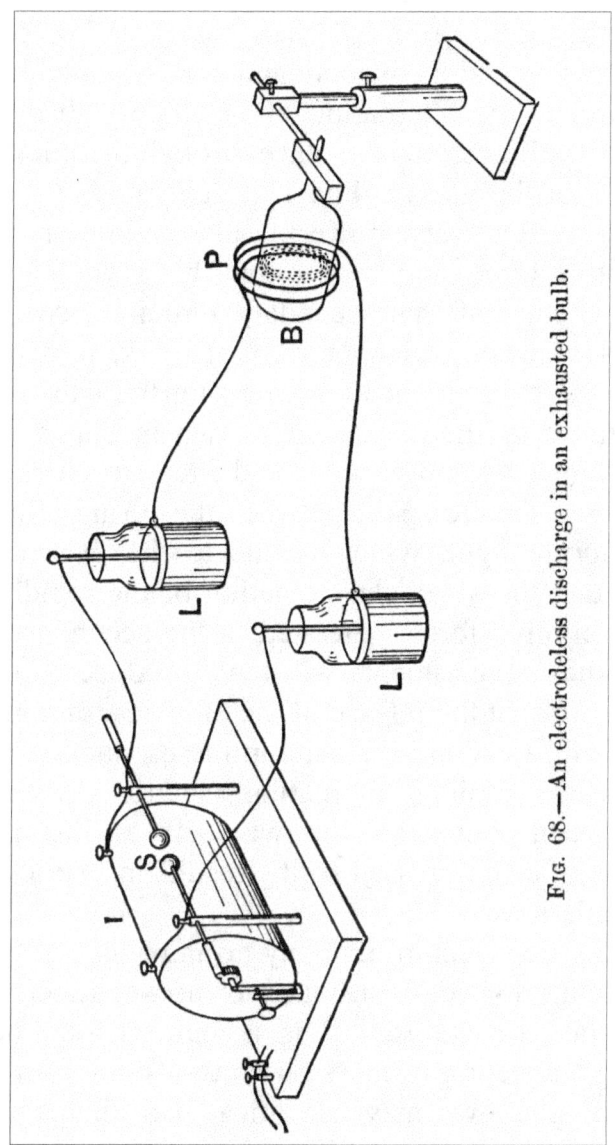

Fig. 68.—An electrodeless discharge in an exhausted bulb.

The production of these electrodeless discharges in rarefied gases has been particularly studied by Professor J. J. Thomson.

Another experiment illustrating what is called the inductive transformation of electrical oscillations is in the arrangement commonly called a Tesla coil. Such a coil is now before you. It consists of a long coil of insulated wire which is placed in the interior of a tall glass vessel, and on the outside of this glass vessel is wound another insulated and much longer wire. If the alternating or oscillatory discharge of a Leyden jar is allowed to take place through the thicker wire in the interior of the glass cylinder, it generates in the outer or secondary wire a very powerful alternating or oscillatory electromotive force, and we see that this is the case by connecting the ends of this secondary circuit to two insulated brass balls, between which a torrent of sparks now passes. We may vary the experiment by connecting the ends of the secondary circuit of the Tesla coil to two insulated concentric rings of thin, bare, brass wire, and then, when the room is darkened, we see the space between these rings filled with a brilliant purple light, which is due to the discharge taking place through the air under the action of the rapidly oscillatory electromotive force generated in the secondary circuit. I trust that these experiments will have produced a conviction in your minds that the release of the electric strain in the glass *dielectric* of a Leyden jar results in the production of electric oscillations or rapidly alternating electric currents in the metallic circuit connecting the two surfaces, just as the sudden release of a compressed spring results in a series of mechanical oscillations.

We may here remark that any arrangement of two metallic plates with a sheet of insulator or non-conductor between them is called a *condenser*. Thus, a condenser can be built up by coating a sheeting of glass on its two sides with tinfoil, or in place of glass we may use mica, paraffin paper, or any other good non-conductor. We may even use air at ordinary pressures; and thus, if two metal plates are placed near to one another in air, the plates being both insulated that is, supported on non-conductors, this arrangement constitutes what is called an air condenser. An air condenser, therefore, is virtually only a kind of Leyden jar in which the glass is replaced by air, and the tinfoil by two stout metal plates. I must now proceed to describe and show you a particular kind of air condenser which was invented by the late Professor Hertz, and, in consequence, is called a Hertz oscillator (see Fig. 69). It consists of two square or round metal plates which are carried on glass or ebonite legs; and these plates have short, stout wires attached to them, ending in brass knobs.

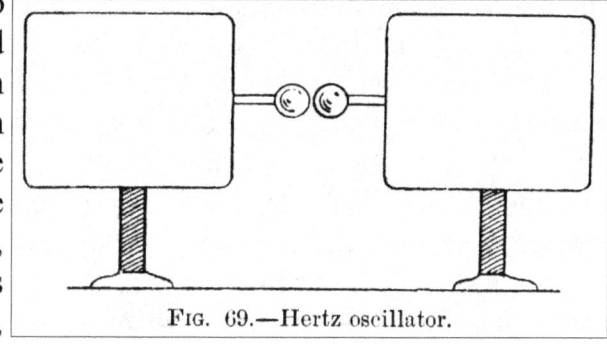

FIG. 69.—Hertz oscillator.

If these plates are placed in line with one another, they constitute an air condenser of a very peculiar kind, the two brass plates correspond with the tinfoil surfaces of a Leyden jar, and the air all round them corresponds with the glass of the jar. Supposing the plates are so arranged that the brass knobs are about ¼ inch apart, or rather less, if then we connect these two brass plates to the secondary terminals of an induction coil or electrical machine capable of giving long sparks in air, we shall find, when the electrical machine or induction coil is set in action, that a very bright crackling spark passes between these little knobs, and with proper experience it is easy to adjust the distance from the knobs so that this spark is an oscillatory spark. Under these circumstances, what is taking place is as follows: In the first place, an electromotive force is acting between the two plates, and creating an electric strain in the air all round them along certain lines, and also between the two knobs. The air, and all other gases like it, possess this peculiar property, that whilst at ordinary pressures they are nearly perfect non-conductors, yet, nevertheless, if they are subjected to more than a certain electric pressure, they pass instantly into a condition in which they become very good conductors. Accordingly, if we progressively increase the electromotive force acting between the plates, up to a certain point the whole arrangement acts like a Leyden jar; but there comes a moment when the air between the knobs breaks down and passes from a non-conductive to a conductive condition. The two plates then resemble at that moment the surfaces of a charged Leyden jar which are connected together by a good conductor, and, as we have already seen, under those circumstances the discharge is oscillatory, and the electric strain in the non-conductor, or dielectric, viz. the air around the plates, dies away by a series of rapidly alternating electric strains in opposite directions.

Now, at this point I must recall to your recollection that, in speaking about the production of air waves, I pointed out that one condition essential to the production of an air wave was that there must be a very sudden application or release of the air-pressure, such as is caused by an explosion or escape of compressed air. We cannot produce an air wave by moving any object such as a fan slowly to and fro through the air. In order to produce an air wave we must strike the air a very sudden blow, or, which comes to the same thing, we must apply and remove a very sudden pressure to the air; and under these circumstances we start into existence an air wave, which travels away from the vibrating or rapidly moving body, and continues its journey out into surrounding space.

I want to show you that, in the case of the Hertz oscillator, these very sudden reversals of electric strain in the air or space round about it, which take place at the moment when the oscillatory spark passes between the knobs, creates in a similar manner what is called an *electric wave*, which travels out into the space around. The point you must appreciate is, that just as an air wave conveys away to distant places a rapidly alternating compression made in the air by a vibrating body at a particular place, so an electric wave conveys away to distant places an alternating electric strain, which is originated at some point in the medium by the oscillatory discharge of some form of condenser. Before, however, we can demonstrate this fact, we must have some means for detecting the influence of what we call an electric wave. You will remember that, in the case of experiments with air waves, I used a sensitive flame in order to make evident to you the presence of waves in the air which you could not see, so here I must use an appropriate detector for electric waves, the operation of which will render evident to us the existence in the space round our electric oscillator of the electric waves we cannot see.

Time will not permit me to discuss all the different forms of electric-wave detector which have been invented. For our present purposes we must limit ourselves to the description of one plan, which depends on the remarkable fact that finely powdered dry metal or metallic filings are non-conductors of the electric current until they are subjected to an electromotive force exceeding a certain value, when the metallic filings at once pass into a conductive condition.

If you recall the remarks made just now in connection with the special electrical properties of air and other gases, you will notice that there is a remarkable similarity between the electrical behaviour of air at ordinary pressures to electromotive force, and that of a loose mass of metallic filings. Both the air and the metallic filings are non-conductors as long as the electromotive force acting on them does not exceed a certain value, but if it exceeds this critical value, they pass at once into a conductive condition. The fact that pieces of metal in loose contact with one another behave in a similar manner was discovered more than twenty years ago by the late Professor D. E. Hughes, who, as you may perhaps know, was the inventor of a printing telegraph, the microphone, and many other most important electrical instruments. Professor Hughes was a great genius, and in many respects in advance of his age. He it was who undoubtedly discovered that an electric spark has the power of affecting at a distance the electric conductivity of a metallic junction consisting of two metals in loose contact.

The peculiar behaviour of metallic filings under electromotive force, and under the influence of electric sparks at a distance, was subsequently rediscovered by Professor Branly; and the effect of an electric oscillatory spark in changing the conductivity of a light metal contact was also rediscovered by Sir Oliver Lodge, and the phenomena investigated by many other observers. I can show you the experiment on a large scale in the following manner:—

I have here a number of aluminium discs, the size of sixpences, stamped out of thin metal, and these are arranged in a sort of semi-cylindrical trough between two terminal screws, so that the discs are very lightly pressed together. Under these circumstances the pile of metal discs is not a conductor, and it will not pass the electric current from a battery which is joined up in series with an electric bell and the pile of discs (see Fig. 70). Supposing, however, that I make an oscillatory spark in proximity to this pile of metal discs, as I can do by tak-

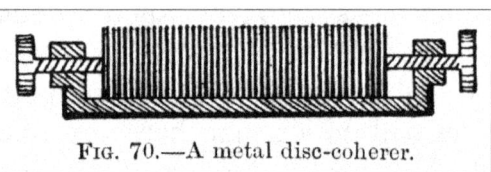

FIG. 70.—A metal disc-coherer.

ing the discharge from a large Leyden jar near it; the pile of discs at once becomes a conductor; the electric current from the battery can then pass through it, and the bell rings. Such an arrangement has been named by Sir Oliver Lodge a *coherer*, because, under the action of the oscillatory spark, the discs cohere or stick together. We can separate the discs by giving them a sharp rap, and then the operation can be again repeated.

A much more sensitive arrangement can be made by taking a small box of wood through the bottom of which pass two nickel wires which are parallel to one another, but not in contact. In this box is placed a small quantity of very finely powdered metallic nickel or nickel filings, and if the quantity

## ELECTRIC OSCILLATIONS AND ELECTRIC WAVES.

of these filings is properly adjusted, it is possible to make an arrangement which possesses the property that there is no conductivity between the two nickel wires under ordinary circumstances, but that they become conductively connected to one another the moment an oscillatory electric spark is made in the neighbourhood. We shall speak of this contrivance as an *electric wave indicator*, and we shall employ it in subsequent experiments to enable us to detect the presence of an electric wave.

We must then return for a moment to the consideration of the production of electrical oscillations in circuits of various kinds. I trust it has been made plain to you that if two metallic surfaces, separated by a non-conductor such as air or glass, are acted upon by an electromotive force, the non-conductor becomes electrically strained. Another way of stating this is to say that a positive charge of electricity exists on one metal surface, and a negative charge on the other. The only objection which can be raised to expressing the facts in this manner is that it fastens attention rather upon the conductors than upon the insulator, which is the real storehouse of the energy. If these two metal surfaces are then connected together by a conductor of low resistance, the charges disappear by a series of oscillations, and the result is an electric current in the conducting circuit connecting the plates, which rushes backwards and forwards in the circuit, but gradually diminishes in strength until it completely dies away. You may picture to yourselves the electrical effect as analogous to the following experiment with two air-vessels: Supposing we have two strong steel bottles, into one of which we compress a quantity of air, and in the other we make a vacuum by pumping out nearly all the air. These vessels would correspond with two conductors, one charged with positive electricity and the other with negative. Imagine these vessels connected by a wide pipe in which is placed a tap or valve, which can be opened suddenly so as to permit the air to rush over from the full vessel to the empty one. If this is done, it is a matter of experience that the equality of pressure between the two vessels is not at once established, but in virtue of the inertia quality of the air, it only takes place after a series of oscillations of air in the pipe. In rushing over from the full vessel to the empty one the air, so to speak, overshoots the mark, and the state of the vessels as regards air-pressure is exactly interchanged. The air then rushes back again, and it is only after a series of to-and-fro movements of the air in the pipe that an exact equality of pressure in the two vessels is attained.

The electrical actions which take place in connection with an electric discharge between two conductors, one of which is charged positively and the other negatively, are exactly analogous to the above-described experiment with two air-vessels, one of which has air in it under compression, and the other has had the air removed from it. You will notice, however, that the oscillations of the air in the pipe in the air-vessel experiment depend essentially upon the fact that air is a substance which has *inertia*, or mass, and you will naturally ask what is it which has inertia, or its equivalent, in the electrical experiment? The answer to this question is as follows: Every electric circuit has a quality which is called *inductance*, in virtue of which an electric current cannot be started in it instantly, even under any electromotive force, and conversely when the current is started it cannot be immediately brought to rest. From the similarity of this quality of the circuit to the inertia of ordinary material substances, it has been sometimes called the *electric inertia* of the circuit. The word "inertia" really means inactivity, or laziness, but the term as used in mechanics implies something more than mere inactivity. It involves the notion of a persistence in motion when once the body is set moving.

When a material substance is in motion it possesses energy, and has the power of overcoming up to a certain point resistance to its motion. This energy-holding power, or capacity for storing up energy of motion, which is characteristic of all material substances, is a consequence of their inertia. The fact is otherwise expressed by stating that the *mass* of a material substance is one element in the production of energy of motion.

An electric current in one sense resembles a moving substance, for it is an exhibition of energy in association with matter. The current-energy is measured by the product of two factors: one is half the square of the current-strength, and the other is the inductance of the circuit. The analogy between the two cases may be more exactly brought out by pointing out that the energy of motion of a moving body is measured by the product of its mass and half the square of its velocity. Hence it follows that the power of overcoming resistance, or, in other words, of doing useful work or mischief, which is possessed by a heavy body in motion is proportional, not simply to its speed, but to the square of its speed. If a bullet, moving with a certain speed, can just pass through one plank 1 inch thick, then, when moving with twice the speed, it will pass through four such planks, and if moving with three times the speed, through nine planks of equal thickness. The energy of an electric current is similarly measured by the product of the inductance of the circuit and half the square of the current-strength. In the same or equal circuits two currents, the strengths of which are in the ratio of 1 to 2, have energies in the ratio of 1 to 4. The greater, therefore, the inductance of an electric circuit, the greater is the tendency of an electric current set flowing in it to run on after the electromotive force is withdrawn. The inductance of a circuit is increased by coiling it into a coil of many turns, and decreased by stretching it out in a straight line.

The important idea to grasp in connection with this part of the subject is that, just as there are two forms of mechanical energy, viz. energy of mechanical strain and energy of motion, so also there are two forms of electrical energy, viz. energy of electro-static strain and electric-current energy.

If, for instance, we bend a bow or extend a spring, this action involves the expenditure of mechanical energy, or work, and the energy so spent is stored up as energy of strain, or, as it is called, distorsional energy in the distorted bow or spring. When, however, the bow communicates its energy to the arrow or the spring to a ball, and so sets these in motion, we have in the flying arrow or ball a store of energy of motion. If a slip of steel spring is fixed at one end, and then set in vibration, we have a continual transformation of energy from the motional to the distorsional form. At one moment the spring is moving violently, and at the next it is bent to its utmost extent; and these states succeed each other. The store of energy in the vibrating spring is, however, gradually frittered away, partly because the continual bending of the steel heats it, and this heat dissipates some of the energy; but also because the spring, if vibrating quickly enough, imparts its energy to the surrounding air, and creates air waves, which travel away, and rapidly rob the vibrating spring of its stock of energy.

In a precisely similar manner all electrical oscillation effects depend upon the fact that electric energy can exhibit itself in two forms. In one form it is electro-static energy, or energy of electric strain. In this form we have it when we charge a Leyden jar. The glass is then, as explained, in a state of electrical strain, and its condition is analogous to that of a stretched spring. The same holds good when we have two conductors insulated from each other in air. We have then an electrical strain in the air. It is important, however, to notice that, since a perfect vacuum can support electric strain, it follows that, in the cases where air or glass constitute this non-conductor, or dielectric, of a condenser, the whole of the energy cannot be stored in the material substance, the glass or the air. The real storehouse of the energy is the æther, as modified by the presence of the ordinary matter in the same place.

When we discharge the Leyden jar or condenser, the electro-static energy in the dielectric disappears, and we obtain in its place an electric current in the connecting conductor; and this, as described, is an exhibition of energy in another form. If the resistance of the connecting conductor is small, then we have electrical oscillations established which consist in an alternate transformation of the energy from an electro-static form to the electric-current form.

At each oscillation some energy is frittered away into heat in the conductor, and if the conductor and condenser have a special form, energy may be rapidly removed from the system by the electric waves which are formed in the surrounding æther or dielectric. These waves consist in the propagation through the medium of lines of electric strain, just as an air wave consists in the propagation through the air of regions of air-compression, or a water wave consists in the propagation of an elevation on the surface.

Returning again to the discussion of the production of electrical oscillations, it is necessary to consider a little more in detail the manner in which we can create an electrical oscillation in what we have called an *open electric circuit*. Let me begin with an experiment, and it will then be easier for you to understand the particular points to be explained.

Before me are two long brass rods, each of them about 5 feet in length, and the ends of these rods are provided with polished brass balls (see Fig. 71). The rods are placed in one line and supported on pieces of ebonite, and are so fixed that the two balls are separated from one another

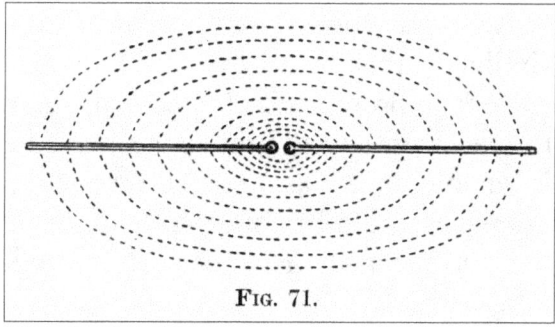

Fig. 71.

by a space of about ¼ inch. The two rods constitute, therefore, two insulated conductors. These rods are connected by coils of wire with the terminals of an instrument called an induction coil, which I shall not stop to describe, but which you may regard as a kind of electrical machine for producing electromotive force. If we set the induction coil in action, it creates between its terminals an intermittent but very powerful electro-motive force, which gradually increases up to a certain value, at which it breaks down the conductivity of the air-gap between the two balls. Let us think carefully what happens as the electromotive force of the induction coil is increasing. One of the rods is in effect being electrified with positive, and the other with negative, electricity, and these charges are increasing in magnitude. The two rods constitute, as it were, the two coated surfaces of a kind of Leyden jar, or condenser, of which the surrounding air is the non-conductor. Accordingly, by all that has been previously explained, you will easily understand that there is an electric strain in the air which exists along certain lines, called lines of electro-static strain, and this state in the air is exactly similar to the condition in which the glass of a Leyden jar finds itself when the jar is charged. If we were to delineate the direction of this electric strain by lines drawn through the space around the rods, we should have to draw them somewhat in the fashion represented by the dotted lines in Fig. 71. As the electrical state of the rods gradually increases in intensity, a point is reached at which the air between the balls can no longer maintain this strain, and it breaks down and passes into a conductive condition. The state of affairs round the rods is then similar to that of a Leyden jar being discharged. An electric current is produced across the air-gap, moving from one rod to the other, and the intensely heated air in between the balls is visible to us as an electric spark. This spark, if photographed, would be found to be an oscillatory spark. The electric current in the rods cannot continue indefinitely: it gradu-

## ELECTRIC OSCILLATIONS AND ELECTRIC WAVES.

ally falls off in strength, but as it flows it creates in the space around the rods an electric strain which is in the opposite direction to that which produced it, although taking place along the same lines.

After a very short time, therefore, the electrical conditions which existed at the moment before the air broke down are exactly reproduced, only the direction of the strain is reversed. In other words, the rod which was positively electrified is now negatively, and *vice versâ*. Then this state of strain again begins to disappear, producing in the rod an electric current, again in the reverse direction; and so the energy, which was originally communicated to the space round the rods in the form of an electric strain, continually changes its form, existing at one moment as energy of the electric current passing across the spark gap, and the next moment as energy of electric strain. We may ask why this state of things does not continue indefinitely, and the answer to that question is twofold. First because the rods possess a property called electrical resistance, and this acts towards the electric current just as friction acts towards the motion of material substances; in other words, it fritters away the energy into heat. So at each reversal of the electric current in the rod a certain quantity of the original store of energy has disappeared, due to the resistance.

There is, however, a further and more important source of dissipation of energy, and this is due to the fact that an electrical oscillation of this kind taking place in a finite straight circuit, or, as it is called, an open electric circuit, creates in the space around an electric wave. The rapid reversal of the electric strain in the air results in the production of an electric wave, just as in the case of an explosion made in air, the rapid compression of the air results in the production of an air wave. It is not easy for those who come to the subject for the first time to fully grasp the notion of what is implied by the term "an electric wave."

In the first lecture, you will perhaps remember, I pointed out that the production of a wave in a medium of any kind can take place if the medium possesses two properties. In the first place, it must elastically resist some change or distortion, and, in the second place, when that distortion is made it must tend to disappear if the medium is left to itself, and in so doing the displacement of the medium must overshoot the mark and be reproduced in the opposite direction, owing to some inertia-like quality or power of persistence in the medium.

It would lead us into matters beyond the scope of elementary lectures if we were to attempt to summarize all the evidence which exists tending to show that the phenomena of electricity and magnetism must depend upon actions taking place in some medium called the *electro-magnetic medium*. All the great investigators at the beginning of the last century, when electrical and magnetic phenomena were beginning to be explored, came to this conclusion, and in the writings of Joseph Henry, of Ampere, and of Faraday we find references again and again to their conviction that the phenomena of electricity imply the existence of a medium exactly in the same way as do the phenomena of optics. It is only, however, in recent years that we have had evidence before us, some of which will be reviewed in the next lecture, which affords convincing proof that the luminiferous æther and the electro-magnetic medium must be the same. The consideration of the simplest electrical effects is sufficient to show that, if this medium exists, it possesses at least two properties, one of which is that it offers an elastic resistance to the production of electric strain in it by means of electromotive force. A question which is sure to arise in the minds of those who consider this subject carefully is, "What is the nature of an electric strain"? And the only answer which we can give at the present moment is that we must be content to leave the question unanswered. We do not know enough yet about the mechanical structure of the electro-magnetic medium, or æther, to be able to pronounce in detail on the nature of the change we call an electric strain. It may be a motion of some kind, it may be a compression or a twist, or it may be something totally different and at present unthinkable by us, but, whatever it is, it is some kind of change which is produced under the action of electromotive force, and which, disappears when the electromotive force is removed.

Clerk-Maxwell, to whom we owe some of our most suggestive conceptions of modern electricity, coined the phrase *electric displacement* to describe the change which we are here calling an electric strain. One essential element in Maxwell's theory of electricity is that an electric strain or displacement, whilst it is being made or whilst it is disappearing, is in effect an electric current, and it is for that reason sometimes spoken of as a displacement current. We have seen that every electric circuit possesses a quality analogous to inertia, that is to say, when a current is produced in it it tends to persist, and it cannot be created at its full value instantly by any electromotive force.

Just as we cannot, at the present moment, pronounce in detail on the real nature of electric strain, so we cannot say whether that quality which we call inductance of a circuit is dependent upon a true inertia of the electromagnetic medium or on some entirely different quality more fundamental.

It may be remarked, in passing, that there is a strong tendency in the human mind to seek for and be satisfied with what we called mechanical explanations. This probably arises from the fact that the only things which we can picture to ourselves in our minds very clearly are movements or changes in relative positions. If we can in imagination reduce any physical operation to some kind of movement or displacement taking place in some kind of material, we seem to arrive at a kind of terminus of thought which is more or less satisfactory. We invariably aim at being able to visualize an operation concerning which we are thinking, and it requires some mental self-control to be able to content ourselves with a general expression which does not lend itself readily to visualization. There are plenty of indications, however, that this mental method of procedure, and this endeavour to reduce all physical operations to simple mechanics and to movements of some kind, may in the end be found to be unjustifiable; and the time may arrive when we may be more satisfied to explain mechanical operations in terms of electrical phraseology rather than aim at dissecting electrical effects into mechanical operations. Thus, for instance, instead of speaking of electric inertia, it may be really more justifiable to speak of the inductance of ordinary matter. The final terms in which we endeavour to offer ourselves an explanation of physical events are in all probability very much a matter of convenience and custom. We may, however, for present purposes rest content by thinking of the electro-magnetic medium as in some sense like a heavy elastic substance which is capable of undergoing some kind of strain or distortion, the said strain relieving itself as soon as the distorting force is withdrawn; but, in addition, we must think of the medium as possessing a quality analogous to inertia, so that as distortion vanishes it overshoots the mark, and the medium only regains its state of equilibrium at the particular point considered, by a series of oscillations or alternate distortions, gradually decreasing in amount. Any medium which possesses these two qualities has, in virtue of explanations already given, the property of having waves created in it, and what we mean by an electric wave is a state of electric strain which is propagated through the æther with a velocity equal to that of light, just as an air wave consists of a state of compression which is propagated through the air with a velocity of 1100 feet a second.

To sum up, we may then say that whenever rapid electrical oscillations are created in open circuit, such as the two rods above described, the arrangement constitutes a device for creating an impulse or effect in the surrounding space called an *electric wave* in the æther or electro-magnetic medium; just as an organ-pipe or piano-string or other musical instrument constitutes a device for creating waves in the air by means of mechanical oscillations. The existence of these electric waves, and their transference to distant places, can be rendered evident by their action as already described upon finely powdered metals. An apparatus which shows this effect very well is now arranged before you. At one end of the table I have a pair of rods connected to an induction coil, constituting a Hertz radiator, the action of which has just been described. At the other end of the table are two similar long rods, but their inner ends are connected to two small plates of silver, which form the sides of a very narrow box, and between these plates is placed a very small quantity of metallic powder. The construction of this little box is as follows: A thin slip of ivory has a little gap cut out of it (see Fig. 72), and on the two sides of this slip of ivory are bound two silver plates bent in the shape of the letter **L**,

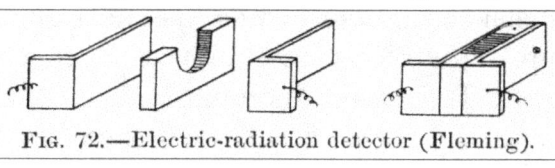

FIG. 72.—Electric-radiation detector (Fleming).

forming, therefore, a very narrow box with silver sides. The two silver plates are connected to the two long rods. As already explained, the metallic filings or finely powdered metal are not in their ordinary condition an electric conductor. Accordingly, if we connect to one of the silver plates one terminal of a battery joined in series with an electric bell, the other end of the bell being connected to the second silver plate, this battery cannot send a current through the bell, because the circuit is interrupted by the non-conductive metallic powder in the little box. Supposing, then, that we cause a spark to pass between the balls of the radiator, and start an electric wave. When this electric wave reaches the long rods connected to the receiving arrangement, it sets up in these rods a sudden electromotive force, and this electromotive force, as already explained, if of sufficient magnitude, causes the loose mass of metallic filings to pass from a non-conductive to a conductive condition. At that moment, therefore, the battery is able to send an electric current through the bell, and to cause it to ring. We can, however, stop the ringing by giving the little box containing the metallic filings a tap, which separates them from one another and interrupts the electric conductivity. The function of the two rods connected with the receiver is not quite the same as the function of the two rods connected to the radiator. In order to create a vigorous electric wave, we must have a radiator which possesses what is called considerable electric capacity, and also considerable inductance, and we can only do this in general by using long rods. On the other hand, at the receiving end the efficacy of the rods is due to the fact that they, so to speak, add together the electric strain taking place over a considerable distance; in other words, the electromotive force which is set up in the receiving circuit is dependent on the length of the rods. The longer, therefore, these rods, the greater is the distance at which we can obtain the effect which is shown to you with a given spark-length.

One point it is important to notice, and that is, that the rods of the receiver must be parallel to the rods of the radiator if we are to obtain any effect at a distance. If we turn the rods of the radiator round so that they are at right angles to those of the receiver, you see that no sparks produced at the radiator balls cause the bell in connection with the receiver to ring. The reason for this is because the electric strain, which is propagated out into the space, exists in a direction parallel to the radiator rods all along a line drawn perpendicular to the rods through the spark-gap. The receiver rods will not have electromotive force produced in them by this travelling line of electric strain unless they are parallel to its direction.

It is to be hoped that the above explanations have afforded indications of what is meant by an electric wave. On the other hand, there may be many who find it exceedingly difficult to derive clear ideas when the subject is presented to them clothed in such general terms as we have been obliged to use.

It may assist matters, therefore, if, before concluding this chapter, a word or two is said on the subject of recent investigation into the inner mechanism of an electric current and an electric strain. It is impossible to do this, however, without making mention, in the briefest possible way, of modern researches into the constitution of matter. If you can imagine yourselves furnished with a little crystal of ordinary table salt, chemically called chloride of sodium, and the means of cutting it up under an immensely powerful microscope, you might go on dividing it up into smaller and smaller pieces. If this process could be continued sufficiently far, we should ultimately obtain a very small fragment of salt, which, if still further divided, would yield two portions of matter not alike and not salt. This smallest possible portion of salt is called a molecule of sodium chloride. Chemical facts teach us that this molecule is made up of two still smaller portions of matter, which are called respectively atoms of chlorine and sodium.

We have good reason to believe that all solids, liquids, and gases are composed of molecules, and these are built up of atoms, few or many.

In the case of some substances, such as *salt*, the molecule is very simple and composed of two atoms. In other substances, such as albumen or white of egg, the molecules are very complicated and composed of hundreds of atoms. The word atom means something which "*can-not be cut*," and until comparatively recent time the opinion was held that atoms of matter were the smallest indivisible portions of matter which could exist.

More than twenty-five years ago, Sir William Crookes showed, by numerous beautiful experiments, that in a vacuum tube, such as you have seen used to-day, a torrent of small particles is projected from the negative terminal when an electric current is passed through the tube. This stream of particles is called the cathode stream, or the cathode radiator. Within recent times, Professor J. J. Thomson has furnished a proof that this cathode stream consists of particles a thousand times smaller than chemical atoms, each particle being charged with negative electricity. These particles are now called *corpuscles*, or *electrons*.

It has been shown that these electrons are constituents of chemical atoms, and when we remove an electron from an atom we leave the remainder positively electrified. An atom can, therefore, by various means be divided into two portions of unequal size. First, a very small part which is charged with negative electricity, and, secondly, a remaining larger portion charged with positive electricity These two parts taken together are called ions, *i.e.* wanderers. The negative ions, or electrons, or corpuscles, taken together constitute what we call negative electricity, and up to the present no one has been able to show that the corpuscle can be unelectrified. Hence the view has been expressed that what we call electricity is a kind of matter, atomic in structure, and that these negative ions or corpuscles collectively are, in fact, the atoms of the electric fluid. These corpuscles can move freely in the interior of some solids, moving between the molecules of the solid just as little dogs can run about in and amongst a crowd of people in a street. In these cases the substance is called a conductor of electricity. In other substances the movement of the corpuscles is more restricted, and these constitute the various kinds of so-called non-conductors.

The corpuscle, being a small charge of negative electricity, creates in all surrounding space a state called *electric force*. It is impossible to expound this action more in detail without the use of mathematical reasoning of a difficult character. Suffice it to say that this electric force must be a particular condition of strain or motion in the æther. If the corpuscle is in rapid motion, it creates in addition another kind of strain or motion called magnetic force. The electric force and the *magnetic force* are related to each other in free space in such a manner that if we know the difference between the values of the electric force at two very near points in space, we are able to tell the rate at which the magnetic force is changing with time in a direction at right angles to the line joining these near points in space. We cannot specify in greater detail the exact nature of these states or conditions which constitute magnetic force and electric force, until we know much more than we do at present about the real nature of the æther. The two fundamental qualities of the æther are, however, its capacity to sustain these states we call the magnetic force and the electric force.

The electrons of which we have spoken not only give rise to electric and magnetic force when in movement, but they are themselves set in motion by these forces. Thus electric force at any point moves electrons placed at that spot, and an electron in motion is affected and has its direction of motion changed when magnetic force acts on it.

Leaving further remarks on the relations of atoms, electricity, and æther until the end of the last lecture, we may conclude the present one by explaining the manner in which the observed facts connected with a Hertz oscillator are interpreted in terms of this electron hypothesis of electricity.

Take the simple case of two long insulated metal rods separated by a spark-gap. The process of charging one rod positively and the other negatively consists in forcing more corpuscles, or negative ions or electrons, into one conductor and removing some from the other. Any source of electromotive force, such as a dynamo or induction coil, is, on this hypothesis, a sort of *electron-pump*, which pumps electrons from one conductor and puts them into another. One conductor, therefore, gains in electron-pressure, and the other loses.

## WAVES AND RIPPLES

The excess of electrons in one conductor endeavour to escape, and a strain is produced on the electrons or atoms in the surrounding dielectric or air, which may be looked upon as the effort of the electrons, more or less tethered to the atoms, to escape. The air in the spark-gap is subjected to the most intense strain, and when this reaches a certain intensity some of the electrons are torn away from their atoms, and the air in the gap then becomes a conductor. The excess of electrons in one conductor rush through the channel thus prepared, and this constitutes an electric current. The first rush carries over too many electrons to equilibrate the electron-pressure, and hence the first torrent of migrating electrons in one direction is followed by a back-rush in the opposite one, this again in turn by another in the original direction, and so the equality in the number of electrons in each conductor is only established after a gradually diminishing series of to-and-fro rushes of electrons across the air-gap. This action constitutes a train of electrical oscillations. At the same time that these operations are going on in and between the conductors, the electrons attached to the atoms of the air or other dielectric all around are being violently oscillated. These oscillations may not proceed to such an extent as to detach electrons from their atoms, but they are sufficient to create rapidly reversed electric and magnetic forces. It appears that the very rapid movement to and fro of an electron causes a wave in the rather, just as the rapid movement of the hand through water causes a wave in water, or the vibration of the prong of a tuning-fork creates a wave in the air.

The electron has some grip on the æther, such that the sudden starting or stopping of the electron makes a disturbance which we may popularly describe as a *splash in the æther*. Hence, if a large number of electrons are suddenly started into motion in the same direction, the effect on the æther is something like casting a multitude of stones on the surface of still water, or the simultaneous action of a number of small

## ELECTRIC OSCILLATIONS AND ELECTRIC WAVES.

explosions in the air. Anything, therefore, which, so to speak, lets the electrons go gradually, or softens the first rush, is inimical to the production of a vigorous electric wave. On the other hand, anything which causes the first rush of electrons from one conductor to another across the air-gap to be very sudden is advantageous, and results in a powerful wave. Experience shows that the nature of the metal surfaces, whether polished or rough, has a great influence on the wave-making power of the radiator. If the spark- balls or surfaces are rough and not polished, it seems to tone down the violence of the first electron rush, and the wave-making power of the oscillator is not so great as if the balls are polished.

At this point, however, it will be best to withhold further discussion on points of theory until we have considered the facts to be brought before you in the next lecture, showing that the electric radiation manufactured by means of electric oscillations is only one variety of a vast range of æther waves, some forms of which are recognizable by us as light and radiant heat.

# CHAPTER VI.

# WAVES AND RIPPLES IN THE ÆTHER.

HAVING in the last chapter explained the nature and mode of production of electric oscillations, and shown that when these take place in an open electric circuit or long straight rod they give rise to certain actions at a distance, rendered evident by the changes taking place in the conductivity of metallic powders, we have now to present the outlines of a proof that these actions are really due to a wave-motion of some description set up in the rather, which in nature is essentially the same as that which constitutes the agency we call light.

We shall begin by studying a few of the epoch-making discoveries we owe to the celebrated Heinrich Hertz, announced in a series of famous researches with which he surprised and delighted the scientific world in the years 1887 and 1888. These investigations opened a new and remarkable field of experimental work.

The precise form of apparatus used by Hertz in these researches is, however, unsuited for lecture demonstration, and I shall use on this occasion some arrangements of my own, which are only convenient modifications of appliances previously employed by other experimentalists. The devices

## WAVES AND RIPPLES

here shown are, however, very convenient for public demonstrations.

This apparatus consists of two parts, a part for generating electric waves, which we shall call the radiator, and a part for detecting them, which is called the receiver.

The radiator consists of a zinc box, A (see Fig 73), which is provided with hollow trunnions, and can be fixed to a suitable stand and turned in any direction. The box has an open end to it, and in its interior there are two brass rods about 4 inches long, each terminating in brass balls, S, 1 inch in diameter. These rods are thrust through corks fixed in the end of two ebonite tubes, which pass through the hollow trunnions of the box. The rods have their ends attached to very closely wound spirals of gutta-percha-covered wire contained in the ebonite tubes. These spirals are called *choking coils*. When the balls are arranged in the interior of the box in their proper position, they are about $\frac{1}{16}$ inch apart, and the rods to which they are attached are in line with each other.

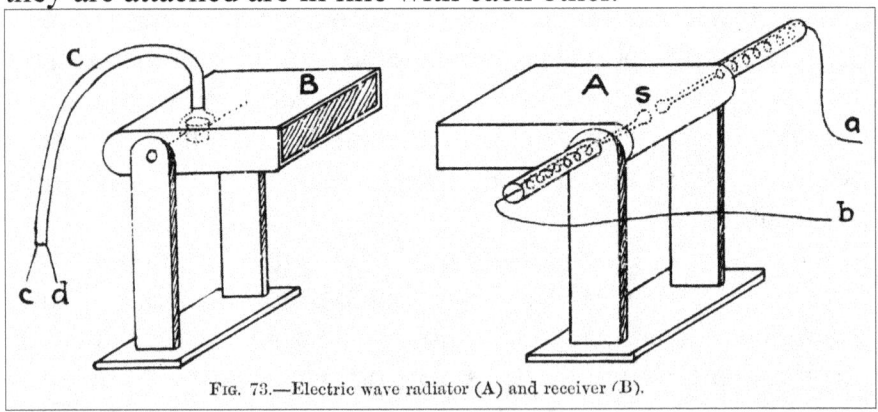

FIG. 73.—Electric wave radiator (A) and receiver (B).

The outer ends of the choking coils are connected to an induction coil or electrical machine, say a small Wimshurst machine, suitable for producing electric sparks about 2 or 3 inches in length. If then sparks are taken between the balls, we have an arrangement which is, in fact, a small Hertz oscillator or radiator. It has been fully explained in the last chapter that the action of the induction coil or electrical machine is first to create a difference in the electric condition of the balls, such that one is positively electrified and the other negatively. The balls and rods and the surrounding air, as already explained, then form a sort of Leyden jar or condenser, and in virtue of the electromotive force the air is electrically strained around the balls. When this strain reaches a particular value, the air between the balls passes at once into a conductive condition, and we have a discharge which is oscillatory in nature produced between the conductors. We may consider that the electrical charges on the two rods rush backwards and forwards, setting up on the rods an oscillatory surface electric current, and that this is accompanied by a very rapid reversal of the strain in the surrounding non-conductor or dielectric. This state of affairs results in sending out into space an effect called an electric wave.

Turning, then, to the receiver B (Fig. 73), we notice that this consists of a similarly shaped metal box, having in it a board to which are fixed two short nickel wires. These are crossed without touching in the interior of a small ebonite box (see Fig. 74). The wires are just covered inside the box with a very small quantity of fine nickel filings. To the end of the zinc receiver-box is fixed a long lead pipe, in the interior of which are two insulated wires, $c$, $d$.

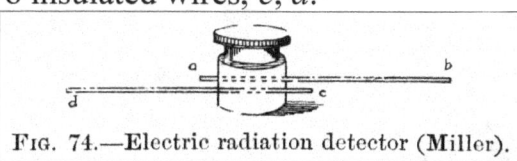

FIG. 74.—Electric radiation detector (Miller).

These wires are joined to the extremities of the nickel wires in the receiver-box and then, passing through the lead pipe, they enter another metal box which contains a battery and electric bell. The pinch of nickel filings in the small ebonite box is not an electric conductor in its ordinary condition, and hence the electric circuit, including the battery and bell, is not complete. If, however, an electric oscillation is set up in the nickel receiver-wires, the mass of metal particles connecting them at once becomes a conductor, because little metallic granules stick or cohere together. The battery is thus able to send an electric current through the circuit, which includes the coherer, and the electric bell is caused to ring. It may be mentioned that in the actual apparatus employed the arrangement is not quite so simple. The coherer would be permanently injured if we were to attempt to send through it an electric current strong enough to ring an electric bell. Hence we associate with the coherer a contrivance called a *relay*. A single voltaic cell, E (a dry cell) (see Fig. 75), is joined up in series with the coherer C and this relay R The latter is a sort of switch or circuit-closer of such kind that when a very feeble current passes through it it closes a second circuit through which a much stronger current can pass. The transition of the nickel filings from a non-conductive to a conductive condition is, therefore, only the means by which a very small current of electricity is allowed to pass through the circuit of an electro- magnet which forms the circuit of the relay. This action causes a piece of iron to be attracted, and this again in turn closes another circuit, and so enables the current from a second battery, F, of five or six cells to actuate the

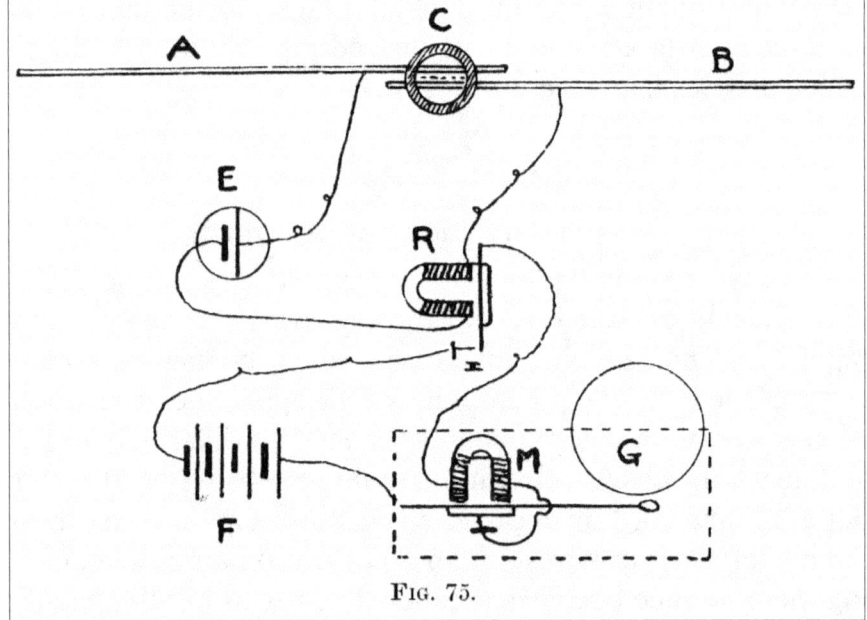

Fig. 75.

electric bell G. The arrangement of the two batteries, the relay coherer, and bell will be understood by studying the diagram of connections in Fig. 75.

The really important condition in securing success in the performance of the experiments made with this apparatus is that the long wires which connect the receiver-box with the metal box containing the bell, battery, and relay shall be entirely enclosed in a lead pipe without joint, which is soldered at one end into the receiver-box and at the other into the battery-box. Another practical point is that these wires, where they enter the battery-box, must have included in their circuit two little coils of insulated wire of a good many turns, which are called "choking coils." A third element of success is that the coherer or sensitive conductor shall be sensitive enough, but not too sensitive. This condition can only be obtained by a process of trial and failure. Being provided with these two pieces of apparatus, we can now proceed to exhibit a series of experiments of great interest.

In the first place, let the and receiver-box be placed a few feet apart with their open mouths facing each other, like two guns arranged to fire down each other's throats. Then, if all is in order when we make an electric spark between the two balls of the radiator, the electric bell in connection with the receiver will begin to ring, showing that the coherer in the receiver-box has been affected and made conductive by the electric wave sent out from the radiator-box. If a smart rap is then given to the receiver-box the clinging metallic filings in the ebonite box will be separated again and, the circuit being interrupted, the bell will stop ringing.

This being done, the radiator-box is then turned a little on one side by rotating it round its hollow trunnions like a gun until the open mouths of the two boxes no longer face each other. It will then be found, on repeating the former experiment, that the bell will not ring when a spark is made between the balls. A little experimenting will show that the action which affects the coherer is propagated out from the radiator-box in straight lines like the light from a lamp, and that we are here dealing with something which has all the character of radiation. In the next place, let the receiver- and radiator-boxes be again arranged with their open mouths facing each other. We make a spark and again secure the responsive action of the bell. We shall now proceed to prove that this effect, which is called *electric radiation*, passes quite freely through certain substances, but is more or less completely stopped by others. For instance, if we hold a sheet of iron, tinfoil, or even paper covered with silver leaf between the open mouths of the radiator and receiver, we find that the bell of the receiver will not ring even when a rapid series of oscillatory sparks are made in the radiator. These sheets of metal, thick or thin, are quite *opaque* to the electric radiation proceeding from the spark-balls. On the other hand, we find a sheet of paper or card, a wooden board, a sheet of glass, a slab of wax or bitumen, sulphur, marble, or slate, are all quite pervious or transparent, and when held between the radiator and receiver do not hinder at all perceptibly the action of the former on the latter. We conclude, therefore, that some bodies are opaque and some transparent to the electric radiation. But the classification does not agree with the classification as regards opacity or transparency for light. Wood, marble, and pitch are optically opaque, but electrically transparent. The general law, however, which decides the question of opacity or transparency for electric radiation, is as follows: *All good electrical conductors are opaque to electric radiation, and all good insulators or non-conductors are transparent.*

Hence we see at once why metal sheets are opaque, and wood, wax, or glass transparent, to the electric radiation from the spark-balls.

We may go one step further. If we take some sheets of perforated zinc or wire gauze, or even a large packet of pins, or paper bag full of iron filings, we shall find that all these bodies are practically opaque to the electric rays. Moreover, we can show that not only is the above law true for solids, but it holds good for liquids as well. I have provided here a number of flat glass bottles which are filled with various liquids, salt water, fresh water, solution of soda, paraffin oil, olive oil, turpentine and methylated spirits.

If we test an empty glass bottle between the radiator and receiver, we can assure ourselves that the bottle itself is transparent to the electric radiation.

If, then, we take the bottles containing the various liquids and test them one by one between the radiator and the receiver, we find that the bottles containing the paraffin oil, the olive oil, and the turpentine are transparent to the electric radiation, but that the bottles containing the salt water, the fresh water, the solution of soda, and the methylated spirits are all opaque. The oils and liquids similar to them are all good non-conductors, whereas water and various aqueous solutions are fairly good conductors of electricity, and hence these liquids, although they are all about equally transparent to light, behave very differently to electric radiation. As regards the electric ray, a bottle full of pure water is as opaque to the electric radiation we are here using as it would be to light if it were filled with black ink.

Experiment shows that every object containing water, or which is wet, is exceedingly opaque to the electric radiation we are employing. Thus, for instance, if I take a dry duster folded in four, and hold it in the path of the electric ray, you see that it is quite transparent, and that the bell attached to the receiver rings as easily as if there were no duster there at all. If, however, we dip the duster in water, and then hold it between the radiator and receiver, we find that the wet duster is perfectly opaque.

The human body consists largely of water which exists in the tissues, and hence it is not surprising to find that the hand or any part of the body placed between the radiator and receiver intercepts the electric ray. You see, if I hold my hand in front of the radiator, that nothing is able to escape from it, when sparks are made between the balls, which can affect the receiver. In the same way it can be shown by experiment that the human head is perfectly opaque in fact, much more opaque than an equally thick block of wood; and this opacity to the electric ray is due in a veritable sense to the water in the brain. All dry animal tissues, such as leather, bone, gelatine, and flesh, if dry, are very transparent to electric radiation of the kind we are now using, but if these objects are made thoroughly wet, then they become intensely opaque.

We can, then, proceed to show that this electric radiation can be reflected, just like light or sound, by metal or other conducting surfaces, and that the law of reflection of the electric ray is the same as the law of reflection for rays of light or sound. If we place the radiator A with its mouth upwards, still preserving the receiver B in a horizontal position, it is possible to adjust the two very near to one another, but yet so that the radiation from the radiator does not affect the receiver. If I now hold a metal plate, P, at an angle of 45 above the mouth of the radiator, you will notice that the bell at once rings, thus showing that the electric radiation has been reflected into the receiver-box (see Fig. 76). Also we find that a very small deviation from the angle of 45 is sufficient to prevent the

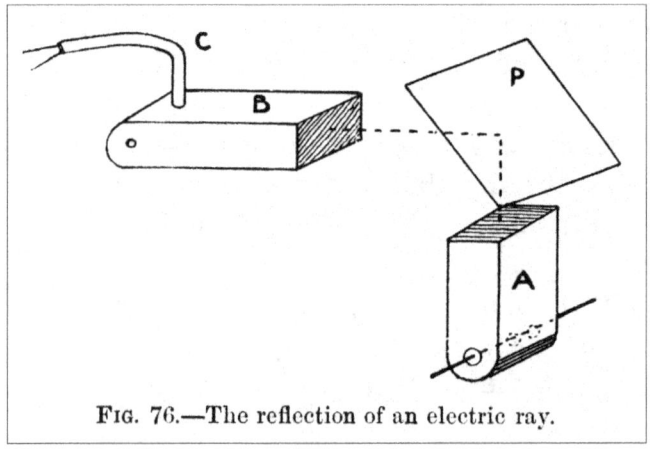

FIG. 76.—The reflection of an electric ray.

effect. Careful experiments in the laboratory show that the electric ray is reflected according to the optical law, viz. that the angle of reflection is equal to the angle of incidence. We find that any good conducting surface will, in this manner, affect the electric radiation. Thus I can reflect it from a sheet of tinfoil or even from my hand, and the fact that I can, so to speak, take hold of this electric radiation, and deflect it in different directions by the palm of my hand, produces in the mind a very strong conviction that we are dealing with something of a very real nature in experimenting with this electric radiation.

It will be in your remembrance that, in the chapter in which we were dealing with waves in the air, I showed you a very interesting experiment illustrating the refraction of rays of sound by means of a carbonic acid prism, and I have now to bring before you an exactly analogous experiment performed with electric radiation. Here, for instance, is a prism made of paraffin wax, a substance which you have already seen is transparent to the electric ray. If we arrange the radiator- and receiver-boxes at an angle to one another, it is possible so to adjust them that the electric radiation projected from the radiator-box A just escapes the receiver-box B, and does not therefore cause the bell to ring (see Fig. 77). When this adjustment has been made we introduce the paraffin prism P into the path of the electric ray, and if the adjustments are properly made, we find that the electric ray is bent round or refracted, and that it then enters the receiver-box and causes the bell to ring. This experiment was first performed by Hertz with a very large pitch prism, but his apparatus was too cumbersome for lecture purposes, and the smaller and more compact arrangement you see before you is therefore preferable for present purposes.

I have it in my power to show you a still more remarkable experiment in electric refraction. It is found that dry ice is very transparent to these electric rays, but if the ice is wetted

# WAVES AND RIPPLES

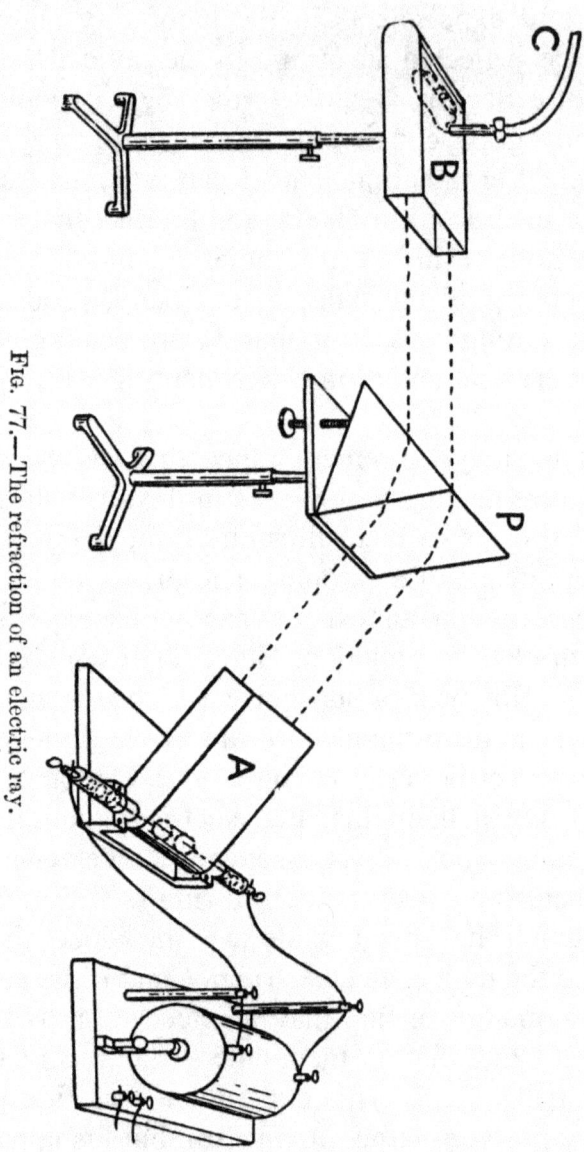

FIG. 77.—The refraction of an electric ray.

on the surface, then, as you have already learnt, the film of moisture is opaque. We have had constructed for the purposes of this lecture a prism of ice by freezing water in a properly shaped zinc box. This prism is now being arranged between the radiator and the receiver, and its surfaces must next be dried carefully with dusters and white blotting-paper to remove every trace of moisture. When this is done we find we can repeat with the ice prism the same experiment performed just now with the paraffin prism, and we can refract the electric ray. If you will recall to your memory the statements which were made in connection with the refraction of rays of sound and waves of water, you will remember that it was pointed out that the refraction of a ray of sound and the bending of a train of water waves was due to the passage of the waves in the air or in the water from a region where they were moving quickly to a region in which they were compelled to move more slowly; and it was furthermore shown that this bending must take place whenever a plain wave of any kind passes in an oblique direction from one region to another region where it undergoes an alteration in velocity. In other words, it was shown that the bending or refraction of the direction of motion of a wave, whether in air or water, is a proof that there is a difference in its velocity in the two places bounded by the surface at which the refraction takes place. If this bending takes place in such fashion that the ray is bent towards the perpendicular line drawn to the bounding surface, which is the same thing as saying if the line of the wave is bent so as to make a less angle with the bounding surface after it has passed from one region to the other, then it shows that the wave-motion travels more slowly after it has passed the bounding surface than before.

If we now return to the consideration of the electric experiment with the prism of paraffin or ice, we shall find that this, properly interpreted, gives us a proof that the electric radiation travels more slowly in paraffin wax or ice than it does in air, and the ratio between its velocity in air or in empty space and its velocity in any non-conductor is called the *electric index of refraction* for that non-conductor. This index can be determined by making two measurements. First, that of the refracting angle of the prism; and secondly, that of the deviation of the ray.[26] I have made these two experiments for the prisms of paraffin and ice in my laboratory, and I find the electric refractive index of paraffin to be 1.64, and the electric refractive index of ice to be 1.83.

In connection with the refraction of rays of sound, it was pointed out that a curved surface has the power to diverge or converge rays of sound, and you will remember that we employed a sound-lens for converging the rays of sound diverging from a whistle, just as an ordinary burning-glass, or double convex lens, can be employed to bring the rays of sunlight to a focus. We shall now attempt a similar experiment with the electric ray. A block of paraffin is fashioned into the shape of a semi-cylinder, flat on one side and convex on the other, and this plano-convex paraffin lens has a convex surface having a radius of 6 inches. If I place the radiator A and receiver B about 4 feet apart, then by making a few little adjustments it is possible to so arrange matters that the radiation which proceeds from the radiator is not powerful enough at a distance of 4 feet to sensibly affect the coherer and make the bell ring (see Fig. 78). If, however, I adjust the paraffin lens **L** halfway between, I shall converge this electric radiation to a focus just about the place where the coherer is

---

26 In the case of the paraffin prism the refracting angle (i) was 60°, and the deviation of the ray (d) was 50°. Hence, by the known optical formula for the index of refraction (r), we have—

$$r = \frac{\sin\frac{i+d}{2}}{\sin\frac{i}{2}} = \frac{\sin 55°}{\sin 30°} = 1.64$$

For the ice prism the refracting angle was 50°, and the deviation 50°; accordingly for ice we have—

$$r = \frac{\sin\frac{50+50}{2}}{\sin\frac{50}{2}} = \frac{\sin 55°}{\sin 25°} = 1.83$$

See "Cantor Lectures," Society of Arts, December 17, 1900. J. A. Fleming on "Electric Oscillations and Electric Waves."

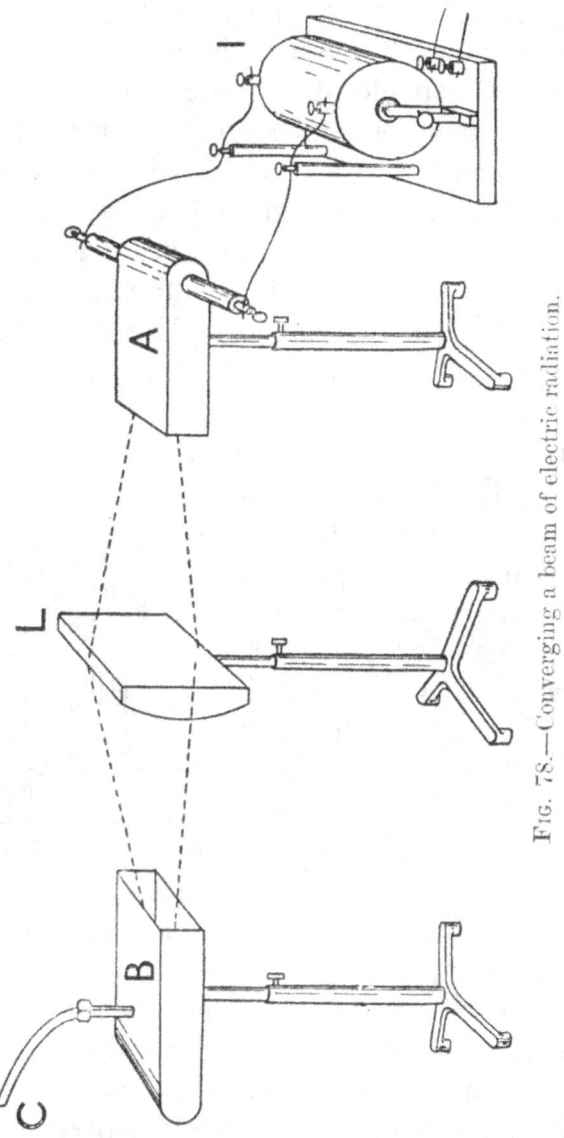

Fig. 78.—Converging a beam of electric radiation.

situated, and the consequence is that on making sparks between the balls of the radiator, we find that the bell attached to the receiver at once rings.

We have, therefore, here brought to a focus, by means of a paraffin lens, the electrical radiation just in the same manner that an ordinary burning-glass focuses the rays of light and heat of the sun, and enables us to light with it some paper or a cigar. "We have, therefore, indubitable proof in all these experiments that we have something proceeding from the radiator which is capable of being reflected or refracted just like the rays of sound or ripples on the surface of water; and, moreover, we find that this electric radiation passes through some substances but not through others. There is, therefore, a strong presumption that we are here dealing with something which is similar in nature to light, although it cannot affect the eye. In order that we may complete the proof we must show that this radiation is susceptible of interference. This proof may be partly obtained from the consideration of the following facts connected with the opacity or transparency of wire grating to the electric radiation :—

I have here a wooden frame across which are strained some wires about a quarter of an inch apart (see Fig. 79). If we hold this frame or grid in front of the radiator so that the direction of these wires is at right angles to the direction of the radiator rods which carry the balls, we find that the grid is quite transparent to the electric radiation, but if we turn the grid round so that the wires of the grid are parallel to the radiator rods, we find at once that the grid becomes perfectly opaque. The same experiment can be prettily shown by means of a paper of pins. Here are some large carpet pins arranged in rows in paper, and if I hold this paper of pins in between the radiator and receiver with the pins parallel to the radiator, it is perfectly opaque to the electric ray, but if I turn it so that the pins are at right angles, it is quite transparent. The same experiment succeeds with a paper of ordinary pins, but not so well with a paper of midget pins.

FIG. 79.

The explanation of this action of a grid is as follows: You have already seen that an alternating current in one electric circuit can produce another alternating current in a secondary circuit placed parallel with the first. It is not difficult to show, either experimentally or from theory, that when the primary current is an electrical oscillation that is, a very rapid alternating current the current in the secondary circuit is also an electrical oscillation of the same frequency or rapidity, but that the currents in the two circuits, primary and secondary, are always moving in opposite directions at the same moment. Accordingly, if we hold a grid in front of the radiator, the wires of the grid have what are called *induced oscillations* set up in them, and these induced oscillations themselves create electric radiation. Accordingly, it is clear that if a grid of this kind is held near to a radiator with the wires of the grid parallel to the radiator rods, we have two sets of radiations produced which, at any point on the side of the grid furthest from the radiator rods, must neutralize one another, and therefore destroy each other's effect. Hence it is possible to cause the electric radiations proceeding from two electric circuits parallel with each other to destroy one another at a distant point; and we may, therefore, make use of the same arguments as in the case of a similar experiment with light to prove that this electric radiation must be a wave-motion.

It would occupy too much of our time, and it would involve the discussion of matters which are rather beyond the scope of elementary lectures, if we were to enter into a complete analysis of all the arguments proving that this electric radiation, which proceeds from an electric oscillator, is really a wave-motion. I may, however, mention one fact, which has been the outcome of an enormous amount of experimental research, and that is, that the velocity of this electric radiation through space is identical with that of light. It has already been mentioned that a ray of light flits through space at the rate of 1,000,000,000 feet, or nearly 186,500 miles a second. By suitable and very ingenious arrangements, physicists have been able to measure the velocity of electric radiation, and have found in every case that its velocity of propagation is precisely the same as a ray of light.

Let us, then, summarize briefly what we have learnt. We find that when we set up an electrical oscillation in an open circuit consisting of two metallic rods placed in one straight line, we have proceeding from this circuit an electrical radiation which is capable of being propagated through space, which moves in straight lines, can be reflected and refracted, can exhibit the phenomena of interference, and moreover which is propagated with exactly the same velocity as light. Is it possible to resist the conclusion that this effect which we call electric radiation, and the similarly behaving physical agency which we call light, must both be affections of the same medium? It is hardly necessary to occupy time with experiments in showing that a ray of light can be reflected and refracted by mirrors and prisms, and converged or diverged by transparent lenses. These are simple optical facts, and if you are not familiar with them it will be easy for you to make their acquaintance by studying any simple book upon optics; but I should like to draw your attention to the fact that, in addition to rays of light and electric radiation, we are acquainted with another kind of radiation, which is also susceptible of being refracted, and that is commonly called *dark heat*.

Supposing that we take an iron ball and make it red hot in a furnace, then, in a perfectly dark room, we see the ball glowing brilliantly, and we are conscious by our sensations that it is throwing off heat. Let us imagine that the ball is allowed to cool down to a temperature of about 500 C.; it will then just cease to be visible in a perfectly dark room, but yet if we hold our hand or a thermometer near to it, we can detect its presence by the dark radiant heat it sends out. Experiments show that even when the ball is brilliantly incandescent, nearly 98 or 99 per cent, of all the radiation it sends out is dark heat, and only 1 or 2 per cent, is radiation which can affect the eye as light. It is quite easy to show that this dark heat can be reflected just like light. If I fix this red-hot ball in the focus of a metallic mirror and lift up ball and mirror nearly to the ceiling and then place upon the table another convex, polished, metallic mirror, the top mirror will gather up and project downwards the radiation from the iron ball and the bottom mirror will converge that to a focus. If then we fix a red-hot ball in the focus of the upper mirror and allow it to cool until it is just not visible in the dark, we shall find that we can still ignite a piece of phosphorus or some other inflammable substance by holding it in the focus of the bottom mirror, thus showing that the dark radiation from the iron ball is susceptible of reflection just as are rays of light or electric rays. In fact, if time permitted, it would be possible to show a whole series of experiments with dark radiant heat which would prove that this radiation possesses similar properties of luminous or electric radiation in its behaviour as regards reflection, refraction, and interference.

A vast body of proof has been accumulated that all these forms of radiation are merely varieties of one and the same thing, and that the only thing in which they really differ from one another is in what is called their wave-length. At this point I will remind you once more of that general law which connects together the velocity of propagation of a wave-motion, the wave-length and the frequency. It is expressed in the formula: *wave-velocity* (V) *equals frequency* (n) *multiplied by wave-length* ($\lambda$), or in symbolical language—

$$V = n\lambda$$

Accordingly, if the velocity of propagation can be determined, and if the frequency or periodicity of the wave-motion is known, then the wave-length can be found from the above simple rule; or conversely, if the velocity of propagation and the wave-length are known, the frequency is determined.

# WAVES AND RIPPLES

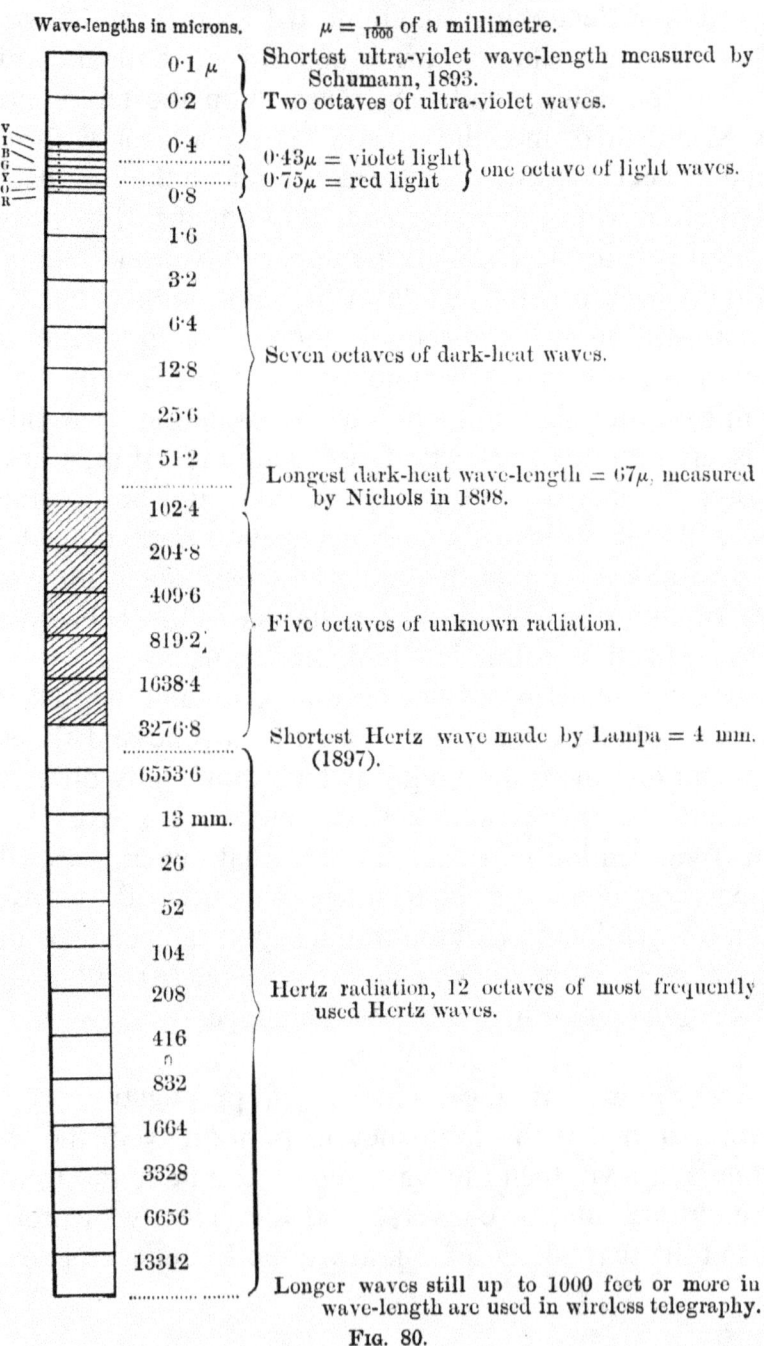

Fig. 80.

The wave-length of various kinds of monochromatic (one-colour) light can be easily determined by means of Young's experiment on interference. If the distance between the two small holes from which the two streams of light emerge is measured, and if the distance from them to the screen and also the distance of the first dark baud from the central line is determined, it is then very easy to calculate the difference in the distances from the two holes to the dark band. This difference, however, must, as already explained, be equal to one-half wave-length of the light employed. Experiments made in various ways have shown that the wave-length of yellow light is not far from the fifty thousandth part of an inch.

Hence as the velocity of visible light is 186,500 miles per second, or 1000 million feet, or 12,000 million inches per second, whilst the wave-length is something like $\frac{1}{50000}$ inch, it is clear that the frequency, or number of light waves which enter the eye per second, must be reckoned in *millions of millions*. In fact, it ranges from 400 to 700 billions. There is a certain difference of opinion as to what is meant by a billion. We here use the word to signify a million times a million, a million being a thousand times a thousand.

The following table shows us the frequency or number of waves per second, corresponding to light rays producing colour-sensations of various kinds:

VIBRATION RATES OF ÆTHER WAVES AFFECTING THE EYE AS LIGHT.

| Colour sensation. | Vibrations per second. |
|---|---|
| Deep red | 400 billions. |
| Red-orange | 437 ,, |
| Yellow-orange | 457 ,, |
| Yellow | 509 ,, |
| Green | 570 ,, |
| Blue-green | 617 ,, |
| Blue-violet | 696 ,, |
| Violet | 750 ,, |

Investigation has shown that the quality in a light ray which causes it to affect our eye with a particular colour-sensation is its wave-length, whereas the quality which affects our eyes as brightness or brilliancy is due to the amplitude of the waves. It is somewhat difficult to realize at first that, outside of ourselves, there is no such thing as colour. Colour is a sensation produced when æther waves of a certain wavelength enter the eye and fall on the retina. If the retina is stimulated 400 billions of times per second, we experience a sensation of redness, and if it is stimulated 700 billion times per second, we experience a sensation of blueness; but externally, there is no such thing as red and blue, there is only a difference in wave-frequency. It is astonishing when we learn for the first time that 400 millions of millions of times per second something in the back of our eyes is moved or stimulated whenever we look at a lady's red dress, a surgeon's red lamp, or the red petal of a geranium flower.

You will notice, on referring to the above table of frequencies, that the range of sensibility of the human eye is very much smaller than that of the ear. Our eyes are wonderful instruments for detecting wave-motion in the æther, and our ears are appliances for detecting wave-motion in the air. The ear, however, is, as explained in a previous chapter, sensitive to air-vibration forming musical tones which lie between 30 and 30,000 per second, and these numbers are in the ratio of 1000 to 1, and cover a range of about ten octaves. The eye, how-ever, is only sensitive to æther-vibrations which lie in frequency between 400 and 700 billions per second, and these numbers are in the ratio of nearly 2 to 1, or comprise only *one* octave.

The question, of course, immediately arises What are the properties of æther waves the frequency of which lies outside the above limits?

Scientific investigation has made us acquainted with a vast range or gamut of æther-vibrations, and we are able to summarize our present knowledge as follows:

The physical effect we call light, and that which we have up to the present moment merely called electric radiation, are

## WAVES AND RIPPLES IN THE ÆTHER.

really identical in nature, and both consist in waves propagated through the space-filling æther, the only difference between them is in wave-length and wave-amplitude. In between these two classes of radiation comes a third, which is called the dark-heat radiation, and beyond the limits of visible radiation we are acquainted with another group of æther waves which cannot affect the eye as light, but which from their power to affect a photographic plate, is called *actinic radiation*. Hence, briefly speaking, four great groups of æther waves are known to us, called respectively

1. Actinic, or photographic rays.
2. Luminous, or light rays.
3. Ultra-red, or dark-heat rays.
4. Electric, or Hertz rays.

Convincing proof has been afforded that these various rays are essentially the same in nature, and that they consist in periodic disturbances or waves propagated through the æther in every case with the velocity of 186,500 miles, or 1000 million feet, or 30,000 million centimetres per second.

We may, therefore, say that these classes of æther waves differ from each other only in the same sense in which a bass note in music differs from a treble one; that is, the difference is a difference in frequency.

Just, therefore, as we have a gamut, or scale of musical tones, or air-vibrations of increasing frequency, so we may arrange a gamut or scale of æther waves progressively placed according to their vibration-rates. Our present knowledge concerning æther waves can best be exhibited by arranging in a chart a series of numbers showing the wave-lengths of the waves with which we are so far acquainted. As a limit of length we shall take the one-thousandth part of a millimetre. Most persons know that a millimetre is a thousandth part of a metre, and is a short length nearly equal to one twenty-fifth of an inch. The thousandth part of a millimetre is called a *micron*, and is denoted by the symbol $1\mu$. This last is therefore an exceedingly short length, nearly equal to one twenty-five thousandth part of an inch.

Following, also, the musical nomenclature, we shall speak of all those waves included between two wave-lengths, one of which is double or half the other, as an octave. Thus all the various waves whose wave-lengths lie between 1µ and 2µ length are said to be an octave of radiation. As a preliminary to further discussion let us consider, in the first place, the simple facts about the radiation which affects our eyes as light.

The light which comes to us from the sun is not a simple thing. It consists of æther waves of many different wave-lengths mingled together. Sir Isaac Newton first revealed to us the compound nature of white light by his celebrated experiment with a glass prism, and his optical discoveries were the starting-point for our information on this subject. If a beam of sunlight is allowed to fall on a glass prism, the rays of light of different wave-lengths which compose it are each bent or refracted to a different degree. In free space æther waves of various wave-lengths all travel, as far as we know, at the same rate. This equality in speed is, however, disturbed the moment the waves enter a transparent material substance such as glass. The velocity of propagation is then reduced in all cases, but it is generally more reduced for the shorter waves than for the longer ones; and as a consequence the rays of shorter- wave lengths are more bent or refracted than the rays of longer wave-length. We have, therefore, a dispersion of the component rays, or a sorting out or analysis of the mixture of rays of various wave-lengths, and if we receive the light on a screen after passing through the prism we have a band of coloured light called a spectrum, which consists of a series of patches of light each of a different wave-length. The component rays of the original beam of light are spread out fan-fashion by the prism. We may note, in passing, that it is not every transparent body when fashioned into a prism which thus analyzes the light into a fan-shaped beam with rays of various wave-lengths arranged in the order of their wave-lengths. The substances which behave as does glass or water when made into prisms are said to exhibit *normal dispersive power*. There are, however, some bodies, such as iodine or an alcoholic solution of fuschine, which exhibit *anomalous dispersion* and refract some longer waves of light more than some shorter ones. The arrangements for forming a normal spectrum are as follows: We pass a beam of light from the electric lamp through a lens, and place in front of this lens a metal plate with a narrow vertical slit-shaped opening in it. At a proper distance in front of the slit we place another lens, and project upon the screen a sharp image of the slit in the shape of a bar of white light. Placing a hollow glass prism filled with bisulphide of carbon in front of the last lens, we find that the various rays in the white light are dispersed, and we produce on the screen a band of rainbow-coloured light, called the spectrum. This spectrum is in reality a series of differently coloured images of the slit placed side by side. By making use of the principle of interference as disclosed by Young, it is possible to make a measurement of the wave-length of the rays of light which produce the sensation of various colours when they fall upon the eye. Thus the wave-length of those æther waves which produce the sensation of deep red is $0.75\mu$, and that of the waves producing the sensation of violet when they fall upon the retina of the eye is $0.43\mu$. The whole of the visible spectrum is therefore included within a single octave of æther radiation. Within these limits any change in the wave-lengths makes itself felt in our eyes as a change of colour. It is commonly said that there are seven colours in the spectrum red, orange, yellow, green, blue, indigo, and violet. As a matter of fact, a highly trained eye can discover about a thousand different tints in the spectrum of white light. Time will not allow us to enter into any discussion of what is called colour-vision and the theory of sensations of colour. The fact I wish to impress upon you here is that, outside of ourselves, there is no such thing as colour. The rays of light which produce these sensations of colour when they enter the eye differ from one another only in wave-length and wave-amplitude. Hence there is a complete analogy between light of different colours and sounds of different pitches or tone. Red light differs from blue light only as a bass note in music differs from a treble note. Hence you must distinguish very carefully between a ray of light in itself, and the sensation it produces when it falls upon the retina of the eye. Our eyes are gifted with a marvellous power of detecting slight differences between the wave-length and the amplitude of the rays which may stimulate two adjacent portions of the retina of our eyes.

That range of sensibility is, however, very limited. Supposing we allow a ray having a wave-length greater than $0.75\mu$ or less than $0.43\mu$ to enter the human eye. It produces no sensation of light at all. Accordingly, if we form a spectrum with sunlight, we find a tolerably sharp limit to the visible spectrum. Supposing, however, we allow the spectrum to fall upon a sensitive photographic plate, we find that the plate will be chemically acted upon far beyond the limits of the visible violet end of the spectrum. Hence we learn that beyond the violet there is radiation of a kind which is invisible to the eye, yet can affect a photographic plate. This is called the *ultra-violet*, or *actinic* radiation.

Schumann, in 1893, measured waves in actinic radiation of a wave-length as short as $0.1\mu$, or one two hundred and fifty thousandth part of an inch, and hence we may say that we are acquainted with at least two octaves of invisible ultra-violet or actinic radiation, or æther waves have wave-lengths lying between the limits $0.1\mu$ and $0.4\mu$.

In a similar manner very delicate heat- detecting instruments or thermometers called bolometers, or thermopiles, show us that beyond the visible-red end of the normal spectrum there is radiation called the *ultra-red* radiation, or *dark-heat*, which cannot affect the eye.

The wave-length of dark-heat radiation has been measured up to a limit of 67μ by Professor Rubens and Professor Nichols in 1897 and 1898. Accordingly, we can assert that beyond the red end of the spectrum we are acquainted with six octaves or more of ultra-red radiation, viz. that lying in wave-length between 0.75μ and 67μ.

We may represent the above facts in another way as follows: In most pianos the keyboard extends over a range of seven or eight octaves. Imagine a piano having a keyboard with nine octaves, and that each key was labelled to correspond with a light wave of a particular length. At the extreme treble end let the first key be labelled 0.1, and at the extreme base end let the last key be labelled 51.2. Then the various octaves will be comprised between the keys marked 0.1, 0.2, 0.4, 0.8, 1.6, 3.2, 6.4, 12.8, 25.6, and 51.2 (see Fig. 77).

Suppose that each key when struck caused some kind of electric radiator to emit an æther wave whose wave-length reckoned in microns or thousandths of a millimetre, is indicated by the number on the key. Of all this great gamut of æther waves only the notes of one octave, viz. the third from the treble end, the wave-lengths of which lie between 0.4μ and 0.8μ, affect the retina of the human eye as light.

Those waves in the two octaves higher up, that is, of wave-length less than 0.4μ, are able powerfully to affect a photographic plate, and so, indeed, do some of the waves in the visible octave. We may, in fact, say that all the æther waves with which we are acquainted, the wave-length of which is less than about 0.5μ, are able to make an impression upon a photographic plate. These rays, whatever their wave-lengths, are called the actinic rays.

On the other hand, all the æther waves with wave-length greater than about 0.8μ, and for six octaves further down, can only be recognized by their ability to heat a delicate thermopile or other heat-measuring instrument. They cannot affect the eye, and they have little or no effect in decomposing silver salts and impressing a sensitive photographic surface.

It should be noted, however, that whilst there are more or less definite limits to the wave-lengths of the eye-affecting radiation, and probably also to the actinic, or photographic radiation (radiation of some wave-lengths being both visible and actinic), rays of every wave-length are in some degree thermal, or heat-producing. The term *dark-heat radiation* is, however, generally restricted to radiation of that wave-l ength which is non-visible and non-actinic. This mode of presenting the facts will call your attention again to the narrow limits of sensibility of the human eye as compared with those of the ear.

The above-mentioned range of wave-lengths does not, however, exhaust our powers of æther-wave production. If we skip over six octaves lying below the limits of the longest dark-heat wave with which we are acquainted, we should arrive at a wave whose wave-length is about 4000µ, or 4 millimetres. At this point we encounter the shortest æther waves which have yet been made by means of electrical oscillations in the fashion first discovered by Hertz.

It is not possible to define exactly the wave-length limits of radiation as yet made by means of electrical oscillations. Lampa has experimented with æther waves made by the Hertz method, the wave-length of which was not more than 4 millimetres. Professors Lodge, Rhigi, Bose, Trouton, the author, and many others, have carried out quasi-optical experiments with electrically made æther waves, the wave-length of which ranged from a few millimetres to several inches. Hertz's own work was chiefly done with æther waves from 1 or 2 feet to 30 or 40 feet in wave-length. More recently, æther waves of 800 to 1000 feet in wave-length have been employed in wireless telegraphy. Perhaps we shall not be wrong in saying that we are acquainted with sixteen or seventeen octaves of æther-wave radiation which is made electrically, and is usually called the Hertz radiation.

Between the radiation of greatest wave-length which proceeds from hot or incandescent bodies such as the sun, the electric arc, or a hot ball, and that of the shortest wave-length which has been created by means of electrical oscillations set up in some form of Hertz oscillator, there is a range of six octaves of æther waves which, so far as we know, have not yet been manufactured or detected. Herein lies an opportunity for much future scientific work. We have to discover how to create and recognize these interconnecting wave-lengths. From the fact that all Hertz waves travel with the same speed as light, and from our ability to imitate, as you have seen, the well-known optical phenomena with Hertz radiation of short wave-length, the great induction has been made that all æther waves have the same essential nature, and that invisible actinic rays, light rays, dark-heat rays, and Hertz rays are all of them æther waves of various wave-lengths and amplitudes. Thus we see, as Maxwell long ago predicted, that light in all probability is an electro-magnetic phenomenon, and therefore all optical effects must be capable of receiving an electro-magnetic explanation. The inclusion thus made of the whole science of Optics within the domain of Electricity and Magnetism is one of the grandest achievements of Physical Science. It stands second only to Newton's great discovery of universal gravitation, which reduced all Physical Astronomy to pure Dynamics, and showed that the force concerned in the falling of a stone is identical with that which holds the planets in their orbits, and controls the motions of galaxies of suns.

At the end of the last chapter it was explained that these Hertz radiations are created in the æther by the suddenly starting, stopping, or reversing the motion of crowds of electrons, which are, as it were, instantly released from a state of pressure or tension, and set moving inside a straight insulated conductor, which forms an open electric circuit. The radiations we call light and dark heat are probably, therefore, started in a similar manner by vibrations of the electrons which form parts of, or which build up, atoms. There are many physical phenomena which seem to show that the electrons which we can detach from atoms in a high vacuum tube are capable of vibrating freely in definite periods when in connection with their atom. If the atoms are able to move freely, and if each is practically independent, as is the case in a gas, and if they are then caused to radiate by any means, the radiation emitted by the vibration of these electrons consists of certain definite wave-lengths. Hence, when we form the spectrum of an incandescent gas, we find it to consist of several detached bright lines, each corresponding to one particular wave-length, and we do not obtain a uniformly graduated band of coloured light. If an atom is struck by colliding with another, and then left to itself, it appears as if the electrons which compose it and form part of it are set in vibration, and each executes its oscillation in some definite period of time. An atom has, therefore, been compared to a "collection of small tuning-forks," which, if rudely struck, would result in the emission of a set of air-wave trains, each one corresponding in wave-length to one particular tuning-fork which emitted it. Hence, if we could administer a blow to such a congeries of tuning-forks, and then analyze the compound sound, we should obtain a sound spectrum consisting of separated tones in other words, a bright line spectrum of the complex sound. Supposing, however, that we have a mass of atoms much more closely in contact, as in the case of a solid body, the continual collisions between the atoms and the closer contact between them cause the vibrations of the electrons to be "forced," and not "free." Hence the electrons are compelled to execute all varieties of irregular motion, and these predominate over their regular free natural vibrations. Accordingly, the waves emitted are of a large variety of wave-length, and when the radiation is analyzed by a prism, we obtain a continuous spectrum, or band of many-coloured light, as the result of the separation of the rays of different wave-lengths present in it.

It is this fact which renders our present method of creating artificial light so excessively uneconomical.

All our practical methods for making light consist in heating a solid body in one way or another. In the case of the electric light we heat electrically a carbon rod or filament, or else, as in the Nernst lamp, a rod composed of magnesia and the rare earths. In the case of the lime-light we heat a cylinder of lime. In an ordinary gas or candle flame we heat small particles of carbon, and the same is the case even in the sun itself.

But this process manufactures not only the single octave of radiation which can affect our eyes as light, but a dozen other octaves of radiation to which they are insensible. Hence it follows that of the whole radiation from a gas flame, only about 3 per cent, is eye-affecting light, the remainder is dark heat. In the case of an incandescent electric lamp, this *luminous efficiency* may amount to 5 per cent., and in the electric arc to 10 or 15 per cent. There is, however, always a great dilution of the useful light by useless dark heat.

The proportion of the light or eye-affecting radiation to the dark heat in the total radiation from any source of light increases with the temperature, but it is not always merely a question of temperature. Thus the electric arc is hotter than a candle flame, and the sun is hotter than the electric arc. Hence, whilst the luminous rays only form 3 parts out of 100, or 3 per cent, of the radiation of a candle, they constitute 10 to 15 per cent, of those of the electric arc, and more than 30 per cent, of those of the sun. On the other hand, the glow-worm and the fire-fly seem to have possession of a knowledge and an art which is as yet denied to man. It has been shown by Professor Langley and Mr. Very that nearly the whole of the radiation from the natural torch of the fire-fly is useful light, and none of it is useless dark heat. Hence these photogenic (light-producing) insects have the art, which we have not, of creating *cold* light, or unadulterated luminous radiation.

At the present moment in ordinary incandescent or glow-lamp electric lighting we require to expend an amount of power, called one horse-power, to produce illumination equal to that of 250 candles. Supposing, however, that all our power could be utilized in generating merely the rays useful for vision, or which can impress our eyes, we might be able to create by the expenditure of one horse-power more than twenty times as much illumination, that is, a light equal, perhaps, to 5000 candles.

These figures show us what rewards await the inventor who can discover a means of generating æther waves having wave-lengths strictly limited to the range lying between the limits 0'4/z and 0'7/u, without, at the same time, being obliged to create a vast multitude of much larger waves which are not useful for the purpose of rendering objects visible to us. For the purposes of artificial illumination we require only the æther waves in this one particular octave, and nothing else.

This increase in the efficiency of our sources of artificial illumination is only likely to be brought about when we abandon the process of heating a solid substance to make it give out light, and adopt some other means of setting the electrons in vibration.

It is almost impossible to discuss the subject of æther waves without some reference to the most modern utilization of them in the so-called wireless telegraphy. Without entering upon the vexed questions of priority, or on the historical development of the art, we shall simply confine our attention here to a consideration of the methods employed by Signor Marconi, who has accomplished such wonderful feats in this department of invention.

We have already seen that when two insulated conductors are placed with their ends very near together and are then electrified, one positively and the other negatively, and then allowed to be suddenly connected by an electric spark, they constitute an arrangement called an electrical oscillator If the conductors take the form of two long rods placed in one line, and if their contiguous ends are provided with spark-balls separated by a small gap, we have seen that we have shown that, under the above-mentioned conditions, electric currents of very high frequency are set up in these rods. For creating these oscillations, an instrument called an induction coil or spark-coil is generally employed. You will understand the arrangements better if a brief description is given first of the spark-coil itself as used in wireless telegraphy.

The appliance consists of a large bundle of fine iron wires, which are wound over with a long coil of insulated wire. This forms the *primary coil*. It is enclosed entirely in a tube of ebonite. One end of this coil is a *contact-breaker*, which automatically interrupts an electric current flowing from a battery through the primary coil (see Fig. 81). A *hand-key* is also placed in the circuit to stop and start the primary current as desired. Over the primary coil is a very long coil of much finer silk-covered copper wire, called the *secondary coil*. The length of this coil is very considerable, and may amount to many miles. The secondary coil is divided into sections all carefully insulated from each other. Another import-

Fig. 81.—A 10-inch induction coil for wireless telegraphy (Newton).

ant part is the *condenser*. This consists of sheets of tinfoil laid between sheets of waxed paper, alternate tinfoil sheets being connected. The arrangement forms virtually a Leyden jar, and one set of tinfoils is connected to one side of the automatic break, and the other to the adjacent side. When, therefore, the primary circuit is interrupted by the break, the condenser is at that moment thrown into series with the primary coil. The rapid interruption of the primary current causes a secondary current in the fine-wire coil. The automatic contact-breaker makes from ten to twenty such interruptions per second. At every "break" of the primary a very high electromotive force is generated in the secondary circuit, which may amount to many hundreds of thousands of volts. This very high secondary electromotive force is able to cause an electric discharge in the form of a spark between brass balls connected to the secondary circuit terminals. Coils are generally rated by the length (in inches) of the spark they can produce between brass balls about ½ inch in diameter. The coil most commonly used in wireless telegraphy is thus technically termed a "10-inch induction coil", from the length of the spark this particular type of coil can produce.

If the insulated brass balls, called the spark-balls, connected to the secondary terminals, are placed an inch or so apart, and the hand-key in the primary circuit is closed, a battery connected to the primary circuit will send a rapidly interrupted current through the primary coil, and a torrent of sparks will pass between the spark-balls. The primary current of the 10-inch coil is usually a current of 10 amperes, supplied at a pressure of 16 volts.

If the hand-key is raised or pressed, it is possible to make long or short torrents of secondary sparks.

Suppose, then, that we connect to the secondary spark-balls two long insulated rods, and place the spark-balls about ¼ inch apart. On pressing the hand-key, we obtain a peculiarly bright crackling spark between the balls, which is an oscillatory spark, and at the same time, as already described, electrical oscillations are set up in the rods and electric waves given off. We may represent to ourselves these electrical oscillations in the rods as similar to the mechanical vibrations which would be set up in a long elastic wooden rod, clamped at the middle and set in vibration at the ends. Or we may consider them similar to the fundamental vibrations of an open organ-pipe, the middle of the pipe corresponding with the middle of the rod. In comparing the mechanical vibrations of the rod or the acoustic vibration of the air in the organ-pipe with the electrical oscillations in the long rods, we must bear in mind that the displacement of the rod or the air in the organ-pipe at any point corresponds with electrical pressure, or potential, as it is called, at any point in the long oscillator. Hence, bearing in mind the remarks in the fourth lecture, it will be evident to you that just as the length of the air wave emitted by the open organ-pipe is double the length of the pipe, so the length of the electric wave thrown off from the pair of long rods is double their total length.

Instead of using a pair of rods for the electrical oscillator, it was found by Mr. Marconi to be an improvement to employ only one insulated rod, held vertically, and to connect it to one spark-ball of the coil, and to connect the opposite spark-ball to a metal plate buried in the earth. Then, when the spark-balls are placed a little apart and the hand-key pressed, we have a torrent of oscillatory sparks between the "earthed ball" and the insulated rod ball. This sets up in the rod electrical oscillations, which run up and down the rod. It is easy to show that there is a strong electric current passing into and out of the rod by connecting it to the spark-ball by means of a piece of fine wire. When the sparks are taken, we find this wire will become hot, it may be red hot, or sometimes it may be melted.

By applying the principles already explained, it is not difficult to demonstrate that in the case of an oscillator consisting of a single rod connected to one spark-ball the electric waves thrown off are in wave-length four times the length of the rod.

The electrical actions taking place, therefore, are as follows: At each interruption of the primary current of the spark-coil there is an electromotive force created in the secondary circuit, which gradually charges up the insulated rod until it attains a state in which it is said to be at a potential or electrical pressure of several thousand volts. The spark then happens between the balls, and the rod begins to discharge.

This process consists, so to speak, in draining the electric charge out of the rod, and it takes the form of an electric current in the rod, which has a zero value at the top insulated end, and has its maximum value at the spark-ball end.

Also, when the oscillations take place, we have variations of electric pressure, or potential, which are at a maximum at the upper or insulated end, and have a zero value at the spark-ball end. From the rod we have a hemispherical electric wave radiated. In the language of wireless telegraphists, such a simple insulated rod is called an insulated *aerial*, or an insulated *antenna*.

A simple insulated aerial has, however, a very small electrical capacity, and it can store up so little electric energy that the whole of it is radiated in the first oscillation. Hence, strictly speaking, we have no train of electric waves radiated, but merely a solitary wave or electric impulse. The effect on the æther thus produced corresponds to the effect on the air caused by the crack of a whip or an explosion, and not to a musical note or tone as produced by an organ-pipe.

We can, however, make an arrangement which is superior in electric wave-making power, as follows:—

The vertical rod, or antenna, A, is not insulated, but is connected by its lower end with one end of a coil of insulated wire, S, wound on a wooden frame (see Fig. 82). The other end of this last coil is connected to a metal plate, e, buried in the earth. Around the wooden frame is wound a second insulated wire, P, one end of which is connected to one spark-ball of the induction coil, and the other end to the outside of a Leyden jar, L, or collection of jars. This double coil on a frame is called an oscillation transformer. The inside of this condenser is connected to the second spark-ball of the induction coil I. When these spark-balls S are placed a short distance apart, and the coil set in action, we have a torrent of oscillatory electric sparks between these balls, and powerful oscillations set up in one circuit of the oscillation-transformer. These oscillations induce other oscillations in the second circuit of the oscillation- transformer, viz. in the one connected to the aerial. The oscillations produced in the air-wire, or aer-

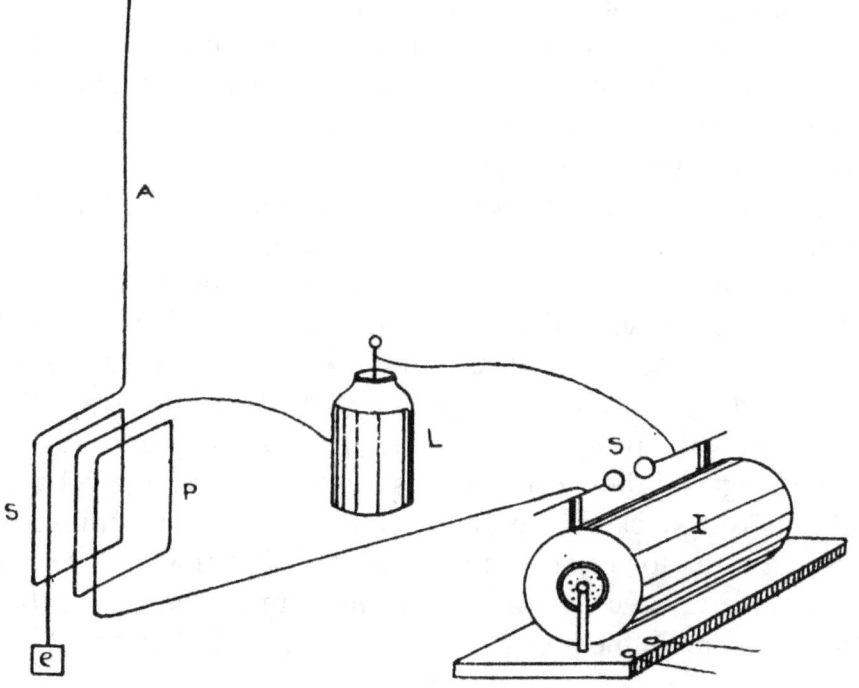

FIG. 82.—Transmitter for wireless telegraphy.

ial, are therefore induced, or secondary oscillations. The aerial wire, or antenna, has therefore a much larger store of electric energy to draw upon, viz. that stored up in the Leyden jars, than if it was itself directly charged by the coil.

In order, however, to obtain the best results certain adjustments have to be made. It has already been explained that every open electrical circuit has a certain natural time-period for the electrical oscillations which can be set up in it. This is technically called its tune.

If we administer a blow to a suspended pendulum we have seen that, if left to itself, it vibrates in a definite period of time, called its natural period. In the same manner, if we have a condenser or Leyden jar having electrical capacity which is joined in series with a coil of wire having electrical inertia or inductance, and apply to the circuit so formed a sudden electromotive force or impulse, and then leave the circuit to itself, the electric charge in it vibrates in a certain definite period, called its natural electrical periodic

The aerial, or antenna, is simply a rod connected to the earth, but it has a certain inductance, and also a certain electrical capacity, and hence any metal rod merely stuck at one end in the earth has a perfectly definite periodic time for the electrical oscillations which can be produced in it. We may compare the rod in this respect with a piece of steel spring held at one end in a vice. If we pull the spring on one side, and let it vibrate, it does so in accordance with its natural time-period for mechanical vibrations. The sound waves given out by it have a wave-length equal to four times the length of the spring. In the same manner the fundamental wave-length of the electric waves emitted by an "earthed aerial," or rod stuck in the earth, when an electric impulse is applied to its lower end, and electrical oscillations are set up in it, have a wave-length equal to four times that of the rod. Hence to obtain the best result the circuit, including the aerial

A, must be "tuned" electrically to the circuit including the Leyden jar L.[27]

A consideration of these arrangements will show you that if the hand-key in the primary circuit of the induction coil is pressed for a long or short time, we have long or short torrents of sparks produced between the secondary balls, and long or short trains of electric waves emitted from the aerial, or earthed vertical wire.

### The Morse Alphabet.

| | | | | | |
|---|---|---|---|---|---|
| A | ·— | J | ·——— | S | ··· |
| B | —··· | K | —·— | T | — |
| C | —·—· | L | ·—·· | U | ··— |
| D | —·· | M | —— | V | ···— |
| E | · | N | —· | W | ·—— |
| F | ··—· | O | ——— | X | —··— |
| G | ——· | P | ·——· | Y | —·—— |
| H | ···· | Q | ——·— | Z | ——·· |
| I | ·· | R | ·—· | | |

### The Morse Numerals.

| | | | |
|---|---|---|---|
| 1 | ·———— | 6 | —···· |
| 2 | ··——— | 7 | ——··· |
| 3 | ···—— | 8 | ———·· |
| 4 | ····— | 9 | ————· |
| 5 | ····· | 0 | ————— |

Full stop ·· ·· ··
Signal for calling up ——— ———

Whenever we have any two different signals, we can always make an alphabet with them by suitable combinations of the two. In the well-known Morse alphabet, with which every telegraphist is as familiar as we all are with the printed alphabet, the sign for each of the letters of the alphabet is composed of groups of long and short symbols, called dots and dashes, as follows: Each letter is made by selecting some arrangements of *dots* or *dashes*, these being the technical names for the two signs. The Morse code, as used all over the world, is given in the table below—

---

27 See Appendix, Note B.

The process of sending a wireless message consists in so manipulating the key in the primary circuit of the induction coils that a rapid stream of sparks passes between the secondary balls for a shorter or for a longer time. This gives rise to a corresponding series of electric waves, radiated from the aerial. The dash is equal in duration to about three dots, and a space equal to three dots is left between each letter, and one equal to five dots between each word. Thus, in Morse alphabet the sentence "How are you?" is written

```
─ ─ ─ ─   ─ ─ ─ ─ ─ ─   ─ ─ ─ ─ ─   ─ ─   ─ ─ ─   ─
   H            O              W         A       R       E
─ ─ ─ ─ ─   ─ ─ ─ ─ ─ ─   ─ ─ ─ ─
     Y             O              U
```

We have, in the next place, to explain how the signals sent out are recorded.

At the receiving station is erected a second insulated aerial, antenna, or long vertical rod, A (see Fig. 83), and the lower end is connected to the earth through a coil of fine insulated wire, P, which forms one circuit of an oscillation-trans-

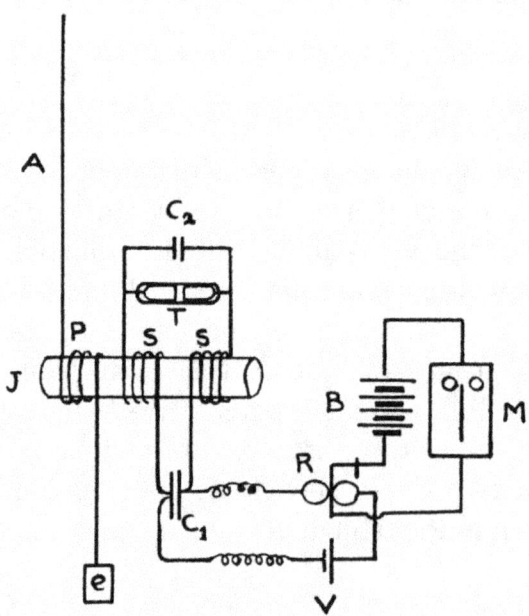

FIG. 83.—Marconi receiving arrangement for wireless telegraphy.

former. The secondary circuit, S, of this oscillation-transformer, which is called a *jigger*, is cut in the middle and has a small condenser, $C_1$, inserted, consisting of two sheets of tinfoil separated by waxed paper (see Fig. 83), and to the ends of this circuit is connected the coherer, or metallic filings tube, T, which acts as a sensitive receiver. The Marconi sensitive tube (see Fig. 84) is made as follows. A glass tube about ¼ inch in diameter and 2 inches long has two silver plugs put in it, and these are soldered to two platinum wires which are sealed into the closed ends of the tube. The ends of the plugs are cut in a slanting fashion and made very smooth. These ends very nearly touch each other. A very small quantity of very fine metallic powder consisting of nineteen parts nickel and one part silver is then placed between the plugs. The quantity of this powder is scarcely more than could be taken up on the head of a large pin. The glass tube is then exhausted of its air and sealed. The tube is attached to a bone rod by means of which it is held in a clip.

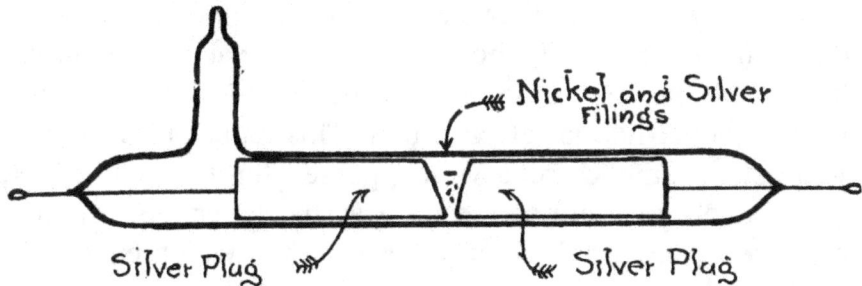

FIG. 84.—Marconi coherer.

To the two sides of the above-mentioned condenser are connected two wires which lead to a circuit including a single voltaic cell, V, and a relay, E. The relay is connected to another **circuit** which includes a battery, B, and a piece of apparatus called a *Morse printer*, M, for marking dots and dashes on a strip of paper.

The working details of the above rather complicated system of apparatus devised by Signor Marconi would require for its full elucidation a large amount of explanation of a technical character. The general reader may, however, form a sufficiently clear idea of its performance as follows:—

When the electrical waves from the distant transmitting station reach the aerial at the receiving station, they set up in it sympathetic electrical oscillations. The most favourable conditions are when the two aerials at the distant stations are exactly similar. These electrical oscillations, or rapid electric currents, set up an electro-motive force in the secondary circuit of the oscillation-transformer, and this acts, as already explained, upon the metallic filings in the coherer-tube and causes it to become an electrical conductor. The cell attached to the relay then sends a current through the conductive circuit so formed and operates the relay. This last contrivance is merely a very delicate switch or circuit-closer which is set in action by a small current sent through one of its circuits, and it then closes a second circuit and so enables another much larger battery to send a current through the *Morse printer*. The printer then prints a *dot* upon a moving strip of paper and records a signal. One other element in this rather complicated arrangement remains to be noticed, and that is the *tapper*. Underneath the coherer-tube is a little hammer worked by an electro-magnet like an electric bell. This tapper is set vibrating by the same current which passes through the Morse printer, and hence almost as soon as the latter has begun to print, the sensitive tube receives a little tap which causes the metallic filings to become again a non-conductor, and so arrests the whole of the electric currency. If it were not for this tapper, the arrival of the electric wave would cause the printer to begin printing a line which would continue. The *dot* is, so to speak, an arrested line. If, however, trains of electric waves continue to arrive, then dots continue to be printed in close order, and form a *dash* on the paper strip. It will thus be seen that the whole arrangements constitute an exceedingly ingenious device of such a nature that a single touch on the hand-key at one station causing a spark or two to take place between the spark-balls makes a dot appear upon a band of paper at the distant station; whilst, if the hand-key is held down so that a stream of sparks takes place at the transmitting station, a dash is recorded at the receiving station. The means by which this distant effect is produced is the train of electric waves moving over the earth's surface setting out from one aerial and arriving at the other.

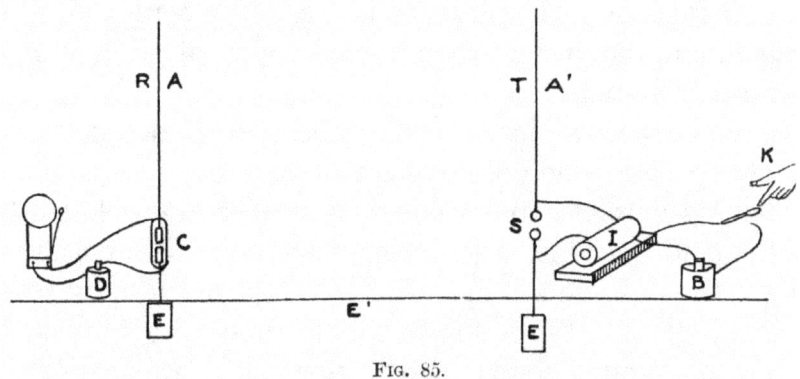

FIG. 85.

The reader who has difficulty in following the above Fig. 85. explanations may perhaps gather a sufficiently clear notion of the processes at work by considering a reduced, or simplified, arrangement. Imagine two long insulated rods, A, A' (see Fig. 85), like lightning-conductors set up at distant places. Suppose each rod cut near the bottom, and let a pair of spark-balls, S, be inserted in one gap and a coherer or sensitive tube, C, in the other. At one station let an electrical machine have its positive and negative terminals connected to the two spark-balls, and at the other let a battery and electric bell be connected to the ends of the coherer. Then, as long as the coherer remains in a non-conductive condition, the electric bell does not ring. If, however, a spark is made between the balls, in virtue of all that has been explained, the reader will understand that the coherer-tube becomes at once conductive by the action of the electric wave sent out from the transmitter-rod. The battery at the receiver-rod then sends a current through the coherer, and rings the bell.

All the other complicated details of the receiver are for making the process of stopping the bell and beginning over again self-acting, and also for the production of two kinds of signals, a *long* and a *short*, by means of which an alphabet is made. In order that we may have *telegraphy* in any proper sense of the word, we must be able to transmit any *intelligence* at pleasure, and not merely one single arbitrary signal. This transmission of intelligence involves the command of an *alphabet*, and that in turn requires the power of production of two kinds of signals.

It remains to notice a few of the special details which characterize Mr. Marconi's system of wireless telegraphy. In establishing wireless communication between two places, the first thing to be done is to equip them both with aerials. If one station is on land, it is usual to erect a strong mast about 150 feet high, and to the top of this is attached a sprit. From this sprit a stranded copper wire is suspended by means of an insulator of ebonite, so that the upper end of the wire is insulated. The lower end of the wire is led into a little hut or into some room near the foot of the mast in which is the receiving and transmitting apparatus.

If the apparatus is to be installed on board ship, then a similar insulated wire is suspended from a yardarm or from a sprit attached to a mast. Each station is provided with the transmitting apparatus and the apparatus, and the attendant changes over the aerial from one connection to the other so as to receive or send at pleasure.

In the case of long-distance wireless telegraphy, the aerial is not a single wire, but a collection of wires, suspended so as to space them a little from each other. Thus in the case of the first experiments made by M. Marconi across the Atlantic, the aerial erected on the coast of Cornwall consisted of fifty stranded copper wires each 150 feet in length suspended in a fan-shaped fashion from a long transverse stay upheld between two masts. The wires were spaced out at the top and gathered in together at the bottom.

The question which almost immediately occurs to most people to ask is how far it is possible to prevent the electric waves emanating from one station affecting all receiving instruments alike within a certain radius. The answer to this is that considerable progress has been made in effecting what is called "tuning" the various stations. In speaking of acoustic resonance it has been pointed out that a train of air waves can set up vibration in other bodies which have the same natural period of vibration. Thus, if we open a piano so as to expose the strings, and if a singer with a strong voice sings a loud true note and then stops suddenly, it will be found that one particular string of the piano is vibrating, viz. that which would give out if struck the note which was sung, but all the rest of the strings are silent. It has been pointed out that every *open electric circuit* has a natural electrical time-period of vibration in which its electric charge oscillates if it is disturbed by a sudden electro-motive force and then left to itself. If the two aerials at two stations are exactly alike, and if the various circuits constituting the oscillation-transformers in the transmitting and receiving appliances are all adjusted to have the same electrical period, then it is found that the stations so tuned are sympathetic at distances vastly greater than they would be if not so tuned. Hence it is possible to arrange wireless telegraph apparatus so that it is not affected by any electric waves arriving from a distance which have not a particular time-period.

Mr. Marconi has even shown that it is possible to receive on the same aerial, at the same time, two different messages on separate receiving instruments from two distant but properly tuned transmitting stations.

No doubt considerable improvements are still possible, but even as it is electric-wave wireless telegraphy has shown itself to be of the greatest utility in effecting communication between ship and ship, and ship and shore. Its value in enabling intelligence to be transmitted from lightships or lighthouses to coast stations cannot be over estimated. One very remarkable feature of the apparatus as arranged by Mr. Marconi is the small space it occupies. It is in this respect most admirably adapted for use on board ship. It only requires a long, insulated, vertical wire which can easily be suspended from a mast, and the whole receiving and transmitting apparatus can be placed on board ship in a small cabin. Employing the sensitive tube and Marconi receiving arrangements, messages can easily be sent 150 miles over the sea-surface by means of an aerial 150 feet high and a 10-inch induction coil.

It is a curious fact that better results are obtained over a water-surface than over land. Two similar stations with the same appliances can communicate at two or three times greater distance if they are separated by sea than if they are on land and have no water between. This is connected with the fact that electric waves are not able to pass through sea-water, but can diffuse through dry earth. The sea-surface acts somewhat like an optical reflector or mirror, and the electric waves glide along its surface. The rotundity of the earth within certain limits hardly makes any perceptible effect upon the ease of communication. The waves emanating from an aerial 150 feet high are about 600 feet in length, and there is, therefore, a considerable amount of bending or diffraction. A large amount of nonsense has been written in the daily newspapers on this point. It is a familiar fact, as already explained, that a wave-motion, whether on water or in air, spreads round an obstacle to a certain extent. Thus an interposing rock or wall does not form a sharply marked *sound-shadow*, but there is some deflection of the air waves by the edge of the obstacle. The amount of bending which takes place depends on the length of the wave.

If we take two places on the sea-surface 200 miles apart, the surface of the sea at the halfway distance is just 5 miles above the straight line joining the places. In other words, the rotundity of the earth interposes a mountain of water 5 miles high between the places. The electric waves used in wireless telegraphy have a wave-length of about 600 to 1000 feet, or say five or six to the mile. Hence the interposition of an object, the height of which is one-fortieth of the distance, is not sufficient to make a complete *electric shadow*. If we were, for instance, blowing a trumpet creating air waves 5 feet long, the interposition of a cliff between two places a mile apart, but so situated that the cliff protruded to the extent of 40 yards across the line joining them, would not cut off all sound. There would be diffraction or diffusion enough of the air waves to enable the sound to be heard round the corner. In the same manner the electric waves are, so to speak, propagated round the corner of the earth. More remarkable still, they have been detected, when sufficiently powerful, at a distance of 2000 miles across the Atlantic Ocean, and in this case they must have travelled round a protuberance which is about 140 miles in height.

A good conception of the relative speeds of water waves, air waves, and æther waves can be gained by considering the time each of these would take to cross the Atlantic Ocean, travelling in its own medium. Suppose we could, at the same moment, create a splash in the sea near England sufficiently great to cause a wave which would travel over the surface of the Atlantic at the speed of many ocean waves, say at 30 miles an hour. To cover a distance of 3000 miles this water wave would then require 100 hours. Imagine that we could, at the same moment, make a sound loud enough to be heard across the same ocean, travelling at the rate of 1100 feet a second, or about 700 miles an hour, the sound wave would cross from England to the coast of the United States in about four hours. If, however, we were to make an æther wave it would flit across the same distance in about the sixtieth part of a second.

If you have been able to follow me in these descriptions, you will see that the progress of scientific investigation has led us from simple beginnings to a wonderful conclusion. It is that all space is filled with what we may call an ocean of æther, which can be tossed into waves and ripples just as the air we breathe is traversed in all directions by aerial vibrations, and the restless sea by waves and ripples on the water-surf ace. We cannot feel or handle this imponderable æther, but we have indubitable proof that we can create waves in it by suddenly applying or reversing something we call electric force, just as we are able to produce air or water waves by the very sudden application of mechanical force or pressure. These æther waves, when started, not only travel through the ocean of æther with astonishing speed, but they are the means by which enormous quantities of energy are transferred through space.

From every square yard of the sun's surface energy is cast forth at a rate equal to that produced by the combustion of eleven tons of best Welsh coal per hour, and conveyed away into surrounding space by æther ripples, to warm and light the sun's family of planets. Every plant that grows upon the earth's surface is nourished into maturity by the energy delivered to it in this way. Every animal that basks in the sunlight is kept warm by the impact of these æther waves upon the earth. All the coal we possess buried in the earth's crust, and in this age of steam forming the life blood of the world, has been manufactured originally by æther ripples beating in their millions, in long-past ages, upon the vegetation of the primeval world.

But in another way the æther serves as a vehicle of energy in the form of an electric current. Every electric lamp that is lighted, every electric tram-car that glides along, is drawing its supply of energy through the æther. The wire or conductor, as we call it, serves to guide and direct the path of the energy transferred; but the energy is not in but around the wire. We have lately learnt to make what we may best describe as billows in the æther, and these are the long waves we employ in wireless telegraphy. But in telegraphy, whether with wires or without, we are merely manipulating the æther as a medium of communication, just as in speech or hearing we use the air.

We therefore find our physical investigations lead us to three great final inquiries, when we ask What is the nature of electricity, æther, and energy? Already, it seems possible, we may obtain some clue to an answer to the first question, and find it in a study of the electrons, or tiny corpuscles which build up atoms. Concerning the structure of æther, physical investigation, which has revealed its existence, may be able to analyze a little more deeply its operations. But the question, What is Energy? seems to take us to the very confines of physical inquiry, where problems concerning the structure of the material universe seem to merge into questions concerning its origin and mystery. In its ultimate essence, energy may be incomprehensible by us, except as an exhibition of the direct operation of that which we call Mind and Will. In these final inquiries into the nature of things, the wisest of us can merely speculate, and the majority but dimly apprehend.

We must not, however, travel beyond the limits of thought proper for these elementary lectures. Their chief object has been to show you that the swiftly moving ocean waves, which dash and roll unceasingly against the coast-lines of our island home, are only instances of one form of wave-motion, of which we find other varieties in other media, giving rise to all the entrancing effects of sound and light. In these expositions we have been able to do no more than touch the fringe of a great subject. Their object will have been fulfilled if they have stimulated in you a desire to know more about these interesting things. Every star and flower, every wave or bird that hovers over it, can tell us a marvellous story, if only we have eyes to see, and ears to hear. We may find in the commonest of surrounding things a limitless opportunity for intelligent study and delight. When, therefore, you next sail your boat upon a pond, or watch ducks or swans swimming, or throw stones into a pool, or visit the sea-side, may I hope that some of the matters here discussed will recur to your minds, and that you will find a fresh meaning and new interest in these everyday objects. You may thus, perhaps, receive an impulse attracting you to the study of some chapters in the "Fairy Tale of Science," more wonderful than any romance woven by the imaginations of men, and open to yourselves a source of elevating pleasure, which time will neither diminish nor destroy.

# APPENDIX.

**NOTE A (see p. 18).**

THE distinction between the individual wave-velocity and a wave-group velocity, to which, as stated in the text, attention was first called by Sir G. G. Stokes in an Examination question set at Cambridge in 1876, is closely connected with the phenomena of beats in music.

If two infinitely long sets of deep-sea waves, having slightly different wave-lengths, and therefore slightly different velocities, are superimposed, we obtain a resultant wave-train which exhibits a variation in wave-amplitude along its course periodically. If we were to look along the train, we should see the wave-amplitude at intervals waxing to a maximum and then waning again to nothing. These points of maximum amplitude regularly arranged in space constitute, as it were, waves on waves. They are spaced at equal distances, and separated by intervals of more or less waveless or smooth water. These maximum points move forward with a uniform velocity, which we may call the velocity of the wave-train, and the distance between maximum and maximum surface-disturbances may be called the wave-train length.

Let v and v' be the velocities, and n and n' the frequencies, of the two constituent wave-motions. Let $\lambda$ and $\lambda'$ be the corresponding wave-lengths. Let V be the wave-train velocity, N the wave-train frequency, and L the wave-train length. Then N is the number of times per second which a place of maximum wave-amplitude passes a given fixed point.

Then we have the following obvious relations:

$$v = n\lambda, \; v' = n'\lambda', \; N = n - n' = \frac{v}{\lambda} - \frac{v'}{\lambda'}$$

Also a little consideration will show that

$$\frac{L}{\lambda'} = \frac{\lambda}{\lambda - \lambda'}$$

since $\lambda$ is nearly equal, by assumption, to $\lambda'$. Hence we have—
$$\frac{1}{L} = \frac{1}{\lambda} - \frac{1}{\lambda'}; \text{ and also } V = NL$$

Accordingly —
$$V = \frac{N}{\dfrac{1}{L}} = \frac{\dfrac{v}{\lambda} - \dfrac{v'}{\lambda'}}{\dfrac{1}{\lambda} - \dfrac{1}{\lambda'}}$$

Let us write $\dfrac{2\pi}{k}$ instead of $\lambda$, and $\dfrac{2\pi}{k'}$ instead of $\lambda'$; then we have—
$$V = \frac{vk - v'k'}{k - k'} \qquad . \qquad . \qquad (\text{i.})$$

And since k and k', v and v' are nearly equal, we may write the above expression as a differential coefficient; thus—
$$V = \frac{d(vk)}{d(x)} \qquad . \qquad . \qquad (\text{ii.})$$

Suppose, then, that, as in the case of deep-sea waves, the wave-velocity varies as the square root of the wave-length. Then if C is a constant, which in the case of gravitation waves is equal to $\dfrac{g}{2\pi}$, where g is the acceleration due to gravity, we have—
$$v^2 = C\lambda, \text{ or } v^2 = \frac{g}{2\pi}\lambda$$

or $\lambda = \dfrac{2\pi}{k}$, hence—
$$vk = \frac{2\pi C}{v}$$

Hence if we differentiate with respect to $v$, we have—
$$\frac{d(vk)}{dv} = -\frac{2\pi C}{v^2}$$

# APPENDIX.

Again, $k = \dfrac{2\pi}{\lambda} = \dfrac{2\pi C}{v^2}$; therefore—

$$\frac{d(k)}{dv} = -2\frac{2\pi C}{v^3}$$

Hence, dividing the expression for $\dfrac{d(vk)}{dv}$ by that for $\dfrac{d(k)}{dv}$, we have

$$V = \frac{d(vk)}{d(k)} = \frac{v}{2}$$

In other words, the wave-train velocity is equal to half the wave-velocity. This is the case with deep-sea waves. Suppose, however, that, as in the case of air waves, the wave-velocity is independent of the wave-length. Then if two trains of waves of slightly different wave-length are superposed, we have k and k' different in value but nearly equal, and v and v' equal. Hence the equation (i.) takes the form

$$V = v$$

In other words, the *beats* travel forward with the same speed as the constituent waves. And in this case there is no difference between the velocity of the wave-train and the velocity of the individual wave. The above proof may be generalized as follows:

Let the wave-velocity vary as the nth root of the wave-length, or let $v^n = C\lambda$; and let $\lambda = \dfrac{2\pi}{k}$ as before. Then—

$$v^n = \frac{2\pi C}{k}, \text{ and } vk = \frac{2\pi C}{v^{n-1}} = 2\pi C v^{-(n-1)}$$

also $k = \dfrac{2\pi}{\lambda} = \dfrac{2\pi C}{v^n} = 2\pi C v^{-n}$

Hence $\dfrac{d(vk)}{d(k)} = \dfrac{(n-1)v^{-(n-1)-1}}{nv^{-n-1}} = \dfrac{n-1}{n}v$

or $V = \dfrac{n-1}{n}v$

That is, the wave-train velocity is equal to $\dfrac{n-1}{n}$ times the wave-velocity.

In the case of sea waves $n = 2$, and in the case of air waves $n =$ infinity.

If *n* were 3, then $V = \frac{2}{3} v$, or the group-velocity would be two-thirds the wave-velocity.

## NOTE B (see p. 243).

Every electric circuit comprising a coil of wire and a condenser has a definite time-period in which an electric charge given to it will oscillate if a state of electric strain in it is suddenly released. Thus the Leyden jar L and associated coil P shown in Fig. 82, p. 241, constitutes an electric circuit, having a certain capacity measured in units, called a microfarad, and a certain inductance, or electric inertia measured in centimetres. The capacity of the circuit is the quality of it in virtue of which an electric strain or displacement can be made by an electro-motive force acting on it. The inductance is the inertia quality of the circuit, in virtue of which an electric current created in it tends to persist. In the case of mechanical oscillations such as those made by vibrating a pendulum, the time of one complete oscillation, T, is connected with the *moment of inertia*, I, and the mechanical force brought into play by a small displacement as follows: Suppose we give the pendulum a small angular displacement, denoted by $\theta$. Then this displacement brings into existence a restoring force or torque which brings the pendulum back, when released, to its original position of rest. In the case of a simple pendulum consisting of a small ball attached to a string, the restoring torque created by displacing the pendulum through a small angle, $\theta$, is equal to the product $mgl\theta$, where *m* is the mass of the bob, *g* is the acceleration of gravity, and *l* is the length of the string. The ratio of displacement ($\theta$) to the restoring torque

# APPENDIX.

$mgl\theta$ is $\dfrac{1}{mgl}$. This may be called the displacement per unit torque, and may otherwise be called the pliability of the system, and denoted generally by P. Let I denote the moment of inertia. This quantity, in the case of a simple pendulum, is the product of the mass of the bob and the square of the length of the string, or $I = ml^2$.

In the case of a body of any shape which can vibrate round any centre or axis, the moment of inertia round this axis of rotation is the sum of the products of each element of its mass and the square of their respective distances from this axis. The periodic time T of any small vibration of this body is then obtained by the following rule:—

$$T = 2\pi \sqrt{ \left\{ \begin{array}{c} \text{moment of interia} \\ \text{round the axis} \\ \text{of rotation} \end{array} \right\} \times \left\{ \begin{array}{c} \text{displacement per} \\ \text{unit of torque, or} \\ \text{pliability} \end{array} \right\} }$$

or $T = 2\pi\sqrt{IP}$

In the case of an electric circuit the inductance corresponds to the moment of inertia of a body in mechanical vibration; and the capacity to its pliability as above defined. Hence the time of vibration, or the electrical time-period of an electric circuit, is given by the equation

$$T = 2\pi\sqrt{LC}$$

where L is the inductance, and C is the capacity.

It can be shown easily that the frequency $n$, or number of electrical vibrations per second, is given by the rule:

$$n = \dfrac{5000000}{\sqrt{\left\{\begin{array}{c}\text{capacity in}\\ \text{microfarads}\end{array}\right\} \times \left\{\begin{array}{c}\text{inductance in}\\ \text{centimeters}\end{array}\right\}}}$$

For instance, if we discharge a Leyden jar having a capacity of $\tfrac{1}{300}$ of a microfarad through a stout piece of copper wire about 4 feet in length and one-sixth of an inch in diameter, having an inductance of about 1200 centimetres, the electrical oscillations ensuing would be at the rate of 2½ millions per second.

Any two electrical circuits which have the same time-period are said to be "in tune" with each other, and the process of adjusting the inductance and capacity of the circuits to bring about this result is called electrical tuning. In the case of a vertical aerial wire as used in wireless telegraphy, in which the oscillations are created by the inductive action of an oscillation-transformer as shown in Fig. 82, page 241, the capacity of the Leyden jar in the condenser circuit must be adjusted so that the time-period of the nearly closed or primary oscillation P agrees with that of the open or secondary circuit S. When this is the case, the electrical oscillations set up in the closed circuit have a far greater effect in producing others in the open circuit than if the two circuits were not in tune. The length of the wave given off from the open circuit is approximately equal to four times the length of the aerial wire, including the length of the coil forming the secondary circuit of the oscillation-transformer in series with it.

## Alphabetical Index

## Alphabetical Index

Actinic rays................................................................227
Air...............................................................................
    movement of, in the concert-room........................163
    necessary for production of sound............................91
    particles, mode of motion of, in case of sound wave...............99
    waves..................................................................91
        interference of.............................................123
        length of......................................................101
        nature of......................................................101
        speed of......................................................102
Alphabet used in telegraphy.........................................243
America Cup race, pictures of yachts entered for the...................85
America yacht, the........................................................82
Amplitude.......................................................................7
Anti-node...................................................................138
Apparatus....................................................................
    for detecting electrical waves..................................211
    for exhibiting motion of air in case of sound wave.................96
    for investigating the laws of falling bodies.......................32
Atlantic waves.............................................................
    height of..........................................................8
    length of..........................................................8
Atomic theory.............................................................201
Beam of sound focussed by collodion lens....................116
Beats..........................................................................
    musical........................................................145
Billows..........................................................................1
Bore............................................................................34
Branly, Professor, electric wave detector.......................188
Breaking wave..............................................................26
Canal wave...................................................................29
    velocity..........................................................31
Canal-boat waves..........................................................31

| | |
|---|---:|
| Capillary ripples | 37 |
| Chromatic scale | 144 |
| Clef, musical | 142 |
| Closed organ-pipe | 152 |
| Cloud waves | 27 |
| Coherer | |
|     Lodge | 188 |
|     Marconi | 245 |
| Column of air set in vibration by a tuning-fork | 141 |
| Conclusion | 253 |
| Concords and discords in music | |
|     musical | 144 |
|     nature of difference between | 144 |
| Conditions necessary for production of true wave in a medium | 11 |
| Conductor, electric | 175 |
| Conservation of energy, law of | 21 |
| Conservation of matter, law of | 20 |
| Convergence of an electric ray by a paraffin lens | 215 |
| Cornish, Dr. Vaughan | 28 |
| Corresponding speeds, Froude's law of | 72 |
| Cup Races | 83 |
| Current, electric | 172 |
| Dark heat | 222 |
| Deep-sea waves | |
|     rules for determining speed of | 10 |
|     rules for determining velocity of | 10 |
| Definition | |
|     of a ripple | 37 |
|     of wave-frequency | 7 |
|     of wave-length | 6 |
|     of wave-velocity | 7 |
| Depth of water, effect of, on speed of canal wave | 30 |
| Difference between | |
|     electric conductors and non-conductors | 176 |
|     velocity of a wave and of a wave-train | 17 |
| Discords in music | 144 |
| Dispersion of æther waves | 229 |
| Distances at which sound can be heard | 106 |

# ALPHABETICAL INDEX

Ear, power of, to analyze sound..................................................162
Echelon waves made by a duck..................................................66
Eddies in liquids..........................................................................54
Eddy............................................................................................54
    motion....................................................................................54
    resistance...............................................................................61
Edison phonograph...................................................................126
Elasticity of the air......................................................................98
Electric.............................................................................................
    circuit, open........................................................................193
    conductor and non-conductor.............................................176
    corpuscles..........................................................................202
    current................................................................................172
        alternating....................................................................173
        continuous....................................................................173
        energy..........................................................................192
        nature of.......................................................................172
    displacement......................................................................197
    energy, mechanical analogue of.........................................192
    force....................................................................................203
    index of refraction.............................................................217
    inductance..........................................................................191
    inertia.................................................................................191
    oscillations.........................................................................165
        apparatus for producing...............................................180
        in open circuit..............................................................193
        produce by discharge of a Leyden jar.........................179
    radiation.............................................................................205
        and light, identity in the nature of................................225
    radiation-detector..................................................................
        (Fleming).....................................................................199
        (Miller)........................................................................209
    radiation, velocity of.........................................................222
    ray..........................................................................................
        reflection of.................................................................214
        refraction of.................................................................215
    strain..................................................................................176
    transparency and opacity..................................................212

wave..............................................................................................
    and air wave compared.............................................198
    detector...............................................................................187
    nature of..............................................................................204
    production of......................................................................186
  waves......................................................................................165
Electric or hertz rays...................................................................223
Electro-magnet.............................................................................174
Electro-magnetic medium............................................................196
  theory of light......................................................................233
Electrodeless discharge.....................................................182, 184
  apparatus for producing......................................................182
Electromotive force......................................................................175
Electronic theory of electricity...................................................203
Electrons........................................................................................202
Energy.............................................................................................19
  kinetic.....................................................................................23
  of electrostatic strain..........................................................192
  of motion................................................................................23
  of moving water....................................................................29
  potential..................................................................................23
  two forms of electric..........................................................192
Ether, the......................................................................................171
Experimental..................................................................................
  tank, uses of, in ship-design................................................77
  tanks.......................................................................................75
Experiments illustrating surface tension......................................36
Explosion of guns heard at great distances...............................106
Falling bodies, laws of..................................................................31
Fish, motion of a...........................................................................60
Flame, sensitive...........................................................................112
Flow of liquid.................................................................................
  in non-uniform tubes............................................................59
  in tubes..................................................................................58
  in uniform tubes...................................................................58
Fog-signals...................................................................................108
  influence of wind upon distance at which they are heard.......110
  power absorbed in making.................................................110

## ALPHABETICAL INDEX

Free period of vibration, influence upon force required to move a body.................135
Froude, Mr. William.................71
Froude's.................
    experimental tank.................72
    experiments at Torquay.................72
Gamut.................143
    of æther waves.................231
Gravitation wave.................36
Ground swell.................28
Harmonic.................
    curve.................96
    motion.................95
Harmonics.................139
Hele-Shaw, Professor.................56
    discovery of means of producing irrotational motion in liquids.................57
    investigations on liquid motion.................58
Helmholtz's.................
    investigation into nature of musical tones.................148
    theory on discords and concords.................148
Hertz oscillation.................185
Hertz's researches. Experiments with electric waves, apparatus for.................209
Hughes, Professor, investigations on electric waves, made by.................187
Human ear.................161
Hydraulic gradient.................58
Illustration of difference between wave-velocity and wave-group velocity.................25
Inaudible sound.................123
Index of refraction.................48
Inductance.................190
Induction coil for wireless telegraphy.................237
Inefficiency of present methods of manufacturing light.................236
Inertia of the air.................98
Interference of.................
    air waves.................123
    electric rays.................220

ripples and waves..............................................................43
Irrotational motion.............................................................53
Kelvin, Lord, investigations on ship waves.........................69
Kinetic energy....................................................................23
Krakatoa..............................................................................
    eruption of..................................................................103
    sound produced by the eruption of............................103
Laplace, calculations of, concerning sound-velocity........105
Law connecting velocity and pressure in liquid motion.....60
Length of wave, definition of the term.................................7
Light, velocity of....................................................167, 168
Liquid flow in constricted tube..........................................59
Lodge, Sir Oliver, coherer invented by............................188
Long wave............................................................................7
Longitudinal waves..............................................................6
Luminous..............................................................................
    efficiency....................................................................235
    rays..............................................................................227
Magnetic force..................................................................203
Major third in music.........................................................143
Marconi................................................................................
    aerial wire...................................................................236
    coherer........................................................................245
    experiments with wireless telegraphy across the Atlantic by..248
    system of wireless telegraphy........................... 245, 248
Matter..................................................................................19
Maxwell's electro-magnetic theory of light......................233
Mechanical explanations into electrical phenomenon......198
Methods of manufacturing light........................................235
Minor third in music.........................................................143
Model illustrating.................................................................
    longitudinal wave.......................................................101
    nature of an air wave..................................................100
Models illustrating...............................................................
    wave motion...................................................................4
Morse alphabet..................................................................243
Motion..................................................................................
    harmonic......................................................................95

## ALPHABETICAL INDEX

    irrotational..................................................................................53
    of water in sea waves.....................................................................2
    periodic......................................................................................95
    rotational ..................................................................................53
    tones.............................................................................................
        sharp and flat......................................................................144
    vortex........................................................................................53
Movement of the air in the case of a sound wave........................99
Music, theory of..............................................................................141
Musical.............................................................................................
    beats........................................................................................145
    scales, notes of the...................................................................143
    tones.............................................................................................
        and noise contrasted.............................................................97
        sharp and flat......................................................................144
Natural period of vibration of a body..............................................132
Node................................................................................................142
Non-conductor, electric..................................................................172
Non-resistance to a body moving through perfect liquid................64
Octave.............................................................................................143
Open.................................................................................................
    electric circuit..........................................................................193
    organ-pipe...............................................................................152
Optical proof that a sounding body is in vibration..................92, 93
Organ-pipes......................................................................................
    construction of................................................................152, 154
    distribution of air-pressure in..................................................153
    overtones of............................................................................155
    relation between length of pipe and length of wave................155
Oscillations......................................................................................
    electric....................................................................................165
    of a stretched string................................................................137
Oscillator, hertz...............................................................................185
Oscillatory electric sparks, photographs of....................................180
Over-tones......................................................................................138
Pendulum, isochronism of the........................................................132
Perfect fluid......................................................................................53
Periodic..............................................................................................

    motion.................................................................................95
    time........................................................................................9
Phonograph, action of the.................................................126
Photographic study of the production of waves..............15
Photographs of ripples on a mercury surface....................48
Plane wave..................................................................................50
Potential energy........................................................................23
Power required to propel ships............................................80
Prism for refracting a beam of sound...............................120
Production of a sound wave..................................................98
Quality of sound.....................................................................102
Radiation..........................................................................................
    electric..................................................................................212
    nature of..............................................................................234
    of energy from the sun...................................................252
Rayleigh, Lord, an acoustic experiment with an open pipe by....155
Receiver for wireless telegraphy (Marconi).....................245
Reflection........................................................................................
    of a beam of sound..........................................................117
    of a wave...............................................................................49
    of an electric ray...............................................................215
    of ripples...............................................................................41
Refraction........................................................................................
    explanation of.....................................................................46
    of a beam of sound..............................................118, 119
    of an electric ray...............................................................215
        by an ice prism.............................................................215
    of ripples...............................................................................46
Refractive index........................................................................48
Relation of wave-velocity and wave-length.......................8
Relay, telegraphic..................................................................211
Resistance........................................................................................
    curves of ships...................................................................81
    to a body moving through a fluid, causes of the......61
Resonance................................................................................132
    an experiment on..............................................................141
Ripple................................................................................................
    and wave, distinction between......................................36

## ALPHABETICAL INDEX

    mark..................................................................................................27
    reflection of a.............................................................................40, 41
    scientific definition of a......................................................................10
Ripples.........................................................................................................1
    apparatus for producing.....................................................................39
    in the air..............................................................................................91
    interference of....................................................................................43
    intersecting........................................................................................44
    on a lake, photographs of..................................................................17
    photography of...................................................................................45
        by J. H. Vincent.........................................................................48
    produced by stones thrown into water.............................................14
    velocity of....................................................................................37, 38
Rotational motion......................................................................................53
Russell, Scott, Mr......................................................................................71
    experiments of, on canal-boat waves................................................89
Scale............................................................................................................
    musical, notes of the........................................................................143
    of equal temperament......................................................................144
Sea waves..................................................................................................2
    motion of..............................................................................................2
    relation of velocity and length in case of............................................9
Semitone..................................................................................................143
Sensitive flame, influence of sound upon a...........................................114
Severn bore................................................................................................35
Shamrock II, trials of................................................................................85
Ship.............................................................................................................
    bow wave mode of production.........................................................67
    design..........................................................................................77, 78
        the problem of............................................................................65
    models, the testing of........................................................................75
    resistance, Froude's law of................................................................73
    waves..................................................................................................51
        complete system of....................................................................69
        various systems of......................................................................65
Short wave...................................................................................................7
Sine curve, mode of drawing a.................................................................95
Singing flame...........................................................................................156

Siren..........................................................................................109
Skin friction........................................................................53, 61
   for various classes of ships...................................81
Soap...................................................................................
   film thrown into vibration by air waves..............128
   solution for making bubbles....................................127
Solitary wave.................................................................23
   and the wave-train, difference between...............23
Sound...............................................................................
   and music.....................................................................131
   causes of variation in the quality of......................126
   due to air waves..................................................91, 92
   lens, making of a........................................................115
   prism.............................................................................120
   quality of.....................................................................102
   signals..........................................................................109
   velocity of, in various cases....................................111
Sounding body is in vibration...................................92
Speed..................................................................................
   of a falling body..........................................................31
   of sound......................................................................102
Stationary waves.........................................................138
Stone falling into water, photographs of a............15
Stream-lines...................................................................57
   round an ovoid............................................................64
Stroh violin..................................................................160
Structure of the human ear......................................161
Surface tension of liquid.............................................36
Temperature, effect of, on sound velocity...........104
Tesla coil......................................................................183
Tidal wave......................................................................35
   speed of..........................................................................35
Tides................................................................................35
Time of vibration of a stretched string..................137
Tone...............................................................................143
Torpedo, motion of, in water......................................60
Transference of wave-motion....................................24
Transverse.........................................................................

## ALPHABETICAL INDEX

    ship waves.................................................................................70
    wave............................................................................................6
True wave.........................................................................................
    conditions for producing a.....................................................14
    definition of a........................................................................13
Tubes of flow................................................................................57
    in a liquid...............................................................................63
Utilization of the æther..............................................................252
Various kinds of resistance to a body moving through a fluid........61
Velocity............................................................................................
    of electric radiation..............................................................222
    of light..................................................................................168
    of sea waves, rule for calculating the.......................................9
    of sound................................................................................
        how affected by temperature..............................................104
        in different gases................................................................111
        influence of specific heats on the.......................................105
        measurements of the..........................................................102
        theoretical determination of the..........................................104
    of sound wave......................................................................102
    of waves in air, water, and æther compared.........................251
Vernon Boys, Professor, instructions by, for making soap solution ...............................................................................................127
Vibration rates...............................................................................
    of musical tones...................................................................142
    of various æther waves........................................................225
Vibrations........................................................................................
    forced...................................................................................133
    free.......................................................................................133
    giving rise to musical tones.................................................142
Vincent, Mr. J. H........................................................................46
Violin, improved by Mr. Augustus Stroh....................................160
Violin, structure of...........................................................157, 158
Viscosity of liquids.......................................................................52
Vortex..............................................................................................
    motion....................................................................................53
    ring........................................................................................
        in air......................................................................................55

  production of..................................................................55
Wave..............................................................................................
 amplitude, definition of.........................................................7
 causes of breaking................................................................26
 electric...................................................................................
  nature of an........................................................................165
 frequency................................................................................7
 gravitation.............................................................................36
 group, velocity of a...............................................................18
 length......................................................................................6
 lengths of various kinds of æther waves.............................229
 longitudinal............................................................................6
 motion....................................................................................2
  definition of.........................................................................3
  model....................................................................................4
  model for illustrating.........................................................12
  various kinds of...................................................................4
 produced in the canal...........................................................30
 reflection of a........................................................................49
 resistance...............................................................................61
Waves..........................................................................................1
 and ripples in the æther......................................................207
 conditions of for interference..............................................44
 electric................................................................................165
 in the air................................................................................91
 interference of.......................................................................43
 made by canal-boats, experiments on.................................90
 made by ships.......................................................................51
 on a snow surface.................................................................27
 on clouds...............................................................................27
 produce by high-speed ships...............................................70
 refraction of..........................................................................46
 sea...........................................................................................2
 stationary............................................................................138
 train........................................................................................17
  velocity of..........................................................................18
 transverse................................................................................6
 velocity, a rule for determining.............................................8

## ALPHABETICAL INDEX

Wind, influence of, upon distances at which sounds are heard...108
Wireless.................................................................................................
   telegraphy........................................................................................
      across the Atlantic..........................................................248
      apparatus for...................................................................237
      explanation of.................................................................242
      Marconi's system of........................................................239
      method of conducting.....................................................244
      transmitter for.................................................................241
      utility of..........................................................................249
Worthington, Professor, photographs of splash of drop...........14, 15
Yacht-design, object of.....................................................................83
Yachts entered for the America Cup race, pictures of....................86
Young, Dr. Thomas, investigations of, on interference of light...169
Æther...............................................................................................170
   properties of..................................................................................171
   wave radiation, range of................................................................233
   waves, various kinds of.................................................................227

www.ingramcontent.com/pod-product-compliance
Lightning Source LLC
Chambersburg PA
CBHW070239090526
44586CB00035B/995